D0948146

LOCKDOWN
—ON—
RIKERS

SHOCKING STORIES OF
ABUSE AND INJUSTICE AT
NEW YORK'S NOTORIOUS JAIL

MARY E. BUSER

St. Martin's Press
New York

This is a work of nonfiction. However, except for public officials and institutions, most of the names of individuals and certain of their identifying characteristics have been changed to protect their privacy. In certain instances composites of inmates have been used. Dialogue has been reconstructed to the best of the author's recollection.

www.stmartins.com

Library of Congress Cataloging-in-Publication Data

Buser, Mary E.
    Lockdown on Rikers : shocking stories of abuse and injustice at New York's notorious jail / Mary E. Buser.
    pages   cm
    Includes index.
    ISBN 978-1-250-07784-4 (hardcover)—ISBN 978-1-4668-9016-9 (ebook)
    1. Buser, Mary E. 2. Jails—New York (State)—Rikers Island.
3. Prisoners—New York (State)—Rikers Island. 4. Prison administration—Moral and ethical aspects—New York (State)—Rikers Island. I. Title.
    HV8746.U62N735   2015
    365'.9747275—dc23
                                                                2015007502

Design by Letra Libre, Inc.

Our books may be purchased for educational, business, or promotional use. For information on bulk purchases, please contact the Macmillan Corporate and Premium Sales Department at 1-800-221-7945, extension 5442, or write to specialmarkets@macmillan.com.

First Edition: September 2015

10   9   8   7   6   5   4   3   2   1

*This book is dedicated to the memory of
Jerome Murdough, Jason Echevarria,
and to all those who fight the battle within.
Be it the struggle with alcoholism, drug addiction,
mental illness, or the agony of depression,
may you find your way.*

And to Jerome and Jason, may you rest in peace.

CONTENTS

PREFACE

AT THE END OF A LONG CINDER-BLOCK CORRIDOR, A correction officer in an elevated booth passes the time with a paperback book. Across from the booth, a barred gate cordons off a dim passageway. Along the passageway wall are the words CENTRAL PUNITIVE SEGREGATION UNIT.

The officer looks up as I approach and nods. As acting chief of the Mental Health Department at Rikers Island, I'm a regular over here at "the Bing"—a curious moniker for this five-story tower of nothing but solitary confinement cells, one hundred per floor. They were designed for Rikers Island's most recalcitrant inmates, the ones who have been pulled out of the general population for fighting, weapons possession, disobeying orders, assaulting staff. The officers refer to them as "the baddest of the bad," "the worst of the worst." I'm not so sure about that.

The officer throws a switch, and the gate shudders open. Around a bend, I step into an elevator car. Since the problem inmate is on the third floor, I hold up three fingers to a corner camera that connects to a TV monitor. This is no ordinary elevator—no buttons to push here. The sweaty little box starts lifting, and as muffled wails seep through, my stomach tightens, the way it does every time I'm called over here. Which is often.

Solitary confinement is punishment taken to the extreme. Rikers folklore has it that the term *Bing* was coined to describe the human brain under the strain of solitary—it goes . . . bing! Whether this story is true is unclear, but it makes sense. Solitary confinement induces the bleakest depression, plunging despair, and terrifying hallucinations. The Mental Health Department looms large in these units, doling out antidepressants, antipsychotics, and mountains of sleeping pills. If these inmates didn't have mental health issues before they entered solitary, they do now. But even the most potent medications can only do so much, and when they give out—when human behavior deteriorates into frantic scenes of self-mutilation and makeshift nooses—we're called to a cell door.

The elevator rattles open on the third floor. Ahead, a long tinted window separates two plain doors, each one leading to a fifty-cell wing. Behind the window, correctional staff hover over paperwork. A logbook is thrust out; I sign it and point to the door on the left, "3 South." When the knob buzzes, I pull the door open and step into what feels like a furnace. A long cement floor is lined with gray steel doors that face each other—twenty-five on one side, twenty-five on the other. Each door has a small window at the top and a flap for food trays on the bottom.

At the far end, Dr. David Diaz and Pete Majors are waiting for me. I hesitate for a moment, dreading the walk through the gauntlet of misery. The smell of vomit and feces hangs in the hot, thick air. Bracing myself, I start past the doors, trying to stay focused on my colleagues. Still, I can see the inmates' faces—dark-skinned, young—pressed up against the windows, eyes wild with panic. *"Miss! Help! Please, miss!"* They bang and slap the doors, sweaty palms sliding down the windows. *"We're dying in here, miss, we're dying!"* Resisting my natural instinct to rush to their aid, I keep going, reminding myself that there's a reason they're in here—that they've done something to warrant this punishment. The officers, themselves sweat-soaked and agitated, amble from cell to cell, pounding the doors with their fists, spinning around and kicking them with boot heels, "Shut the fuck up!"

Diaz, a silver-haired psychiatrist, greets me with a weak smile. Pointing to a door that's slightly ajar, he says, "We got a head basher." He hands me the inmate's chart. The label on the manila folder reads "Troy Jackson." "He's been going downhill for a while now," Diaz explains. "I've upped his meds, changed them. We've talked to him, but at this point, we're out of options."

"He's been in for two months now," says Pete, the lanky therapist who works with Diaz. "With *three more* to go."

I wince at the length of punishment. Two entire months spent inside an eight-by-nine-foot cell—just enough room to pace back and forth, about the only activity the cramped quarters allow. No phone, no TV, with one hour of "rec," which amounts to a shackled walk to an outdoor cage to stand alone and glimpse the sky. Although the maximum punishment for any single infraction is ninety days, there's nothing to keep infraction tickets from piling up, which is apparently what's happened in this case.

"All right, let me talk to him," I say, with some vague hope of dispensing calming words that might enable Troy Jackson to hang on a little while longer.

The officer pulls open the creaking door and steps back. Inside, a Black youth stands trembling, beads of sweat dripping from his chin. He's barely out of his teens. Behind him, a little mesh-covered window transforms the day's brilliance into grayness. A dingy sheet is strewn across a cot; across from it is a tiny metal sink and toilet. "Please, miss, please," he whispers. "Help me . . ."

For a moment, Troy Jackson and I stare at one another. In his jeans and T-shirt, he looks no different from every other kid on the street. I can easily picture him shooting basketballs on a city playground or bounding up subway steps headed for school. Instead, he's trapped inside a cement box on Rikers Island. As his eyes plead with mine, blood seeps through his scalp, running down behind his ears. *How could his young life have derailed this badly?* I feel a clutch in my throat and my mind starts swirling back to my earlier days on Rikers, when I would have worked with him, listened to his story, helped him to find a better path for himself. But my days as an upbeat therapist are starting to feel like the distant past. As a newly appointed administrator, I remind myself that I'm not here to get to know Troy Jackson, or even to find out why he's in solitary. I'm here to make sure of exactly one thing: that he remains alive. "Mr. Jackson, I'd like—"

"I can't," he interrupts. "I'm telling you, I can't. Please, miss, please. I'm begging you . . . I'm begging . . ."

The blood is trickling down into his eyes, and I realize that we're well beyond any therapeutic dialogue. "Okay, just give me a minute here, okay?"

Pete, Diaz, and I huddle to the side of the cell, once again finding ourselves at a familiar miserable impasse. Although we have the authority to provide temporary relief in these situations, doing so is hardly a cut-and-dried matter. In the outside world, someone banging his head would be treated with a sense of urgency and alarm. But in here it's different. Behind bars—and especially in the Bing—these drastic acts are common, and the Mental Health Department is under fierce pressure to not give in to the inmates' goal of a reprieve. Of course, it's also up to us to make sure nobody actually dies. I'm still comprehending the reality of my new job, but it's already clear that it entails walking the thinnest of tightropes.

The question before us is whether the breaking point has truly been reached. If we agree that death or severe injury is likely, then Troy Jackson will be bused to a smaller, more specialized unit in another jail down the road. The bus ride alone seems to offer isolation-weary inmates enormous relief. We call it "bus therapy." Once he's a little better, though, he'll be shipped right back here to complete his sentence. Like a weary swimmer treading water but starting to go under, he'll be pulled out long enough to catch his breath, and then thrown back in. I can't help but feel that this has all the earmarks of torture. But I brush the word from my mind. After all, I live in a civilized country that prohibits such things. Besides, I'm still new to this post, and there must be some reasonable rationale for this punishment that I'm missing, although I'm hard pressed to figure out what it could be.

Diaz mops his forehead with a bandanna. "Medical can stitch him up," he says, "but if we put him back in, he'll just tear out the stitches—smash his skull right open—I'm sure of it."

"If we let him out," says Pete, "we're going to get copycats, but if we don't, this is only going to get worse."

As acting chief, they look to me for a final answer. I want to give this kid a break, and I'm relieved that these two veterans of punitive segregation seem to want the same. "I don't think we can let this go any further," I say. "If somebody else tries the same thing, we'll just have to deal with it."

"Agreed," says Diaz.

"Listen," Pete says, "we better do something quick."

A loud moan comes from Jackson's cell, and we rush back in just as the young man's head thuds against the concrete. Blood is freely spilling now, the gash in his scalp revealing a patch of glinting whiteness.

"Please, Mr. Jackson," I say. "We're trying to help you. We're going to get you out. Just give us a chance here! Troy, please!"

But Troy Jackson, beyond words, crumples to the floor.

"You're coming out," says Diaz, leaning over him. "It's over. It's over now!"

"Cap–tain!" the officer shouts. "We got one comin' out."

With our decision made, I start back down to the clinic to begin the mountain of paperwork this transfer requires. On my way out, I move quickly past the cells, past the clamoring fists and pleading palms. In a day or two, we'll be standing at any one of these other doors, faced with another scene of human desperation. Most won't be as lucky as Jackson. For most, we simply offer words of encouragement and walk away, deeming them not yet decompensated enough to warrant the bus trip out. I try not to think about it. One day at a time.

On the ground floor, the big barred gate is inching open to allow a new shift of officers to enter. I bolt through. Wending through cooler corridors, I walk alongside general population inmates who are headed to work details or to the law library. As I pass by the jail's main entryway booth, officers glance up from their paperwork and wave. In some ways it's almost pleasant. I manage a weak smile and with a quivering hand wave back, all the while struggling to blot out the white gleam of Troy Jackson's bare skull.

1

_____

ON A GRAY SEPTEMBER MORNING IN 1991, I STOOD IN front of Bloomingdale's on Manhattan's Upper East Side, eagerly waiting for my ride. As a graduate student at Columbia University's School of Social Work, I was beginning a yearlong internship at Rikers Island. I would report to New York City's notorious correctional complex three days a week to provide emotional and psychiatric support to incarcerated women. While most people would balk at the mere thought of working with criminals, as soon as I learned about this assignment, I was intrigued. It incorporated my most important aspirations: to help the poor and underprivileged and to become a psychotherapist. The fact that the poor and underprivileged in this setting were also accused of crimes barely fazed me. Already in my mid-thirties, I had prior experience, not only with people in emotional distress, but with the incarcerated.

I grew up during the sixties in a middle-class family on suburban Long Island. My father was a lawyer, and my mother was a homemaker and, later, a high school English teacher. Altruism was encouraged, both at home and in the Catholic school I attended. Even though our primary exposure to crime and racial strife came by way of the evening news, we were taught that helping the less fortunate was our responsibility, an ideal I took to heart. But it wasn't only inner-city turmoil that flashed across the TV screen. The whole country was grappling with waves of change during the sixties, and I remember being drawn to the grainy images of the civil rights marches. Even then, I felt strongly about justice and fairness, not yet realizing that years later, despite all the country's strides forward, I would discover a world beyond the reach of the six o'clock news, where inhumanity had found a whole new mode of ugly expression.

As the oldest of seven children in a family that was as loving as it was dysfunctional, I often found myself in the role of listener and peacemaker. Sometimes at the kitchen table my mother would take off her glasses and rub her eyes, and I would listen as she told me how overwhelmed she felt by the day-to-day demands of raising a large family. Then she would replace her glasses, smile, and pat my arm. But I knew she felt a little better for having been heard. Everyone needs to be heard.

In school, I was the one friends brought their troubles to. Whether it was anxiety over grades, fear for a parent battling cancer, or boyfriend woes, I quietly listened, noticing that as my pals talked things through, they usually felt better. Early on, I discovered that simply being heard is a great soother of life's intangible hurts and struggles.

After college, I volunteered at a Boston-based suicide prevention hotline called the Samaritans. No longer was I talking just with family and friends; now I was comforting total strangers. Whether it was an isolated elderly person who needed to talk or a distraught young man thinking about ending it all, I listened, allowing them to express their deepest levels of despair. And like a pipe releasing steam, more often than not their tears dried and their depression lifted. At least for the moment, they found the peace and relief that comes from being deeply heard by another. I couldn't imagine being part of something more important.

And then I decided to take things a step further. The Samaritans operated several outreach programs, one of them being a novel jailhouse program. The program had come about when a rash of suicides at Boston's Charles Street Jail prompted alarm among city officials, who turned to the Samaritans. The result was Lifeline, a program designed to teach a group of inmates the same suicide prevention techniques we used on the hotline. In a setting better known for prisoners yelling "Jump!" to a despondent inmate posturing to end his life, it was hard to imagine incarcerated men coming together like this. But they did. Not only that, but after the Lifeline intervention, the annual suicide rate, which had been approaching double digits, dropped to zero.

I found this astonishing—proof positive of the power of the human connection! I also knew I had to be part of it. The Lifeline team went into the jail every Wednesday night to support the Samaritan inmates, and on a cold winter evening I joined my fellow volunteers on the jailhouse steps for the first time. At twenty-three, I was the youngest in the crew. Nervous but eager, I followed along as guards led us through barred gates until we reached a room where five inmates sat behind a long table. As we took our place across from them, they did not seem particularly threatening but rather ordinary, save for the elaborate tattoos that decorated their forearms. After introductions were made, the Lifeline leader asked the men about their week as "jailhouse Samaritans." They unfolded their crossed arms, and their hard faces softened as they took turns describing how they'd tried to comfort the despairing and suicidal in their own ranks. Of particular concern was a newly arrested inmate named Johnny, who was crying and leaving his food tray untouched. Anthony and Lamar, the most extroverted of the five, had approached him. "We asked him if he wanted to talk a little," said Anthony, "you know—about how he was feeling and stuff."

"He looked kinda surprised," the ponytailed Lamar deadpanned.

"Yeah," Anthony laughed, "to say the least. But he took us up on it, he talked, all right. Flat out told us he was thinking about stringing up a sheet. Then he lost it—cried like a baby. Told us he'd never been arrested before, that he'd lose his job, didn't know how his family was going to get by, and was scared to death. And we just let him talk. We didn't interrupt him."

"And when he was done," said Lamar, "we told him we'd be with him. And he kept on saying, 'Thank you, Thank you.' Later on, he called his wife and looked a little calmer when he got off. He may have even eaten a little. But we're going to keep an eye on him."

"Well done!" said the Lifeline leader. As the rest of us joined in, acknowledging their fine efforts, Anthony and Lamar were beaming. As the evening wore on, I melded into the conversation, and by the time the session ended, I'd almost forgotten where I was. After that night I became a Lifeline regular, and those Wednesday evening jailhouse visits were a cherished part of my week. Although I never did learn why those five men had been arrested, in terms of our particular mission, it didn't matter. But what did matter to me was that I was supporting the goodness and humanity in the world—even in this unlikeliest of places.

My Samaritans experience was so profound that I moved back to New York and cofounded the Samaritans of New York. Without forms to fill out or payment to be negotiated, New Yorkers in emotional distress could call our hotline for a caring human connection. I became the hotline's first executive director and expanded the operation to include a speakers' bureau on suicide prevention and Safe Place, a group forum for those who'd lost a loved one to suicide. I was especially pleased to have assisted the NYPD in producing a suicide prevention film that was shown to all incoming cadets. Yet as fulfilled as I was, six years later I had grown weary of fund-raising, budgets, and board issues. From my paper-strewn desk, I watched our volunteers taking calls from phones that I hadn't answered in years. Hard as it was to leave something I'd helped to create, I needed to get back to what made me feel most alive—working directly with people. But this time, instead of fleeting encounters with hotline callers, I wanted continuity with those in emotional distress. I wanted to see if I might facilitate lasting change.

It was on the heels of my departure from the hotline that I enrolled in the clinical track at Columbia's School of Social Work. In preparation for our first field assignment, we were asked to rank our top three picks among a number of options. As I scanned the predictable list of settings, I spotted "Correctional Facility." As soon as I saw it, I smiled, recalling those Wednesday nights in the Charles Street Jail. The years had done little to dim my memory of the Samaritan inmates. Had they been released? I wondered. If so, how were they faring? What if I was able to help inmates like them in a deeper way? While they may have committed crimes, the incarcerated were still people—people capable of growth and compassion—as the Samaritan inmates had demonstrated. What if I could sit down with them and really listen to their stories? Insightful therapy sessions could lead to change—change that would translate to happier, jail-free lives following release. A win-win for all!

I didn't really need to think about it for long. In the box next to "Correctional Facility," I inked in the number 1.

* * *

I was lost in thought, trying to imagine what the year ahead would bring, when a white Bonneville pulled up. Inside were three of my fellow students, all of whom I'd met during a series of orientations for this unusual assignment. Unlike me, they were none too pleased. In the back was Allison, freshly graduated from college. Allison had battled unsuccessfully for a transfer to a more conventional setting, and as I hopped in next to her, she stared ahead through steel-rimmed glasses, barely managing a smile. In the front was Maureen, a middle-aged woman with short, dark hair who'd raised her family and was fulfilling a lifelong dream of helping the impoverished. Although initially apprehensive about Rikers, once she learned her clientele would be female, Maureen was content. But our driver, Wendy, with a ginger-colored bob and a smattering of freckles, was not. "I never said anything about wanting to work in a jail!"

Wendy was outraged. "And those supervisors! I mean, come on! It's one thing to be forced into this for school, but to *choose it!* Either they're out of their minds or they're *loo–sers!*"

"Yes," Allison agreed, "losers!" Maureen chuckled, and I said nothing.

The supervisors they referred to were members of the Rikers Mental Health staff who had come up to school to meet us. Each of us had been paired off with one of these veterans who would oversee our work in the year ahead. My supervisor was a tall Black woman named Janet Waters. With a stately bearing and a quiet dignity, she smiled shyly when we shook hands. "I think you got yourself a good assignment, Mary," she said in a soft drawl that hinted at her Alabama roots. I liked Janet immediately. Anything but a loser, here was someone with a sense of purpose—exactly what I'd hoped for in a supervisor! I didn't really know what I was getting into, but meeting Janet felt like an affirmation that I was on the right track.

With the Manhattan skyline fading behind us, we crossed the Queensboro Bridge and drove through the tree-lined streets of Queens and its neat brick houses, a rather unlikely route to what was then the largest correctional facility in the nation. Yet not one sign hinted that the massive complex was nearby. With maps to guide us, we found our way to an intersection in the quiet neighborhood of East Elmhurst, where a billboard jutted out, announcing the Rikers entryway. Shields and emblems shaded in the Department of Correction's colors of orange and royal blue flanked either side of the huge sign. Prominent city officials were listed at the top, and underneath were the names of ten jails—nine for men, one for women. Scrolled across the bottom was the Department of Correction's proud motto: "New York's Boldest!"

Around a corner, a long, narrow bridge stretched out over the gray water, guarded by a couple of security booths. A man in a navy blue uniform stepped out as we pulled up. "Good morning, Officer," we chimed, holding up silver beaded chains with our newly issued ID badges attached. We were under strict orders to address correctional personnel as "Officer," or "CO," referring to their title of Correction Officer. Operating in the shadows of the touted NYPD, the jails' keepers bristle at the word *guard* and gripe that they aren't accorded due respect for patrolling New York City's "toughest precinct," especially since they don't carry guns inside the jails. "Remember," we were cautioned at the orientation, "You are guests in *their* house!"

The man did not respond to our friendliness; instead, he leaned into the car window, studying the IDs, carefully comparing our photos to our faces. There would be nothing cursory about this inspection. Without smiling, he stepped back and waved us on.

The narrow span rose up as we drove over the dark waters of the East River. Choppy waves slopped against the pilings, and seagulls cawed and hovered about the lampposts. In the heavy mist, the blinking lights of the runways at nearby LaGuardia Airport were so close that jets hurtling for takeoff appeared to be gunning right for us before angling up sharply and thundering overhead. As we pressed on, the car filled with a rank odor from a sewage treatment plant on the Queens shoreline. We gasped and ran up the windows, fast. "Geez," said Maureen. "If the city was looking for a crummy place to put criminals, they sure found it!"

At the crest of the bridge, we fell silent as the island unfolded like a bland industrial plant. Municipal-type buildings were scattered about, connected by a maze of roadways, each one encircled with chain-link fencing topped with rolls of barbed wire. A belt-type road skirted the perimeter, where security jeeps, throwing off long yellow beams, patrolled the river's edge.

Rikers Island was originally purchased by the city in 1884 from the Ryker family, descendants of seventeenth-century Dutch settlers. For most of its history, the island was little more than an overgrown forest. During the Civil War, it served as a training compound for African American regiments. After that, the island sat empty until 1933, when someone thought it would make an ideal spot to tuck away accused criminals, and the first jail, the House of Detention for Men, was built. For the next twenty years, the accused were ferried across the river to city courts to face their charges. In 1954, landfill enlarged the island from 87 to its present 415 acres. This expansion marked the beginning of Rikers' development into a full correctional complex. In 1966, the three-lane, mile-long bridge was built, eliminating the need for ferries.

As we came off the bridge and onto the island, lines of exiting cars, trunks popped open, awaited inspection before crossing back to Queens. Correction officers in yellow rain slickers were crouched next to the cars, extending long poles with attached mirrors underneath each one, checking for an inmate desperate enough to cling to the undercarriage of a car to make it across the bridge—a grim reminder that this was no industrial plant.

We parked in a stadium-sized lot and walked to Control, a cavernous administrative building that visitors and workers must pass through before proceeding to the jail. Out in front, it was a chaotic scene as a city bus screeched to the curb and throngs of visitors exited, mostly dark-skinned women and frightened-looking children. One woman with a long braid looked up at me as she unfolded a flimsy stroller. With my pale skin and student backpack, I felt a little self-conscious. But she gave me a little smile, and I waved back. During our orientations, we had learned that Rikers is a jails complex. Unlike prisons, which house those convicted of crimes, jails house "detainees," those who may well be innocent of their charges but cannot afford bail as they await trial. Since money is the sole factor in determining whether or not bail is attainable, by default Rikers houses the poor. In most cases, the bail amount is less than $1,000. Most of these women's loved ones—primarily young Black and Hispanic males from New York City's most impoverished neighborhoods—couldn't scrape together even that.

The inside of Control was nothing more than a scattering of graffiti-scarred benches, a cement floor, and a few birds swooping through the rafters. Along the walls, ominous signs warned against cameras, recording devices, drugs, weapons, and other contraband with the threat of arrest for any violation. The idea that someone could be arrested while inside a jail complex struck me as a little funny, but no one here was amused. Long lines of tired visitors holding whimpering babies and lawyers in pinstriped suits waited at clerical windows for the necessary security passes. The four of us proceeded to rear turnstiles, where stone-faced COs once again compared our ID photos to our faces. With their grudging nods, we headed out to a bus depot and climbed aboard an orange-and-blue school bus bound for our destination, the Rose M. Singer Center.

The bus churned down the main roadway, and we pressed our faces to the windows for our first close-up view of this stark "campus." Large brick buildings with strange little slits for windows were situated haphazardly. Some were tucked back amid groves of trees; others sat closer to the road, with long armlike annexes reaching out to the curb. Smaller roadways fanned out from the main artery, accessing jails that were out of view. Each of these jails was governed by its own warden who oversaw a staff of deputy wardens (deps), captains, and a battalion of correction officers. The original House of Detention for Men stood prominently along the curb. A throwback to another era, the dark-brick HDM featured a cement stoop and a little yellow light over the front entrance.

Around a bend, Department of Correction buses were parked inside maintenance garages. As we pressed on, the scent of leavening bread from the island's bakery filled the damp, heavy air. An efficient world unto itself, the island was also strangely quiet, not an inmate in sight. We'd been told that recreation yards are contained within the interiors of the jails, meaning that inmates are never seen on the grounds. And since walking anywhere on the island was strictly forbidden for correctional personnel and civilians alike, the winding sidewalks and grassy lawns were eerily empty, save for flocks of grazing geese.

At an intersection, we waited while a parade of buses, their windows covered in steel mesh, lumbered up from smaller lanes, headed for the bridge. As the caravan swung around the corner, I could just make out the silhouettes of male inmates. Each day, a staggering one thousand detainees are shuttled to city courts for hearings and trials. However, despite high hopes of beating their charges and going home, for most this bleak island is simply the first stop on the way to an upstate prison. Alongside the jails, commercial buses were parked in wait. As cases are resolved, these coach buses travel up the New York State Thruway, delivering the newly convicted to Downstate Correctional Facility in Fishkill, New York, a massive processing center. From there, they are farmed out to one of seventy prisons, where they will serve sentences ranging anywhere from a couple of years to life. And in capital cases, there were those on this island who potentially faced death row.

After the bus traffic cleared, we turned down a tree-lined road that paralleled the river. Through the leaves of the old oaks and maples, the water rippled. Across the way, the Queens shoreline looked small and distant.

The bus ground to a halt in front of a hulking rectangular building, the American flag fluttering high above. "Rose Singer!" shouted the driver. At the jail's entryway, a female CO with fluorescent orange fingernails unlocked the door, checked our IDs, and admitted us into a bare-bones lobby furnished with a magnetometer and a small security desk. The yellow cinder-block walls were dominated by a framed portrait of Rose Singer, the jail's namesake. With a wry smile and upswept gray hair, Rose Singer was a lifelong advocate for incarcerated women. At the jail's dedication in 1988, she was quoted as saying that she hoped this facility would serve as "a place of hope and renewal for all the women who come here." Although a curious sentiment for a jail, as I gazed up at her picture, I thought I would have liked Rose Singer, and took her wish as a good omen for my year ahead.

2

AT THE ENTRYWAY GATE, OUR SUPERVISORS WERE WAIT-
ing. They helped us negotiate the main security booth, and when the
big gate inched open, they led us into the Rose Singer halls, where
looming cinder-block corridors reeked of pine-scented disinfectant.
Barred gates were swung open, and navy blue–uniformed officers
milled about, smoking cigarettes and chatting. There were no inmates in sight. Janet Waters, my superviser, explained that it was
"count time," one of several daily periods when inmates are confined
to their houses to be tallied up to ensure there hadn't been an escape.

Our destination was the clinic, and as we proceeded through
the halls, the officers stiffened at the sight of four unfamiliar faces,
their eyes latching onto our photo IDs. Allison clutched her pock-
etbook tightly, Wendy rolled her eyes, and Maureen made a soft
clucking noise. A light shiver ran down my back. This was not the
Charles Street Jail.

We stopped at a wide double doorway. Next to the entrance
was a plain hinged door. Janet rapped on this smaller door, and it
was snatched open by a stocky CO, big key ring at his waist. "Officer Overton!" Janet beamed. "Say hello to the new students—
they'll be with us for the next year."

But Officer Overton simply glared at us. "Baahhh" was about
all he managed before returning to a corner desk where he kept
watch over the Mental Health section of the clinic.

Janet rolled her eyes. "Don't worry, you'll get used to him."

The clinic's perimeter was lined with small offices for the staff—psychiatrists, psychologists, and therapists of master's degree level in either social work or psychology. Toward the rear was a makeshift conference room. With a rickety wooden table and a buzzing overhead light, this was the assigned space for the students, home base for the year. About the only point of interest were three small mesh-covered windows that ran the length of the outer wall. We threw our bags down and stood up on tiptoe to peer out. But other than a pile of broken cement and a chain-link fence, there was little to see, not even a tiny glimpse of the river. Allison slumped into a tan folding chair, pulled a calendar from her backpack and crossed off our first day, though it had barely begun. "One day down!"

"Oh, girls," Maureen smiled. "It's just going to take a little getting used to."

"Oh, ho!" said Wendy. "There's *a lot* we're going to have to get used to."

After settling in, we split up to meet with our supervisors. As I took a seat in Janet's office—a cramped cinder-block square she shared with a colleague—it occurred to me that jail affords no extra comforts to its civilian workers. But Janet didn't seem to mind. Seated behind a battered metal desk in a smart burgundy suit, she looked as graceful and assured as I'd remembered her back at school. As she poured us some tea, she filled me in. "There's over a thousand women in this jail, Mary—twelve hundred, to be exact—and the Mental Health Department is kept *verrry* busy. These women, they've been pulled away from home, family, children, and a lot of them are coming off drugs. They're in a bad way, and it's our job to get them stabilized, especially to prevent suicides—always a concern in here. We don't get involved in their legal cases; we work independently of the courts. Our mission is to treat these women for however long they're here on Rikers."

"You mean, until they go to trial?" I asked.

"Well . . . until they leave. Very few go to trial, Mary. It's not like TV. They usually accept a plea bargain offer, and then it's off to Bedford Hills Prison."

"Oh," I said, absorbing this surprising bit of information.

"But for however long they're here—weeks, months, or even years—we try to give them the best treatment possible. Most of them have had pretty crummy lives, you'll see."

"Are we talking rehabilitation?" I asked.

"Not exactly. More like stabilizing. We try to stabilize them with medication and therapy to get them out of acute crisis. But that's not to say you won't be doing in-depth work with some of them. It's just a question of how long they're here on Rikers."

As we sipped tea and chatted, a growing din in the corridors was turning into a roar. Janet glanced at her watch. "Count just cleared—they're coming out of their houses now. Off to work, mess hall, the clinic. Let's get started," she smiled. "I'd like to show you the receiving room—it's where the newly arrested are processed, issued IDs, given medical screenings, and assigned beds. There's someone I need to check on. If she needs follow-up, I'll assign the case to you. After that, we'll visit the Mental Observation Unit— it's where we house the suicidal and mentally ill. And while we're there," she said, "I have another case in mind for you."

As Officer Overton unlocked the clinic door, I was so taken with the idea of my own cases that I barely realized we were stepping into halls that were now crowded with inmates. Janet melded easily into a noisy throng that would have reminded me of a high school corridor between classes if not for the officers who stood watch—both male and female. I stuck close to her as we walked alongside women who bore the markings of hard lives—toothless smiles, ripped ear lobes, and jagged scars across their cheeks. The women were mostly young, and all were Black or Hispanic. The attire was jeans, sneakers, and sweats—permissible because they were detainees and therefore presumed innocent. But clipped to each woman's shirt was also a big photo ID with a ten-digit case number beneath the photo.

The crowd seemed unfazed by our presence, although someone recognized Janet. "Hello, Miss Waters!" Janet's response was friendly but restrained.

On the outer edges of the crowd, I noticed emaciated women with ghostlike stares shuffling along in baggy, billowing clothes. Janet leaned down and whispered, "Crack addicts—just arrested. Couple of months in here, off drugs, they'll come back to life, you watch."

I tried not to stare at these eerie figures, but I wondered about Janet's assertion that they would "come back to life" in here. Could they have done so on their own? Maybe jail wasn't such a bad thing for them. Maybe it was just the intervention they needed. I hoped I could be a part of it.

But it wasn't exactly a pleasant intervention. Although street clothes were permitted, hats were not allowed outside the housing areas, and somewhere in the sea of women, a red kerchief was bobbing along. An officer reached out a tattooed arm and snatched it off the head of a startled young woman. "What the fuck you doing?" he roared. "Not in *my jail,* you don't!"

Janet sighed but said nothing, and we continued on, our progress slowed by barred gates that were now shut. At each one, we held up our ID badges to officers who opened them and just as quickly locked them up again. There was no easy movement through the jail, as passageways were sectioned off from one gate to the next.

As we neared the jail's entryway, Janet nodded to the CO who stood guard over the receiving room. As he fussed with keys, I could already hear the clamor on the other side. "Brace yourself," Janet said. The door swung open to reveal cages—floor-to-ceiling bullpens where mobs of disheveled women were pressed in tightly. With arms flailing through the bars, they sobbed and cried out, *"I'm hungry. I need to call my mother. I didn't do anything! I'm cold. Help me!"* Their pleas were directed at officers, seated behind a large console, who never looked up.

The sight of human beings in cages caught me off guard. It felt utterly barbaric, and my knees began to wobble. I glanced at Janet, who seemed unperturbed. Yet I knew she cared. Somehow, Janet managed to go about her work, holding herself above the sad fray. I didn't know how she did it, but if I was really going to do this work, I had to toughen up.

Behind the console was an open rear door. The skies had cleared, a blue sky now beckoned, and a bus sat idling. A line of seven women, each one handcuffed to a single long chain, were being led off the bus. Some wore sneakers, others flip-flops, whatever they'd been wearing at the unexpected point of arrest. With eyes swollen from crying, they looked exhausted and defeated.

"Incoming bodies!" a CO shouted. His colleague eyed the arriving line and shook his head. "Too many goddamned bodies—not enough beds!"

Bodies?

I followed Janet to a nurses' booth where cursory mental health screenings were part of the intake process. A nurse handed Janet a chart. "Her name's Tiffany Glover. First time in, doesn't look good—thought you should have a look."

Off to the side, a single holding pen held the inmate in question. A CO unlocked it and told Tiffany Glover to step out. No older than twenty, with her hair pulled into a ponytail, she reminded me of a deer, her long skinny legs set off by a pair of bony knees. Wearing a T-shirt over her emaciated frame, Tiffany Glover resembled the stick figures in the halls—the crack addicts.

Janet told Tiffany who we were and asked her how she was feeling. But the sad young woman simply stared at the floor.

"We're going to help you," Janet said, eyeing the pink scars that crisscrossed the young woman's forearms.

"I wanna go home," she whispered. "I'm not a criminal."

"Tiffany," said Janet. "I understand this is your first time in jail. Are you having any thoughts of hurting yourself?"

"I wanna go home."

Although it was a safe bet that everyone wanted to go home, with her slumped shoulders, no eye contact, and a propensity for cutting herself, I could see why the drooping Tiffany Glover was a particular concern.

"Tiffany," said Janet, "we're going to help you while you're in here. We're going to transfer you to a special house, and Miss Buser here is going to work with you. We'll give you some medicine so you won't feel so depressed. We're going to help you get through this, okay?"

I tried to offer Tiffany a little smile, but she never looked up. Large teardrops were rolling down her cheeks. Other than being told she could get back on the bus and leave, I don't think anything would have comforted Tiffany Glover in that moment.

From the thick folder that Janet carried with her, she pulled out a transfer form and showed me how to fill it out. She handed it to the officers at the console, instructing them to house Tiffany Glover on the Mental Observation Unit.

As Tiffany was ushered back into the pen, Janet cautioned me about the heightened suicide risk for first incarcerations. "She'll come around, but right now I'd rather play it safe."

As we walked past the pens to leave, a sobbing older woman in a floral housecoat was waving to us frantically. In broken English, she tearfully cried, "*Por favor! Ay dios mio!* I live my sister and my sister son, I take care him—I go get milk before sister go work—she clean office at night, in city—I go corner," she said, her voice starting to break, "*policía, policía* come—they put to wall. Me, me no have drug. I tell *policía*, I buy *leche*, but he say me, 'Shut fuck up!' I get milk," she said pointing to her feet, to the fuzzy blue slippers she was wearing when she ran out for the milk. "My sister, she no phone—she know . . . where I go! *Ay dios mio!*"

"Looks like she was picked up in a drug sweep," Janet said. "Okay, hold on," Janet told her, as she opened up her notebook.

I knew of the infamous drug sweeps that are carried out regularly in the city's poorer neighborhoods as part of the federal "War on Drugs." These sweeps cast a wide net, and it's not unusual for the innocent to be swept up with the guilty. While this woman may have been mixed up with drugs, she could just as easily have been in the wrong place at the wrong time, and, if so, the idea that she could have been plucked off the street like this was frightening.

Janet jotted down her name. "I'll have someone from Social Services call you," she told the woman. "They'll help you write a letter to your sister, so she knows where you are."

"The least we can do," Janet muttered. "I'm sure she's got no money for bail, so she'll sit here for a few months while her case gets sorted out."

A few months! Her sister would find out where she was through a letter! It seemed inconceivably primitive, but there was Janet, jotting it all down.

"Gracias, gracias!" the woman said, wringing her hands together.

I doubt she understood what Janet was saying, but she seemed grateful for this little bit of attention.

While we waited at the exit door, the bar-banging and shouting had grown deafening, and one CO was no longer ignoring it. A short officer with bulging biceps charged out from behind the console and shouted, *"Shut up! Shut up, motherfuckers! Shut the fuck UPPP!"*

The receiving room went stone silent, save for quiet sobbing and the idling bus.

"Come on, Mary, let's go," Janet said. She didn't have to ask twice.

Out in the hall, I said to Janet, "How could he speak to those women like that?"

Janet sighed. "I'm afraid you're going to see a lot in here that'll be upsetting. Some COs are a lot worse than him. But we're not going to change their behavior, Mary. We walk a fine line in here— remember, this is their house, and we're guests. If we're going to do our work in here—and we do a lot of good for these inmates—then there are things we have to overlook. We're going to help Tiffany Glover, and that's what we need to stay focused on."

I saw her point. I would try to keep my eye on the bigger picture.

"Now," Janet said, "Our next stop is the Mental Observation Unit. Ever since the state started shutting down the big psych hospitals, the mentally ill just can't cut it on their own. They get in trouble with the police, usually for petty, stupid things, and they wind up in here. To take care of them, most of the jails on the island have a Mental Observation Unit, or 'MO' as we call it. It's where each jail houses its mentally ill inmates, those with schizophrenia, bipolar disorder, dementia. It's also where we place inmates at risk for suicide."

As we continued through the halls, we passed a series of barred gates that lined the walls. Next to each one was a big black number. "These are the entryways to their houses," Janet explained. "And the number just identifies the house—it's the address, so to speak. The houses, as they're called, are where the women essentially live, where they shower and sleep." At one of these barred gateways that lined the halls, Janet stopped, and my soft-spoken supervisor rapped on the bars. "ON—THE—GATE!" she shouted. As the gate shuddered and started moving, she winked at me. "Jail language." Once inside, we stepped into the "bubble," a Plexiglas booth where we were greeted by a chubby CO in a worn-out swivel chair who passed us a logbook. In front of his desk, a broad picture window looked directly into a cellblock, where mentally ill inmates milled about. "Hello, Miss W," the congenial officer said. Janet introduced me to Officer Timlinson, who took an immediate interest in my jailhouse education. "This is what's called a protected house," he said. "These MO inmates, they don't mingle with general population [GP]. Their meals are brought here, they don't go to the clinic—the doctors and nurses come here, for their own protection. We keep a good eye on them."

We thanked him, stepped out of the bubble, and waited for him to "pop" the door leading onto the MO. Never having been in a psychiatric ward before, I was clutching my notebook tightly. But nothing happened when we walked in. In the middle of an old linoleum floor bordered by a long row of sulfur-colored cell doors, a dozen or so women, looking slightly "off," sat in colored plastic chairs around a big TV set. I immediately recognized these women as those sad but familiar figures often seen on the city landscape, prowling the subways in tattered clothes and standing on street corners ranting and raving to the world and no one—the sorry souls that the rest of us sidestep.

Now, they were stabilized on Rikers Island, rocking back and forth, lightly tapping laceless sneakers to the floor.

"Side effects of their meds," Janet said, referring to the tapping. "But even with the side effects, they're doing a whole lot better than they were out on the streets." She also explained the missing shoelaces. "We take away belts and shoelaces when they're admitted, to thwart any suicide plan." Fixtures that could potentially be used for a hanging also had been removed. As a further precaution, two GP inmates with laced-up sneakers and belted jeans sat at either end of the unit. "Suicide prevention aides," Janet explained. "They alert us to any self-destructive behavior. It's the highest-paying jailhouse job," she added. "Ten bucks for a forty-hour workweek."

Around the shower area there was a little drama as a Mental Health worker tried to persuade a newly admitted patient into showering. Not yet stabilized, the poor woman was filthy. With the promise of a few cigarettes, she relented. "Go on! Don't forget the soap! Soap is your friend!" An officer stood by with clean clothes from the jail's clothes box.

Just like Officer Timlinson, these COs seemed kind and helpful, and Janet told me that these MO officers all had undergone training to understand the special needs of the mentally ill.

"Now, let's see," Janet said, scratching her head. "Let's find Annie Tilden. She's a paranoid schizophrenic who stays to herself, and I'd like you to start working with her."

A CO jumped up to help out. At cell number three, she pounded on the door. "Tilden! You in there?"

A pair of eyes darted out at us through the little window.

"Get dressed and come out!" the officer ordered.

Shortly, Annie Tilden emerged, looking a little woozy, as though she'd been sleeping.

"Hello, Annie," Janet said as we stepped up to meet her.

Annie Tilden said nothing, but simply stared at Janet. Heavyset, with mocha-colored skin and wiry hair pulled back into a clip, she seemed mesmerized.

"How are you feeling today?" Janet continued. "Taking your meds?"

"Yes, Miss Waters," she uttered robotically.

"Good. Now, Annie, I'd like you to meet Miss Buser. She's a student intern and she's going to be working with you."

"Nice to meet you," I offered.

But Annie Tilden just looked at me with a blank expression.

"So," Janet continued, as if Annie had responded, "Miss Buser will be coming to see you. All right then, that's all."

Annie Tilden started back to cell number three, but not before I tried to make some little connection with her. "I look forward to meeting with you!" But she never looked back, and the cell door slammed shut.

"That's okay," said Janet. "A lot of schizophrenics don't do well socially—nothing personal. Your relationship with her will be a lot different than women from GP. Focus on her medication. That's what's most important with the mentally ill. The two of you can go upstairs and talk. There's a couple of empty cells up there that we use for sessions."

I looked up to the second tier, where Mental Health staff were chatting with patients in open-door cells. I hadn't anticipated conducting therapy sessions inside a jail cell, but as Janet looked at me expectantly, I said, "Okay."

On our way out, we passed the rocking women peacefully planted in front of the TV. Janet shook her head. "When I first started working here, we had a few mentally ill inmates here and there, but now, the numbers are huge. They don't belong in here. It's no way for a civilized society to treat its mentally ill. But here they are. Jail's their new home. It's really sad."

3

IN THE DAYS THAT FOLLOWED, MY TOUR OF THE JAIL
continued, and I met more key officers and clinic staff. But it was
an afternoon agenda that I was most excited about, which was accompanying Janet to a support group for new mothers. During our
orientations, we had learned that within the barricaded world of
Rikers Island was a nursery. A pilot program, we were told, one
of only three in the entire country. If a pregnant inmate gives birth
while incarcerated, the baby can stay for a year, the idea being that
it's best for the baby to be with its mother for that first year. After
that, though, the child must leave, before developing an awareness
of its surroundings.

We set out early one afternoon, trekking through the corridors
until we reached what was obviously the nursery entrance, a door
with a Mickey Mouse decal and the civility of a doorbell. Janet
pushed the bell, and a female officer unlocked the door and led us
down a narrow passageway where the delicate sounds of newborns
echoed strangely off the concrete and steel. The passage opened into
a softly lit, carpeted nursery, where kerchiefed mothers, most little
more than teenagers, tended to their babies, bottle-feeding the infants, changing diapers, and patting the babies' backs. Others were
sitting in a glass-walled "living room," tots on their laps. Outside
the living room, neat rows of cribs were filled with stuffed animals
and crocheted blankets. The cell doors that lined the walls—the

cells where the mothers slept—were the only feature to remind us where we were.

Nurses' aides kept a watchful eye, and the nursery director supervised the operation from a windowed office. The nameplate on the window read "Camille Baxter, R.N." Janet rapped on Baxter's open door, and the nursery director hopped up from behind piles of papers to greet us. Fortyish, she wore red-framed eyeglasses, a white lab coat, and stylish high heels. She pumped my hand when Janet introduced us. "Welcome!" she beamed. "Glad you're on board. These mothers need all the support they can get. Living in the nursery is a big cut above general population, but it's not an entitlement—it's a privilege. If these girls don't toe the line, they can be expelled and their baby sent home. Before they were arrested, most of them were out on the streets, using drugs, barely able to take care of themselves. Now they're expected to be model inmates, model mothers, model people. It's a tall leap, gets wild in here sometimes, doesn't it, Janet?"

But Janet just smiled and moved to the center of the nursery. "Ladies, group is starting!"

In the living room, we joined the early arrivals, and following Janet's lead, I sat down on the couch alongside the mothers, an arrangement that was cozier than I'd expected. But it felt natural, and I was immediately drawn to the babies, who cooed and gurgled, oblivious to their circumstances. Seated next to me, a dark-haired girl was cradling her baby for me to admire. "This is Teresita, my little pink princess." Adorned in a pink satin headband, Teresita looked up from her bottle to give me a gummy little smile.

"Nice to meet you, Teresita!"

"And I'm Marisol," her mother whispered as the room came to order.

Janet started things off by introducing me to the group, who were semi-interested in my presence. Carmen smiled shyly; Tasha and Swanday, seated together at the end of the couch, shrugged. Addie and Michelle, both fussing with their babies, managed a quick wave. Kim and Josette stifled yawns but still nodded politely.

The gangly Millie, with a neon orange pick planted atop thick tufts of hair, said, "Yeah, hi," without looking up. And in a rocking chair angled off to the side was Lucy, who said nothing. Like the women in the halls, all of these mothers were Black or Hispanic.

"So, how's everyone doing this week?" Janet started.

"Stresssssed," they chimed in unison.

"Very stressed," said Michelle, a slight girl with neat braids. "I don't know what's happening with my case, and I can never reach my lawyer. And I'm grateful to be here in the nursery, of course, but it's one thing after the next: chores, parenting classes, Narcotics Anonymous, nutrition classes—"

"Yeah," Kim agreed. "It's a lot, but we're trying." With a light scar running from ear to mouth, Kim looked old and tired for her short years.

"For me," said Addie, clinging tightly to the little bundle in her arms, "I love Jacy so much, but the longer I have her, the harder it's gonna be to let her go. My lawyer's talkin' about a three-to-six. Jacy'll go to foster care. I just hope my baby gets a good home—that's all."

As Addie bit back tears, a painful silence fell over the room. Addie seemed nice enough. Looking at her round friendly face framed by a white kerchief, I wondered what she could possibly have done to merit such a harsh punishment. And as baby Jacy's tiny hand reached up and cupped her mother's chin, I tried not to think of what the split would mean for this fragile new life.

I glanced at Janet, who was smoothing her skirt, taking it all in. "Well, now," she said, comfortingly, "we just have to take things a day at a time—that's the key here—a day at a time."

"About all we can do, Miss Waters," said Carmen. "But it's so hard; we don't know how our cases are going to turn out, whether we're going home—or to prison. We don't know if we'll be able to hold on to our babies or lose them. Some days it's just so hard."

But not everyone was perturbed. "Well, I know *one* thing," Millie piped up. "Calvin's my sixth, and I'm gonna hold on to *this* one." But while Millie beamed, little Calvin was sliding off her lap.

At the far end of the couch, Tasha and Swanday were whispering, sharing a little laugh at Millie's speech.

"What's so funny?" Millie said, struggling to pull Calvin back up, the orange pick flopping out of her hair.

"Hey," Janet said to Tasha and Swanday, "we're not having private conversations here!"

"What's so funny?" Millie demanded.

"It's okay, Millie," said Janet. "It's okay now."

But it was not okay. Millie jumped up from the couch, Calvin no longer in her lap but dangling from his armpit with Millie gripping him like a ragdoll.

"Millie!" Janet gasped. *The baby!* Janet was on her feet, her clipboard and folders scattering to the floor, long arms outstretched. "Give me the baby, Millie, give me the baby!"

But Millie, shaking in hurt and rage, heard none of it. "Ya rotten bitches," she quivered. "I hate you. I hate all of you!" As she shook her arms for emphasis, the baby also shook.

Janet was inching closer. "Give me the baby, Millie! Give me the baby!" With a calculated lunge, Janet grabbed poor little Calvin, just as Millie was returning to her senses.

Janet handed the shrieking child over to Camille Baxter, who'd rushed in with nurses' aides and an alarmed officer in tow. As Baxter nestled the child against her lab coat, a weeping Millie reached out for her son. *"Cal–vin!"*

"Oh, no, miss!" said Baxter, reeling back. "*Now* you want to be a good mother? Doesn't work like that! Go to your cell—now!"

Millie stormed out, her own wails even louder than her son's cries. The spectacle over, the crowd disbursed and the mood turned somber. Accusing looks were shot in the direction of a subdued Tasha and Swanday. After a few more minutes of strained conversation, Janet opted to end things early. She set out the box of donuts she'd brought along, and the mothers lined up for a sugary treat. "See you next week," a few of them quietly said to me, taking a donut as they walked away.

On our way out, we stopped by the nursery director's office. "I don't know what I'm going to do with her," said a shaken Baxter. "She's always flying off the handle. After this stunt, she should be thrown out of here and sent back to GP. But I hate to do it—her charge isn't that serious and she's got a good shot at a drug program. If I boot her out, it all falls apart."

"Well, wait a minute now," said Janet. "What if we were to work with her? Help her develop some coping strategies, tide her over till she goes to the program?"

Baxter's face lit up. "Hey, couldn't hurt . . ."

"And Mary," Janet said, turning to me, "ready for another case?"

"Yes, sure," I said, taken a little off guard. "That would be fine."

Baxter instructed a nurse to summon Millie, and the sniffling mother reappeared.

"Millie," said Baxter, "how would you feel about meeting with Miss Buser for therapy? You're skating on very thin ice, miss!"

"Yes, that would be good," Millie mumbled.

As I smiled at Millie, I was trying to picture the two of us sitting down together, talking, maybe sharing a little laugh now and then. But as I grasped her limp hand, all I could really think was that this woman had already lost *five* children—and just jeopardized the life of her sixth. What could I say to her—in the space of a few therapy sessions, no less—that could possibly make any difference in this woman's life? Camille Baxter's words started booming in my head: *These girls had been out on the streets, using drugs, barely able to care for themselves* . . . As I looked around at the nursery, at the teddy bears and crib mobiles, my grand hopes of making a difference were dimming, and I began to wonder if this whole nursery program was nothing more than an artificial window imposed on hopeless causes.

I was looking down at the floor, feeling about as bleak as the cold cement walls, when there was a loud rap on the window. I looked up to see a beaming Marisol holding up her little pink princess. She was waving the baby's hand at me, in the same way Dorothy held Toto's paw when they were leaving Oz. Despite my sinking spirits, I laughed. Behind her, the others were feeding and rocking their little ones, smiling and gazing into their babies' eyes with such love that I could almost feel the bond between mother and child. There was so much at stake here—not only for the mothers, but also for these babies. Drug addicts or not, these mothers were first and foremost human beings, and it was far too soon for me to rule out the power of the human spirit. I'd be darned if I was going to let one incident discourage me. I waved back at Teresita and Marisol and resolved that if there was any way to help these women—even if the gains were modest—then I was determined to find it.

4

BY THE END OF THE WEEK, I HAD THREE WOMEN ON A caseload that would eventually build to nine—Annie Tilden, Tiffany Glover, Millie Gittens—and Janet gave me the green light to start. The therapeutic modality we were learning in school was called "insight-oriented" therapy, the general idea being that we were to meet our clients "where they were"—to try to see the world from their perspective, gain their trust, and then to gently help them to broaden their own insights. I was ready to find out where they were.

My first session, I decided, would be with Millie, followed by a trip to the MO to meet with Annie and Tiffany. I asked Officer Overton to summon Millie to the clinic, which was the procedure for contacting our GP "clients." While I waited, I returned to the conference room and reviewed various mental health forms. Wendy and Allison's clients had arrived promptly, and they were already meeting with them in semiprivate booths in view of correctional personnel but just out of their earshot. Despite all their grumbling, both were reluctantly acclimating to jail, and our car ride conversations were now filled with chatter about our developing caseloads. Maureen had been assigned to work with HIV-positive women exclusively, an assignment most would have found unenviable. But Maureen was delighted, which only reinforced my belief in the idea of a "calling" in life. After that, her schedule changed, and we didn't see much of Maureen for the remainder of the year.

After ten minutes had ticked by, I looked out at the crowded inmate waiting area—rows of plastic seats mounted on steel rods, much like those in a bus station—but Millie wasn't there. The women chatted quietly, although someone on an end seat held her face in her hands and wept. All at once a door banged open, and a thirtyish woman in a Tommy Hilfiger T-shirt bolted from a psychiatrist's office. "I can't believe he won't give me any sleeping pills! I'm stressed! I'm having real mental health problems and these people won't help me! What good are they!"

Officer Overton was on his feet, backed up by another CO. "Out!" he shouted, holding the door open. "Get the fuck out now!" yelled the other officer. "Back to your house!" The woman burst into tears and charged out, with Overton slamming the door behind her.

Although we'd been forewarned that sleep meds were a constant inmate request, it was the Mental Health Department's policy not to prescribe them. "We can't just hand them another pill," our supervisors explained. Instead, we were to dispense handouts entitled "Natural Techniques to Fall Asleep," which Janet told me went over like the proverbial lead balloon.

After the commotion died down, I ventured over to Overton's desk to be sure he'd called for Millie. Since our arrival, Overton had maintained a cool distance. We didn't even know his first name—and never would. Of all the information we were learning about life behind bars, we were told that, for security purposes, the first names of correctional personnel are never divulged. While the men were to be addressed as "Officer," with the women we had the option of "Officer" or "Miss."

Despite Overton's aloofness, I hoped things would get a littler friendlier, and it was with a warm smile that I asked him about Millie.

"Yeah, sure, I called her," he growled. "You wanna know why Millie Gittens hasn't come? I'll tell you why—she doesn't wanna come, that's why!"

"Excuse me?"

"Yeah, that's right," he said, looking up at me through horn-rimmed glasses. "She's got better things to do right now—probably busy smoking crack."

"What!"

"Yeah, that's right," he smirked.

I didn't know what to make of this guy, but I wasn't going to let him get the better of me. "Oh, I see. I didn't know the Department of Correction allowed drugs in here. That comes as a big surprise."

"Hey, you never know. Listen, let me clue you in—these inmates, they got a racket going on. They come in for the winter, lay up, eat, get off drugs . . . they come in all scrawny, then they get better and do it all over again."

"Yes—they've really got it made! If only we could all be so lucky! Listen, could you please call the nursery again?"

"Yeah, sure," he said, picking up the phone, grinning all the while.

I returned to the conference room, but when the clinic started emptying out for the afternoon count, I knew my first session with Millie Gittens would have to wait for another day. I was disappointed, but I still had Annie Tilden and Tiffany Glover on the MO, so I secured my ID, ignored Overton's smirk, and prepared to brave the hallways.

When I reached the protective cellblock, the the TV was blaring and a circle of women were parked in front of it. In a far corner, I spotted Tiffany Glover. The despondent waif from the receiving room was up and about, busy sweeping the cement floor. Walking over to her, I said, "Hello Tiffany. Do you remember me from the other day?"

She gave me a quick nod of recognition, but kept sweeping.

"How about if we sit down and talk a little?"

"No, thank you," she managed. "I won't be in here for long. This is all a mistake."

"Yes, well, maybe while your case is getting sorted out, it could be a good opportunity—"

"Listen," she said, stopping to face me. "I am not a *cri–mi–nal*. I'll be leaving soon so there's no point talking."

For someone so depressed, she certainly had a spark in her.

"Well, all right, but if you change your mind, I'm here," I offered, as she scooted away.

Staving off the sting of rejection, I tried to tell myself that it wasn't personal, that talking to me would mean she was actually participating in a jail program, and jail was something that Tiffany Glover wanted no part of. Still, I couldn't help but feel discouraged. First, Millie Gittens was a no-show, and now this snub by Tiffany Glover. Instead of the lively sessions that I'd imagined, I was standing alone on the MO, feeling self-conscious and out of place, gazing up at the second tier, where floor-to-ceiling chicken wire kept the despondent from jumping.

As I contemplated my next move, a slight woman with one eye bigger than the other sauntered up to me. "Did you see the Easter Rabbit last night? Did you?"

The picture of innocence, I couldn't imagine she could be held responsible for much of anything. Hard to believe our answer for her was Rikers Island.

"He was here—right here!" she insisted before running off to spread the news.

My last hope was the robotic Annie Tilden, who was nowhere in sight. Figuring she was asleep in her cell, I asked an officer to rouse her. While I waited, I reviewed my classroom directives on working with the mentally ill: *Stick to basics—medication and hygiene. Avoid emotionally stimulating conversations—they could trigger a decompensation.*

Medication and hygiene. Not too hard—assuming she would even come out and speak to me.

"Miss Buser," said the officer. "Your patient is ready."

Outside her cell stood a groggy Annie Tilden. I approached her a little warily. "Hello, Annie. Do you remember me from the other day?"

She regarded me with a hard stare. "Uh-huh," she finally uttered.

"Good! How about if we go upstairs where we can sit down and get a little acquainted?"

She gave a barely perceptible nod that I took as a yes, and I turned for the staircase, relieved that she was following. She was climbing slowly, though, clutching the waistband of her beltless jeans and taking care not to step out of her open sneakers.

"Take your time," I said.

As we reached the top, I noticed there were no other sessions in progress. We would be alone up here, which suddenly didn't seem like such a great idea. Although familiar with the mentally ill from a distance, I'd never actually spoken with one of these fragmented human beings. But there was no turning back now. I awkwardly entered an empty cell and sat down behind a little desk, with Annie Tilden taking her place across from me.

I folded my hands on the desk and cleared my throat. "So, Annie," I said, cheerfully, "I understand that you're taking medication. Do you feel it's working for you?"

She began a slow rocking motion, which I found a little unnerving. She also seemed to be glaring at me, but I told myself it only appeared that way because of her illness.

Finally, she said, "Yes."

"That's good—very good, great. And do you take it when you're supposed to? At the times the doctor has—"

"Yes."

"And are you having any problems with the meds? Any side—"

"No."

"Oh, okay. That's good." I fished around for something more on the topic. "You do realize, of course, that it's very important for you to continue to take them, otherwise . . ."

"Yes."

Well, that was it. The medication topic had been exhausted in less than one minute. Annie Tilden was rocking rhythmically now, her eyes boring straight into me, awaiting my next question. I flipped through my notebook, stalling as I considered topic number two—hygiene! Was I really supposed to ask this woman, whom I'd known for all of five minutes, how often she bathed? *No way!* The discussion of hygiene, which had seemed so plausible in the classroom, fell apart in real life.

Outside our makeshift office, laughter and snippets of conversation echoed up to the second tier. On an impulse, I decided to veer off the prescribed path. Pointing toward the door, I said, "The others are watching TV, playing cards, but you're always in your cell. How come?"

Her eyes narrowed and she rocked harder, back and forth.

I tried a friendly smile, but her mouth never budged. Annie Tilden was definitely glaring at me, and I didn't think it had anything to do with her illness, and even if it did, what difference did it make? An awful silence followed, just the two of us looking at each other. And then it dawned on me that she'd taken the seat closest to the door, a strategic error. I also became acutely aware that officers were nowhere nearby—they were meandering around on the main floor, chatting in the bubble. *What am I doing here?* I thought. *Sitting in a jail cell, no less! And to think—I had requested this!*

Just then, Annie Tilden stopped rocking, sat up straight, and pointed to the doorway.

I braced myself for I knew not what.

"You know what they watch on that TV?" she said.

"Excuse me?"

"You want to know why I stay in my cell, right?"

"Yes . . . *yes!*" I'd almost forgotten my question.

"That TV downstairs—you wanna know what they watch on it? Cartoons—listen."

I tuned in to the sounds from below, and sure enough, Bugs Bunny was chattering away.

"I'm not gonna watch cartoons," she said. "They're like little kids down there."

She might have been mentally ill, but this Annie Tilden was not unintelligent.

"I just want to do my time," she said. "Stay away from the troublemakers around the TV and get out of this place."

Although her tone remained flat and her face, expressionless, there was someone inside, and this someone was telling me about herself. I didn't know if I was supposed to be engaging her like this, but it sure beat going around in circles about medication.

"I'm gonna get released in December," she continued. "I'll be home for Christmas. The others downstairs—I'm different from them."

"How are you different?"

"I wasn't always like this," she asserted. "This is my first time in jail. I didn't always have schizophrenia, you know. I used to be a mail carrier."

"A mail carrier?"

"Bet you're surprised."

I sure was. "Really?"

"That's right. I worked for the Post Office for seven years. Hey, miss—do you know all the words to that saying, "Neither wind nor rain . . . ?""

"No, I don't."

"I didn't think so," she said, and a crooked little smile emerged. "Well, I do."

As she proceeded to recite the iconic postal slogan, I completely forgot I was sitting in a jail cell on Rikers Island. Like two old friends overdue for a reunion, Annie Tilden told me everything, how she had gone from gainfully employed postal worker to Rikers Island inmate. While working for the Post Office, her income was limited, and as a single mother with a mentally handicapped daughter, she hit on the idea of opening her home to a couple of boarders for a little extra money. "They weren't the down-and-out types, you know, so when they started smoking pot, I didn't think it was any big deal, and I started getting high with them. And then they started using harder drugs, and one thing just led to another."

At thirty-seven, Annie Tilden, the hardworking employee and mother of a special needs child, was lulled into the world of drugs. Tragically, these drugs were highly toxic to her brain, causing a drug-induced psychosis. She had no mental illness prior to her drug foray, but the residual effect was paranoid schizophrenia. She'd paid a terrible price for her drug use—her career, her freedom, her sanity. As I absorbed her story, I was struck by the utter devastation that drugs can cause. She was lucky to have come away from this with her life.

"A lot of bad things happened, miss," she acknowledged. "Very bad. But you know something—I gotta look at the positive. My daughter's with my sister, and that's where I'm going when I get out, and I'll never go through this again. I'll never wind up on the streets in rags, talking to myself. I'll always have to take the medication, but I'm going to get my life back—at least as best I can. And while I'm in here I'm not gonna take any chances on anything going wrong. I can watch TV when I get home—and it won't be Bugs Bunny."

Her odd, emotionless delivery never changed, but it didn't matter. I heard her, heard every word she said. I never expected such a connection with a paranoid schizophrenic, but there it was. When the session ended and I made my way back to the clinic, I sailed through the gates with a smile, ignoring the bewildered looks of the COs who opened them and locked them up again.

5

MY WORKDAY PACE WAS PICKING UP, AS WENDY, ALLI-
son, and I were now pitching in with the daily referrals. Inmates in
emotional distress came to the Mental Health Department's attention primarily through medical screenings and alert officers who
generated referral slips that were dropped off to us and placed in
a wire basket. Whether the emotional crisis was the shock of arrest, an AIDS diagnosis, a family death, or the trauma of a heavy
sentence, the basket was always overflowing, our waiting room a
daily mob scene.

Our highest priority was to identify the suicidal and mentally
ill, who were to be transferred out of general population and onto
the Mental Observation Unit; less critical situations called for supportive therapy, an appointment with a psychiatrist for medication,
or some combination of the two. But the appropriate action wasn't
necessarily obvious. Mental dysfunction is not an exact science;
there's nothing like a blood test to pinpoint bipolar disorder, types
of schizophrenia, or degrees of depression. A psychological assessment is largely a judgment call, and in the beginning our supervisors followed our assessments closely, especially after the three of
us started putting almost every person we met onto the MO as a
precaution, creating a mini-crisis. The permanent staff swiftly descended on our conference room. "Ladies! You can't put the whole

jail on the MO. Not everyone who's depressed is suicidal, and not everyone with messy hair is psychotic!" We were learning.

When I sat down to interview these women, I almost forgot they'd been accused of crimes. In a place where they were treated as nothing more than a number and a body, they seemed grateful for a little personal attention and were generally polite and well mannered. Although I needed to complete a lengthy intake questionnaire, I made a point of shaking hands and chatting a little, which helped to establish a rapport that eased the sting of the prying questionnaire a bit. One of the first questions dealt with the reason for arrest. The general responses painted a picture of drug possession, petty theft, prostitution, and shoplifting, or "boosting," as they called it. While I surmised that many were guilty as charged, I had resolved that if I was going to work with the incarcerated, then I needed to leave judgments to the courts and keep my focus on mental status.

As we moved into the "Family Background" section, the stories were painfully similar: growing up in the care of a drug-addicted mother, extension-cord lashings, empty refrigerators, abuse, fear, and neglect. As I took in the sad details, I wondered how I—or anyone, for that matter—would have turned out under similar circumstances. And what of their own children? When we reached this sensitive question, their eyes welled with tears as they confided that their kids were in foster care or, in luckier cases, with family members, often their own mothers—the very same mothers who'd once been addicts themselves. Instances of a formerly drug-addicted mother now raising grandkids would become a familiar theme. Many an inmate would recover from addiction too late to raise her own children, but would eventually straighten out and take over for her children's children, with her adult kids lost to the streets. Among the jail population, this is a tragic but common family scenario as the misery of drug addiction passes from one generation to the next.

I was often surprised by the twists and turns an assessment interview could take, and I was learning the utter importance of refraining from judgment. In one situation, the Social Services Department informed us that the husband of an inmate had been killed in a car accident, and it was up to us to break the news to her. "It's a tough one," Janet said, handing me the referral. "But it's important experience." Armed with a box of tissues, I went out to the waiting area where Daphne Cruz was perched on the edge of her seat, anxious to find out why she'd been summoned to the clinic.

I led her to a session booth and gently told her. But as I passed her the tissues, I was shocked to see that she was suppressing a smile. Her husband had just died in a terrible accident! But I caught myself and pulled back from judgment, resolving to let her tell her story, and I was glad I did.

Putting the tissues aside, I said, "I get the feeling that this isn't really such bad news."

"Oh, yes, yes, it is! It's just . . . terrible," she replied, trying to conceal her obvious joy.

"Look," I said, "it's okay to say how you really feel. It really is."

She probed my face for a moment to see if I meant it. Then she took a deep breath and the smile vanished. "Well, maybe I don't feel bad about it," she whispered. "Maybe I don't feel bad about it at all. Look, miss, I know that sounds terrible, but see, he was terrible—he used to beat me up, bad. He even burned me once with boiling water. Look!" she said, rolling up her sleeves to reveal ugly scars along her upper arms. "I wanted to take out a restraining order, but he said if I did it, he'd kill me—and he would have. I was like a walking dead person. And then a funny thing happened. I got arrested for selling drugs, little nickel and dime bags of reefer. At first, I thought going to jail was the end of the world. But when I got in here, *I was safe!* This is the one place in the world where he couldn't get me. After I was released I made sure I got arrested again, and as long as my son was with my sister, I was fine with it. You know, miss," she whispered, "There's worse things in life than coming to jail. Much worse."

This was not at all what I'd expected, but I understood. "It's over," I said softly. "It's over now."

"I'm free! I'm free!" she said, holding prayerful hands up to the heavens. "Thank you, God—thank you!"

I never saw Daphne Cruz again, and as she walked out of the clinic, I had the feeling that her jail days would soon be over for good.

* * *

Whenever I made a good connection with someone I'd met through the referral process, Janet would assign the case to me, and my caseload was building. Of my original three cases, I was meeting with Annie Tilden regularly, but I was discouraged that Tiffany Glover continued to hold me at arm's length. And I was thoroughly challenged by Millie Gittens, who never showed up. But as soon as Camille Baxter got wind of this, Millie was promptly delivered to the clinic.

"What happened?" I asked her. "Did you get my messages?"

"Yeah, sure I did—and I wanted to come, but Calvin was crying and I couldn't leave him. We can't just walk away, you know!"

There! Her explanation made perfect sense. There was a good reason she hadn't been coming.

As I spread out my intake forms, though, it bothered me that Millie was twisted around in her seat, straining to see who was in the waiting area. But she settled in, readily answering the intake questionnaire. Millie was twenty-seven years old and confided that she'd been arrested for possession of a small amount of "cocaine." As I probed about her drug addiction, her cocaine use seemed more akin to smoking crack, a cheap derivative of cocaine, but even more addictive. Like many of the inmates I'd work with who'd been hooked on crack, I noticed that she was careful to avoid the undignified word itself.

Millie's background was a sad one. Her sisters and brothers, as well as half-sisters and half-brothers, were raised by an overwhelmed grandmother. She had no memories of her father and said her mother wasn't around much while she was growing up.

"She used drugs back then," Millie said softly. "But she doesn't anymore. Now she's taking care of two of my kids and some of my nieces and nephews." When Millie's grandmother became ill, she and her siblings were farmed out to foster care. "That happened when I was nine, and I didn't see two of my sisters again till I was twenty." As she described her foster family experiences, it was apparent that these makeshift arrangements were anything but nurturing, loving, or secure. At fifteen, it was off to group homes until she was on her own at eighteen. Somewhere along the way, she'd dropped out of high school. As she recounted a painful childhood, I felt a deep sadness for Millie, once again wondering how I would have turned out under similar circumstances. I thought of my own mother, the family rock, and then I tried to picture her holding a crack pipe or a heroin needle. It was a preposterous thought, an image impossible to even conjure. Yet this had been Millie's reality.

With the paperwork completed, we sat back to talk. "Have you thought about what happened during that group session?" I asked.

"I sure have!" she retorted. "I shouldn't have gotten blamed for everything when it was those two who started it!" With that, she thrust out her long legs, crossed her arms, and pouted.

Her childish answer was disappointing, indicating a starting point well below what I'd hoped for. "Well, what they did was mean," I agreed.

"That's right."

"But . . . maybe we need to work on your reaction to it. People aren't always going to be nice to us, Millie. Sometimes they're going to get nasty, but we just can't let it get to us that badly. Do you know what I mean?"

"Hey," she said, pulling up straight. "Here's what you could do for me—how about getting me some sleeping pills. Now *that* would really help!"

Suddenly I had an image of Overton's smirk.

"I don't think so, Millie. Not every problem in life can be solved with a pill."

She slumped back again, but I wasn't ready to give up. "Let's back up. Before everything went haywire, you said Calvin was your sixth child, that you wanted to be a good mother to him. That's a good goal—an important one—something we can work on together. Now, being a good mom means keeping your baby safe, right?"

"Uh-huh."

"And the thing is, when you got so upset, you could have dropped—"

"Yeah, well," she interrupted, "maybe I wouldn't get upset if I wasn't so tired all the time. Other girls in here get sleeping pills—I know they do—so how come I can't?"

"I don't know about them, Millie, but I don't think sleeping pills are the answer here."

She stared at the floor. I tried a different angle, looking for something positive where we might make a connection. I praised her for meeting with me, for trying to improve her troubled life. But once pills were ruled out, I was grabbing at air. Still, it was only our first meeting, too soon to become discouraged. As the session ended, I finished up with a cheery, "See you next week!"

But as Millie skulked out of the clinic, I wasn't hopeful.

In contrast to Millie, one of my first promising cases was a woman named Jeanine Bowers. Jeanine had been referred by an officer who noted that she spent her days lying on her cot, weeping and staring at the ceiling. During our initial interview, the neatly kempt twenty-six-year-old tearfully told me she'd been arrested numerous times in the past, and it seemed that this pattern of coming in and out of jail was the source of her despair. "I've been getting locked up since I was fifteen," she whispered. "Going to jail didn't used to bother me. I was always fooling around in the halls—it was all a big joke. But now, when I see older women in here—women in their thirties and forties—looking all beaten up, I say to myself, *That could be me!* The thing is, I'm scared, miss—I'm really scared. I thought I could turn this around any time I wanted, but I haven't been able to do it."

Jeanine Bowers and I made an instant connection. In our first few sessions, time flew by as she told me how she'd attended Narcotics Anonymous meetings and enrolled in GED classes each time she'd been released, hoping to break the jail pattern. "But it always winds up the same—I fall back into drugs and wind up right back in here."

As she and I looked more closely at her backslides, and at how she might line up outside support prior to release, I was delighted with this budding relationship. My work with the motivated Jeanine was exactly what I'd hoped for in coming to Rikers. But I was about to learn one of the cold realities of providing therapy in a jail setting. When I asked Overton to summon her one afternoon, he said, "She's gone."

"Gone?"

"Yeah—she went upstate yesterday morning—prison. She got sentenced. Once they get sentenced, they're not city property anymore, they're state property, and the city's not paying for state property—and you better believe it!"

"Thank you for that!"

I immediately sought out Janet, who explained that once the detainees were sentenced, DOC wasn't going to tell them—or us—their departure date. The date was kept vague as a precaution, to thwart any plan of springing someone from a bus while en route to prison.

From a security standpoint, this policy made perfect sense, but from a therapeutic perspective, it was a disaster. Although deeply disappointed that she was gone, I only hoped that Jeanine would continue therapy in prison. After that, I learned to become attuned to my clients' legal proceedings, now understanding that they could simply disappear.

6

ONE BRIGHT FALL WEEKEND, I WENT OUT TO LONG IS-
land for a family visit, where there was often a crowd gathered
around the Sunday dinner table. My mother was enjoying the first
wave of grandchildren, and as the tots arrived in state-of-the-art
strollers with the latest in child-safety gadgets, I had a flashback
to the woman with the flimsy stroller whom I'd encountered on
my first day at Rikers, and I felt a pang of sadness. Nonetheless, I
was excited to tell everyone all about my unique internship, and it
was a rapt audience that listened as I explained what I had learned:
that Rikers Island is not a prison and that it is not one building,
but rather a complex of ten jails, and just how jails differ from prisons. "Prisons are for those who've been convicted and sentenced,
whereas jails are for pretrial detainees," I explained.

"I had no idea," my mother said. "Jails, prisons—I thought it
was all the same thing."

For my family, like most, Rikers Island was an occasional blurb
on the evening news, its true function just as fuzzy as its exact
location.

But my mother mulled it over a little more, and then looked
puzzled. "But if the detainees haven't been convicted, then why are
they in jail?"

"Because they can't afford bail while they wait for their cases
to resolve."

"Well, that doesn't seem right," she said.

"It doesn't seem right to me either," I agreed. But I didn't really understand the legal system, and so I told them more about what I did know, about the women I'd met, of their sad backgrounds, and of how we were helping them to find their way.

Everyone was interested and supportive, and outside the family, my friends were also enthused. The only sour note came from my father. My parents were separated, and although my father lived in another state, we maintained a close relationship. His blunt take on all this was that it was okay to work in jail for the school year, but after that, "Get the hell out of there." I didn't understand his negativity, but I didn't let it bother me.

*   *   *

The following Monday morning, Janet announced that she was stepping aside as nursery group leader and assigned Allison and me to take over as co-leaders. "I think I'll take a break," Janet said, with a little smile that made me suspicious.

Although initially excited, I found the nursery group to be an uphill battle. Marisol and Addie were eager and interested, but the others less so. Tasha and Swanday never budged from the end of the couch, Millie was off in her own world, Lucy stayed to herself in the rocking chair, and the rest were otherwise distracted. This wasn't at all what I imagined of a therapeutic group, and it certainly didn't measure up to the ideals touted in the classroom: "The group is a vehicle for change!" At the rate things were going here, I didn't see how this could be a vehicle for much of anything. It was quickly obvious that the biggest obstacle to a good discussion was the babies. Sweet as they were, babies cry. Not only did they cry as their mothers fussed with bottles, but they also cried from their cribs, meaning that the mothers were continuously jumping up and running out to the cribs, creating a constant, nerve-wracking distraction.

One afternoon, after yet another challenging session, I had an idea. I stopped off at Camille Baxter's office and ran it by her.

"What if we used women from general population as babysitters? They could tend to the babies so the mothers could attend the group in peace."

Baxter smiled, but with a knowing look. "Babysitter," she said, was already an official job, just one that was hard to fill due to two criteria. "First," she explained, "the babysitter can't be facing a murder charge, which isn't much of an issue—most of these women aren't killers. But it's the second one that gets you: a babysitter can't be here on a drug charge. We've got over a thousand women in this jail, Mary. Months can go by before someone qualifies for the job."

I was stunned. I knew from my assessments that drugs were a huge problem, but I never imagined it to be on this scale.

"Sad, isn't it?" Baxter said.

With the babysitter idea dashed, Allison and I had little choice but to slog through the crying and distractions and try to generate a meaningful discussion. But the dialogue seemed to go around in circles, rarely moving to deeper levels. As much as I hated to admit it, the high point was usually the end, when everybody got a donut. Allison felt we should be serving fruit instead of donuts, but when we put it to a group vote, not one hand shot up in favor of an apple or a banana.

But all was not lost. While everyone was relaxing afterward, someone would often sidle up to me or Allison, eager to talk—just not publicly. Addie sought out Allison, while the pleasant Marisol waited for a moment when I was alone. "Miss Buser," she whispered. "I want to tell you something that I don't want everybody knowing about." Bobbling Teresita on her hip, she said, "I did something that was really hard for me to do—I got tested for HIV. When I was out on the streets, I'll be honest with you, Miss B—I used needles. So I've been really worried that I might have gotten the virus. But I got the results this morning at the clinic. I don't have it—I'm negative! I can't stop smiling. I waited six months before I got tested so I wouldn't get a false negative, but the HIV counselor said it's definite!"

Marisol's relief was understandable. It had only been a decade earlier that the deadly virus that causes AIDS had been identified, and the country was still struggling to understand this baffling new disease. Fear of AIDS loomed large, especially for inmates, a population highly vulnerable to HIV primarily because of drug addiction, which often involves dirty needles and can lead to casual and unprotected sex; both are major modes of transmission. As the newly arrested recovered from drug use, the possibility that they'd contracted AIDS was a constant worry.

"I feel like this is a second chance from God," Marisol asserted. "Now I know that I can get through this jail stuff and stay off drugs when I get out and, well—just be a good mother to Teresita." Smiling down at her baby, she said, "That's all I want in life, Miss B, that's all I want."

And then in a big surprise, the aloof rocking chair mother approached me. With a little gap-toothed smile, Lucy Lopez had a certain attractiveness. "Could we meet privately?" she asked. "I don't want everyone in here knowing my business."

I pulled out my appointment book, and a few days later, I greeted Lucy in the clinic, curious why this distant woman wanted to talk to me.

"Oh, I know you think I'm not paying attention during group," she started off, "but I'm listening, all right."

"Then, why don't you ever say anything?" I asked.

"It's like this, Miss B. I take care of my baby and mind my own business—I stay to myself. I don't want to fool around in here and get all silly, 'cause if I do, I just might forget."

"Forget what?" I asked softly.

Lucy Lopez looked me in the eye. "Miss B," she said, "I'm going to keep it real with you. I'm a crack addict. Hard-core. I'm not going to dress it up like the others do and call it cocaine—no, crack! Now that I'm in here and I can see just how far gone I was out on the streets, it scares the hell out of me! This one time, I was so high that I was laying on a subway platform in the Bronx and my arm was dangling right over the edge. I was looking down at the tracks, they were shiny and so close. And somewhere deep inside of me, a little voice was whispering, *Lucy—what are you doing? You're gonna get killed, you're gonna die*. But there wasn't a thing I could do—I could no more pull myself off of that platform than I could get off drugs and get a job and take care of my son. And then, like in a really bad dream, I could hear the train coming. 'Cept it wasn't any dream," she whispered. "It was getting louder, so what I did was—I shut my eyes, tight as I could. And just when I thought it was gonna all be over, I could feel somebody picking up my legs and dragging me back. That happened to me, Miss B—it happened," Lucy said, her face crumpling into tears. "I need help."

I scrambled for a box of tissues, barely able to believe that this young mother had been sprawled out on a subway platform, inches from a horrific death.

Wiping away the tears, she composed herself. "I gotta believe that getting locked up happened for a reason, that there's a reason God didn't let me get killed that day—and that somehow, my life's gonna get better. I don't know exactly how, Miss B, but I've gotta find a way, 'cause if I don't—when I get out this time, I'm gonna die for real. I will, I know it. That's why I thought I should talk to you. I started going to NA meetings in here, and they have this one saying that keeps going through my head: 'If you do what you've always done, then you'll get what you always got.' And the thing is, I never asked anyone for help before. But maybe this is something I should do different. I hear you when you talk—I just don't like the group. I'd like to meet with you privately, if that's okay."

"Of course it's okay. I'm so glad you're reaching out like this, Lucy."

"Me too," she said, struggling to hold back a new round of tears.

As Overton announced the start of the afternoon count, we set up our next appointment, and Lucy Lopez dashed back to the nursery.

* * *

As I continued meeting more of Rose Singer's inmates, tales like Lucy's were common—young women who'd lived on the edge in a drugged-out haze, now "coming to," growing disconsolate about their lives and frantic about their children. Much of the chatter in the waiting area centered on children, prospects for regaining custody, and dealings with BCW—the hated Bureau of Child Welfare. It was a long road back for most, and while not everyone had Lucy's level of motivation, many did. And for those in denial, the absence of drugs and their continuing incarceration usually brought them around to their sad reality, which is exactly what finally happened to Tiffany Glover, who continued to insist that her arrest and incarceration was one big misunderstanding.

So it was somewhat of a shock when Tiffany was waiting for me one afternoon when I arrived at the MO. "Oh, Miss Buser," she beamed, "Things are going great!"

"They are?"

"Yes, see, I go to court tomorrow and I've been on the phone with different drug programs, and I found one that'll accept me. Not that I need it, but if it gets me out of here, then why not? Gotta do what you gotta do," she laughed. Reaching into her pocket, she pulled out a folded paper. "I got this today—a letter saying I could come. It's a day program. I'm bringing it to court and when I show it to the judge, he'll release me."

"Hold on a second, Tiffany—what does your lawyer say about all this?"

"Oh, him! He's a joke. Every time I try to call him from that card he gave me, I just get a machine and my call's wasted. It makes me realize I gotta take matters into my own hands. This is my life, and I've gotta be in charge of my own life—right?"

"Well, it's a good effort you made here, but it doesn't mean the judge will go for it."

"He's gotta let me go. I gotta think positive. Everyone deserves a second chance."

"Yes, but there's no guarantee—"

"You're just bringing me down," she interrupted. "I'm going home tomorrow! Home!"

Tiffany's spirits were soaring. This was the first time I'd even seen her smile, but I had a bad feeling. Try as I might, I couldn't get her to at least consider the possibility that her plan might not work. As soon as I got back to the clinic, I talked it over with Janet, who feared that if she wasn't released, the soaring spirits would plunge. Janet showed me how to place Tiffany Glover on an enhanced suicide watch.

The next day was Tiffany's big day in court, and I wondered how it was going. The following morning, I scanned the daily census, a thick computer printout of every inmate at Rose Singer. Had she been released, her name would have been gone, but it was still right there.

When I got to the MO, Tiffany's faithful broom was propped up against the wall, but she was nowhere in sight. I tapped on her cell door. Through the window I could see her limp figure lying diagonally across the cot, laceless sneakered feet dangling off the side.

She lifted her head. "Miss Buser?" She slowly righted herself and stumbled to the door.

"I guess things didn't go well in court," I said softly.

She shook her head.

"What happened with the program?"

"What program?" she whispered hoarsely. "I wasn't allowed to say anything and my lawyer wouldn't even tell the judge about it. They want me to take a one-to-three. Oh, Miss Buser, I'm not a bad person. Why am I in jail? I can't take this—I just can't!"

When I suggested we sit down together, she finally agreed. We found an empty cell where she fell into a chair, dropped her face into her lap, and sobbed. "This can't be happening—it just can't. I can't be going to prison. I can't do it—I just can't!"

"Tiffany, I know this feels like the end of the world—"

"It *is* the end of the world. Okay, so maybe I do have a drug problem, but I'm not bad! Why am I being punished like this? I have a baby boy. Who's going to take care of him while I'm in prison? Huh?"

"Who takes care of him now?"

"My mother."

"And who took care of him before you were arrested?"

"I did!"

"Tiffany," I said carefully, "you came in here bone thin. You couldn't have been eating very much, or taking care of yourself. Are you sure you were taking care of a baby?"

"Yes!"

"So it was you who put your son to bed, got him up, fed him, bathed him—every single day—or your mother?"

"No! *Stop!* I love my baby! I love him! I would come home to see him—at least once a week. That was my rule! Once a week!" she cried, pounding her fist on the desk.

As the truth crashed through, her thin shoulders heaved and her face turned the color of scarlet. "I'm going to prison," she sobbed. "Prison! This can't be happening."

"As awful as it feels," I said gently, "it could have been a lot worse than this."

"What could be worse!" she snapped.

"You could have died, Tiffany. You could have been raped—overdosed—murdered—you were vulnerable to a lot of terrible things, things that happen to people every single day."

She sniffled and stared at the floor. "I'll tell you one thing—I'm never going to touch drugs again. Ever! I'm done!"

"That's a good beginning. What do you say you and I keep working on this?"

"I guess that would be okay," she said, looking up at me as though seeing me for the first time. "Guess it couldn't hurt."

"Good," I smiled. "It's about time we got started."

7

JUST AS MY WORK WAS GETTING UNDER WAY IN EAR-
nest, my Rikers mission was threatened by an unlikely health crisis.
Several cases of tuberculosis, a disease thought to be long eradicated
in the United States, had cropped up in the city. When the source of
the outbreak was traced to released inmates, Rikers Island was in
a frenzy. An airborne virus, tuberculosis isn't a threat where fresh
air circulates, but in the stagnant, germ-ridden confines of jail, TB
had found a foothold. Overnight, Rikers Island, normally a vague
footnote to the larger city scene, had jumped to center stage.

The resurgence of tuberculosis made front-page news, and on
our morning drive to work, the three of us read aloud the *New
York Times*'s daily coverage of the outbreak. Our families were understandably alarmed, and Columbia was considering halting the
Rikers program and pulling all the students off the island. Montefiore Hospital, the jail system's health-care vendor, responded
swiftly and aggressively, adding TB testing to the battery of inmate
medical exams.

But it wasn't only the inmates who were to be tested. Tables
sprung up in the jails' lobbies, where officers and civilians stood by
with rolled-up sleeves. Long lines of navy blue uniforms and white
lab coats became a familiar sight, and like everyone else, Allison,
Wendy, and I stood in line and waited. The test, called a PPD im-
plant, is injected under the skin of the forearm. If the skin remains
flat, there's been no exposure to TB. As the needle was slid under

the skin of my arm, the area reddened and a Band-Aid was placed over the puncture wound. For the next few days I couldn't stop checking it, fearful of a rising mass of angry tissue. But the redness disappeared and the skin remained flat. I had not been exposed! Nor had Wendy or Allison. In fact, all the Mental Health staff tested negative.

That news was reassuring, as was the medical department's insistence that the TB cases were isolated and few, and that contracting the disease was highly unlikely. Jailhouse seminars on disease transmission were scheduled daily, where questions were answered and fears quieted. Columbia stepped back cautiously, as did our families. Still, just the idea of tuberculosis was frightening, and the three of us decided on stringent precautions. To keep our workspace air as fresh as possible, the small windows in our conference room would remain open. We were into November now, and with winter approaching, the next few months would be spent in coats. It would be semimiserable, but well worth it. Not everyone, however, was appreciative of our novel strategy. "What are you trying to do," demanded Officer Overton, "freeze out the entire clinic?"

"We're trying to avoid TB."

"Avoid TB, huh? What about pneumonia? Ever hear of that? That's what you're going to get, and that's what you're going to give everybody else! I'm closing this door—if you want to freeze to death, that's your choice!"

But before shutting the door, he took the opportunity to sound off on a few other matters. "Every year, you students come in here thinking you're going to help these inmates. Let me tell you something—they see you coming, they just play you!" And then, looking directly at me: "Did Millie Gittens get her sleeping pills? That's all she wants," he taunted, slamming the door before I could respond.

Overton's impression of the inmates was typical of his fellow officers, and frankly not far from most people's opinions of the incarcerated. One evening after work while the three of us waited for the route bus, a couple of police officers exiting the jail offered us a ride. When we described our work, they said, "You mean you actually *talk to these skels?" Skels* is the term the police routinely use to characterize drug addicts, the homeless, the mentally ill, the down and out. Behind bars, these people are bodies; on the streets, they're skels. Try as we did to defend our jailhouse mission, their only response was a rolling of the eyes and knowing smirks. But their opinions aside, my interest in this work was only deepening. The skels they referred to were Lucy Lopez, lying on the edge of a subway platform; Annie Tilden, lost to a terrifying mental illness; and Tiffany Glover, a scrawny, delinquent mother. Not pretty pictures. But while their behavior may have hit the societal bottom, they were still human beings with the inherent dignity of all life, and with the ever-present possibility for change. And changes they were making. Lucy was battling back against drug addiction, Annie was adjusting to a radical brain change, and Tiffany was tuning in to a dawning awareness. Still, Overton's dig about Millie Gittens did sting—probably because in my heart I knew he was right.

The brighter news, though, was that Millie's mind-set was soundly outnumbered by those who wished to remain drug-free and were prepared to do whatever it took to put drugs behind them and get their lives on track. And as these more motivated women came to their sessions and shared the intimate details of their lives—of the degradation of prostitution, of helplessness in the jaws of addiction, of surviving a fringe-type existence, and of humiliation in the face of scorn and judgment—I felt privileged to be their confidante.

Most of my nine cases were from general population, with a few from the Mental Observation Unit. It was through my work on the MO that I was getting a solid grounding in the nightmare of mental illness. Ever since our first session, when I happily realized that Annie Tilden wasn't readying to throttle me, a bond had developed between us. When I arrived for our sessions, she was no longer in her cell, but waiting for me by the staircase. Together we bounded up to "our office." Despite her insistence that she always took her meds, the daily compliance report showed otherwise. "Well, it *seems* like I take them all the time," she said. I challenged her to do better and we made a contest out of it. And as I became her trusted counselor,

Annie offered me a glimpse into the tormented world of schizophrenia. "Sometimes," she told me, "I'd be lying in bed and a person's head would pop up out of the mattress! And other times this same head would pop up out of my stomach. Now I *know* that heads don't pop out of mattresses and stomachs, but I'm telling you, Miss B, the heads were right there, plain as my hand," she said, holding out her palm. "And it was so scary—terrifying. And the TV? When the news was on, I just *knew* Dan Rather was talking to me—so I would talk back to him. People would run away, but I'm telling you, *it was so real*. Sometimes now, when I'm watching the news and I see Dan Rather, I just shake my head."

I thought about how frightening Annie's pretreatment life must have been. Contrary to popular belief, schizophrenia is not a "split personality," but rather a disturbance in perception, often resulting in auditory, and sometimes visual, hallucinations. I find the very word itself, *schizophrenia,* scary. A cruel condition, it renders the afflicted unable to discern the real from the hallucinated. With such impairment in basic functioning, the schizophrenic can't move past futile attempts at organizing the brain. Without treatment, anything resembling a normal life is impossible. I thought schizophrenia must be a living hell and had all the more compassion for Annie Tilden and the legions like her who struggle with this horrific affliction.

* * *

So far, all of the women I'd met had stories and plights that I could, in some way, empathize with. Honestly, they didn't seem like "real criminals" to me.

But with the assignment of a new case—Rhonda Reynolds, one of the few Rose Singer inmates charged with murder—that was about to change. "A little more of a challenge for you," Janet said.

Janet had already done the initial evaluation and suggested we meet with Rhonda in her house. As we stood in her cellblock waiting for her to emerge, I was chewing on my pen. Janet had been so casual about the murder charge; I supposed that as a jailhouse veteran, very little fazed her. But I didn't have long to fret. An upper cell door popped open and a wiry woman glowered down at us, her hardness softened by an oversized fuzzy blue headband. As she descended, her irritated demeanor transformed to that of a debutante making a grand entrance. Taking her time, she slowly made her way over to us. She gave me a coy little smile and looked squarely up at Janet.

"Hello, Rhonda," said Janet. "I want you to meet Miss Buser. She's a student intern and I'd like the two of you to start working together."

"Uh-huh," said Rhonda in a low, raspy voice.

Inching closer to Janet, I smiled at Rhonda. In turn, she sized me up. "Yeah, you can call me."

Gee, thanks!

With that, Rhonda Reynolds turned away and faded back up the stairs.

"She seems like a tough customer," I commented, resuming my pen chewing.

"Not as tough as she seems," said Janet. "She's facing a lot of time upstate, but she's in complete denial about the trouble she's in. She may be someone you'll work with for just a few sessions, or she could be long-term. Either way, she'll be here long enough for you to find out—it'll take forever for her case to resolve. The wheels of justice move very slowly, Mary, especially for serious charges."

A few days later, Rhonda Reynolds arrived at the clinic for our first session. Along with the fuzzy blue headband, she wore her hair in little girl pigtails. Giggling loudly in the waiting area, she was the center of attention.

"Your client is here," Overton announced, rolling his eyes.

As we settled in, I wasn't exactly sure how to begin, but I needn't have worried. Rhonda Reynolds got right to the point. "I'm here for murder—you believe that? I didn't murder anybody. Let me tell you what happened. A bunch of us were hanging out on the corner, just messing around, and this girl jumps on my back. Everybody's laughing, but it wasn't funny. I *can–not* have anyone crowding me like that. So, I yell at her to get off. When she didn't, I pull out my handy knife and cut her—not hard, just to let her know I wasn't kidding around. When I saw the blood, I told her to wait while I got some peroxide and a Band-Aid. But did she wait? Nooooh! She decided to go home and bleed to death along the way. I told her to wait, but she did what she wanted. Not *my* fault she died."

With that, Rhonda Reynolds sat back and probed my face for a reaction.

She had to be kidding. Her story was ridiculous. Obviously, she'd killed this poor woman. But her denial was rock-solid. If I challenged her, any hope of a relationship would have ended then and there. About all I could think to say was, "Do you always carry a knife?"

"Yes, I carry a knife!" she growled. "Where I live, you need a knife! Being a White girl and all, you wouldn't understand that!"

Ignoring the racial jab, I said, "It must be hard to not feel safe."

"It is! Everybody carries something—you have to! And now I'm in this place and all I feel is stress. Stress, stress, stress! What you need to do is get me sleeping pills."

To this, I explained the department policy, but didn't quite have the nerve to pull out our handout, "Natural Techniques to Fall Asleep." Not this time.

She leaned forward and banged her fists on the desk. "You get me sleeping pills!" And then, pointing both index fingers at me, "That's *your job!*"

She was intimidating, but I held my ground. "I'm sorry, but I can't help you there."

"Well, then, why'm I here?" she said, slumping back.

"What happens when you try to fall asleep?" I asked.

"I have nightmares, that's what. Okay? Nightmares that wake me up."

"What are the nightmares about?"

She hesitated for a moment, then said: "Pools of blood. Okay? Happy now?"

When I asked if the pools of blood meant anything in her waking life, she became withdrawn and refused to answer any further questions. Not nearly as upbeat as she'd been when she'd arrived, the session ended and she flounced out of the clinic, but not before I asked if we could make a follow-up appointment. "I'll think about it!" she snapped.

I had my doubts as to whether Rhonda Reynolds would return, but when I called her the following week, she arrived promptly. In a rerun of the first session, she demanded sleeping pills, referring to the nightmares. When I again tried to probe, she abruptly switched gears, launching into tales of an idyllic childhood filled with birthday parties, Easter baskets, and warm family gatherings. Of course, none of this added up to the woman sitting on Rikers Island charged with murder. But she had her own reasons for portraying this happy image, her own reasons for denying she'd killed someone. I didn't know where any of this was going, but it seemed to me that despite her outward gaiety, Rhonda Reynolds was deeply troubled, and for that very reason I was actually hopeful that we might make some progress. Emotional turmoil, uncomfortable as it may be in the moment, is an impetus for change. Even twelve-step programs talk about "hitting bottom" before any real change can occur. I had the feeling that, for Rhonda Reynolds, the bottom was getting closer.

*   *   *

If emotional angst prompts change, then its absence may have at least partially explained my stalled relationship with Millie Gittens. Despite having lost custody of five children and now being behind bars, which for most people would have been hitting bottom— many times over—when Millie Gittens put her head on the pillow at night, she slept soundly.

As much as I hated to admit it, Millie and I weren't making any progress. She remained fixated on sleeping pills, and that was when she bothered to show up. She rarely made her appointments, showing up just often enough to keep the busy Camille Baxter pla-cated. Determined to make this relationship work, I would storm down to the nursery, only to find her sprawled out on the couch, protesting that she couldn't find anyone to watch Calvin, or that she'd gotten mixed up on dates and times. Always an excuse.

During my weekly hour of formal supervision with Janet, my "Millie struggle" dominated every conversation. Janet suggested various strategies for engaging her, and though I tried them all, nothing worked. Millie's disinterest in therapy flew in the face of my belief that with a little patience, everyone would come around. Yet no matter how hard I tried to forge some kind of therapeutic alliance with her, I was unable to do so. Even worse, I often wound up as her adversary. In one of our infrequent sessions, she revealed how she'd lost her two youngest children to the Bureau of Child Welfare. She told me she'd been living in a hotel in downtown Man-hattan. "I did a lot partying down there," she giggled. "Anyway, middle of the night, my three-year-old gets up, leaves the room, and gets down to the street. The police found him on the sidewalk, so they called BCW and they just took both of them away from me. You believe that?"

"It must have been hard for you to lose your children like that," I said, trying to meet her "where she was."

"It was! It really was. And it was all BCW's fault!"

"Well . . . now . . . do you see a problem with a toddler being alone on the streets at two in the morning?"

"'Course I do! But what are they blaming me for? Huh?"

"You're the baby's mother, Millie. You're responsible for him."

"Now *you* sound just like BCW, and like I told them, don't you think I would have done something—*if I was awake?* Ah, duh!"

"Do you think that maybe the partying might have something to—?"

"No, no, no! I was just asleep—that's all. How'm I supposed to know the baby's goin' out the door if I'm asleep? Duh!"

"But, Millie—"

"Ah, DUH! Ah, DUH!"

With that session, I saw the light. My belief that everyone could be helped was naive. Even the ever-optimistic Janet agreed. "It looks like Millie's just not receptive to help, at least not at this point in her life. The simple truth is that you can't help someone without their participation—no one can."

As soon as Janet deemed the situation hopeless, the floodgates of relief opened up. No more maddening trips to the nursery, no more struggling for magical words that would turn this disinterested person around. Best of all, Janet didn't view it as my fault—something I'd worried about. "You can't help someone without their participation—*no one can.*" A great burden was lifted. The Millie struggle was over.

But not quite. Janet also noted that Millie hadn't been in any trouble since I'd been meeting with her and wanted me to continue doing so. "At the very least, she knows she's being watched—and let's not forget she's going to a program soon. Let's just give her the added support till she leaves."

It was with mixed feelings that I kept Millie on my caseload, still finding it hard to accept that we can't help someone who just doesn't want help.

* * *

But this defeat was offset by a growing sense of competence. As I handled the daily referrals, Janet was looking over my shoulder less as I was making accurate assessments, transferring only those in true need to the more protected Mental Observation Unit.

My mornings were spent with referrals, with afternoons devoted to follow-up sessions. The faces on my caseload came and went—usually to Bedford Hills Prison. But Lucy Lopez, Tiffany Glover, and Annie Tilden had developed into my long-term cases, and as they took wobbly steps forward, I delighted in their progress.

Once Lucy Lopez asked for help, she never looked back. Once a week, she could be heard running down the hall for her session, her jail-issued red plastic slippers slapping hard on the linoleum floor. Lucy always managed to find another mother to babysit her son, underscoring her level of motivation. The challenges she faced were formidable: Lucy's father had been shot and killed when she was two, and her mother had been in and out of jail while she was growing up. She was raised by her grandmother, a solid care-giver. Tragically, her loving grandmother passed away when Lucy was nine, and then it was on to foster care. But the memory of her grandmother's love was Lucy's life preserver, pulling her back from the brink of destruction. "Sometimes," said Lucy, "I feel like I can hear my grandma talking to me—*You can do better than this, Lucy—you can do better!*"

And Lucy was doing better. She pushed herself. Therapy was just the beginning of her personal improvement campaign. She was the first to show up for jailhouse Narcotics Anonymous meet-ings, and she took full advantage of the Mental Health Depart-ment's weekly meditation group. "It really helps! When I get out of jail, and find myself getting uptight and wanting to get high, I'm going to meditate instead. It's just another tool I'm learning," she smiled. When Lucy wasn't immersed in various therapies, she was busy with the Social Services Department regarding another child, her four-year-old son, Junior, who'd been in foster care dur-ing Lucy's years of drug use. Despite Lucy's valiant efforts behind bars, her older child was being readied for adoption. The prospect of permanently losing Junior terrified Lucy, and she was making every effort to prove herself a responsible mother. Social Services was assisting her in negotiating the vast Bureau of Child Welfare, helping her to file petitions and gather letters of recommendation. She was also trying to arrange for a visit with Junior in the Rose Singer visiting room. It was an uphill battle, and with fingernails bitten to the quick, she told me how she lay awake at night, ago-nizing about how all of this would play out. "I worry about how long I'll be sentenced, whether or not I'll get my children back after I'm released, and if I do—hope of hope—then I worry about where we'll live, what I'll do for money. I dropped out of high school and don't have any skills. It's all so scary. But what scares me most is that it's all too late, and that in the end I'll lose my children anyway. And then I get so depressed I don't even want to get out of bed. So I try not to go there. I can't look too far ahead—it's too scary. So what I do is, I just do the best I can every single day, and leave everything else in God's hands. That's all I can do, Miss B, that's all I can do."

Lucy's steely determination was admirable, and I just hoped something good would come her way. Though I kept my thoughts to myself, I had to agree that her future was daunting. Despite Lucy's progress, it was not with open arms that the world would greet an ex-con and recovering crack addict. Still, some things have to be taken on faith, and sometimes the only thing to be done, as Lucy said, was to leave it in God's hands.

Tiffany Glover was more fortunate in that she didn't have to worry about losing her son, who lived with her mother, a woman who prayed for her daughter's recovery. After the drug program fiasco, it was as though a dam broke, and everything bottled up inside Tiffany began to flow. "I cannot believe I was a down-and-out addict—me! You just don't realize what's happening to you when you're in the middle of it," she said, shaking her head. With Tiffany's acknowledgment of her addiction, her mood lightened, so much so that being on the Mental Observation Unit was no longer warranted. Janet noted Tiffany's improvement. "She's doing a lot better, Mary—time for her to go to GP."

Except for severe psychiatric impairment, the MO is temporary, just long enough for sustained emotional stability, followed by a discharge to general population. "It's healthier for them to function in GP," Janet explained. "Not to mention the need to free up beds for the newcomers."

While this policy only made sense, the MO was viewed as a safer, softer haven in jail, and transfers from the protective unit to general population were met with fierce resistance, and in this regard Tiffany Glover was no exception. Although I tried to frame the move as a milestone in her improvement, she didn't buy it. "But I'm afraid of GP!"

"I think you'll do fine," I said. "You and I will continue to meet, but it will just be in the clinic, that's all. You can do it!"

Her eyes welled up with tears and she stared at the floor, her demeanor reverting to that first day in the receiving room. For a moment, I wondered if this really was the right move. But then she bit her lip and nodded.

A day later, her meager belongings packed up in a clear plastic Hefty bag, Tiffany Glover dragged the bag through the corridors as she was led to a GP dorm.

Although the transition to GP was initially difficult, Tiffany began to thrive in her new environment, another plus for her. She made friends with the girl in the next cot, a girl nicknamed Lanky who'd given birth just prior to her arrest. Tiffany told me that Lanky had been so desperate to get high that as soon as her baby was born, she'd jumped out of the hospital bed and run down a side stairwell. Tiffany said Lanky was just now wondering what had happened to her daughter. "At least I never did that!" Tiffany declared.

With wide brown eyes and a full pretty smile, Tiffany Glover stood out as a beauty in the Rose Singer halls. She'd had numerous boyfriends on the outside, many of whom were drug dealers. "That's how I got my fix," she explained.

Reading between the lines, I surmised the arrangement with these men was sex for drugs, an all too common bartering arrangement among the female inmates.

One afternoon, Tiffany arrived for our session with a big announcement: "I want to join STEP."

STEP, an acronym for "Self-Taught-Empowerment-Pride," was a jailhouse drug rehab program. The STEP participants lived in the same dorm and were often seen marching through the halls in military style. Upon completion of the program, certificates were awarded. "Some of the girls told me they have a graduation where your family comes," said Tiffany, "and I was thinking that could be really nice. If I can get through this program, I think it will help me when I go upstate, and I know my mother would be proud of me. They have a new class starting and I'm going to check it out. What do you think?"

I told her it was a wonderful idea, that it was a big step in her recovery. I also told her it was smart to take advantage of any programs jail had to offer. "Time is going to fly by, and when you're released, you want to be ready."

Shortly afterward, Tiffany Glover was transferred to the STEP dorm. She immediately shared the news with her mother, who was thrilled.

Annie Tilden differed from Tiffany and Lucy because of her schizophrenia, but within the constraints of her mental illness, she, too, was progressing. By now, she was fully compliant with her meds and feeling quite proud of herself. The next challenge I gave her was to come out of her cell and socialize a little. She rolled her eyes at the suggestion. "There's too many troublemakers around the TV," she said. Still, I prodded, and I noticed that she began coming out, chatting with a good-natured CO whose brother just happened to be a mailman. With a realistic grasp on both her illness and addiction, Annie was on track for her December release, and for sustained recovery.

For Tiffany, Lucy, and Annie, it seemed to me that arrest had been their salvation, a forced time-out from self-destructive paths. Without the radical intervention of arrest and incarceration, they would never have made such progress. In this regard, I viewed jail as having a valuable purpose, as a window of opportunity for lives that were dangerously out of control.

But not every jailhouse situation was positive. Next door to the clinic was the office of the jail chaplain, Sister Marion Defeis. She was a Josephite, an order of Catholic nuns committed to social justice. Sister Marion had converted her small office into a chapel of sorts. With a cloth-covered table and a simple homespun rug that hung on the cinder-block wall, the room served as a refuge for inmates seeking spiritual solace. A tall woman in her fifties—reserved, refined, and with a deep sense of commitment—Sister Marion worked closely with "mules," women charged with the serious crime of trafficking drugs through city airports. Most who sought out Sister Marion were Spanish-speaking women from South America. Although mules transport drugs—sometimes packed inside condom-like containers and then swallowed—they're not drug dealers per se, but rather tools of the violent drug trade. Living in impoverished third world countries without any type of public assistance made available to them, most were simply trying to survive. Recognizing their desperation, the powerful cartels offered them big money for performing a "small job." In many cases, Sister Marion told me, they weren't "offered" the job but were tricked or forced by calculating husbands and boyfriends.

Although the rewards are high, the stakes are higher—if caught, they would bump up against the harsh Rockefeller laws. In 1973, New York's governor, Nelson Rockefeller, took the nation's newly declared War on Drugs to a new level, signing tough legislation aimed at stamping out the illicit drug trade. The penalty for drug trafficking was a minimum prison term of fifteen years to life, and a maximum of twenty-five years to life. At the time, these laws were hailed as progressive. However, in the ensuing decades, it has become clear that they've failed to stem the flow of drugs, and what was once viewed as progressive was now considered by many as draconian. With her personal relationships with these women, Sister Marion was at the forefront of a growing movement to repeal the laws, traveling to the state capital in Albany to argue that they weren't only cruel, but ineffective.

Although reform would come, it would not be in time for the women who gathered in Sister Marion's chapel in utter despair. Sister Marion's first priority was to help them with basic needs: a pair of socks, new underwear, a long-distance phone call. After their practical needs were met, she would ask them if they wished to pray. When an inner door was propped open, the prayers could be heard, followed by tears and cries for their children: *"Ay dios mio! Mis niños! Mis niños!"* The cries of the women were heartbreaking, and someone usually got up and shut the door.

8

ON A BRISK MORNING IN LATE NOVEMBER, MILLIE GIT-
tens and a bundled-up Calvin were saying their good-byes. The
details for Millie's drug program had been abruptly finalized, and
Camille Baxter and the mothers were gathered around, waiting for
officers to escort Millie and Calvin to the receiving room. Everyone
was wishing her well, although I could also hear the murmurs: "It's
not fair—how come she gets to go to a program?"

I still had mixed feelings about Millie, but as the officers arrived, I just hoped things would somehow work out for her in rehab.

And on the Mental Observation Unit, Annie Tilden was pacing the floor, awaiting the release that would send her home for
Christmas. "Every day I'm in here feels like a year," she said in our
final session.

"It's almost over now," I said. "You're coming down the home-
stretch. Soon, this place will be a memory."

"Hey," she said, "how will you and I be able to meet when I'm
home?"

"Well—we won't, Annie," I responded honestly to the question that had been cropping up of late. "But we'll always have nice
memories, and as long as I know you're taking your meds and staying away from drugs, then I'll know you're fine."

"Like I told you a thousand times over," she sighed. "I'm done
with drugs. And the medicine—you know I'll take it. You think I

want to start talking to Dan Rather again? I mean, he's nice and all. But, no thank you!"

The Monday after Thanksgiving, Annie Tilden's name was gone from the Rose Singer census, and I smiled. She was home now.

In early December, green plastic wreaths popped up on the clinic windows, and in the nursery the mothers put up a small silver tree. Even the dour Overton surprised everyone by bringing in a strand of colored lights that he hung over the inmate waiting area.

Although the festivities were less joyous and more restrained than on the outside, the holiday spirit still permeated the cold concrete walls, and modest party plans were under way. The students were asked to prepare a Christmas party for the mentally ill, and after work one evening, the three of us drove to a convenience store and bought bulk holiday candy, careful to avoid gum and anything in aluminum wrapping. Gum can be used to jam locks, and convincing badges can be fashioned out of aluminum, so both are prohibited.

We filled goody bags with chocolates, peppermints, and hard candy. One of the permanent staff members belonged to a church that donated toothpaste and other toiletries to the mentally ill, and we added these to the bags. The final step was permission for music. Since nothing—even something as innocuous as a tape deck and assorted Christmas tapes—could be brought into the jail without DOC approval, I assumed the job of getting the okay from the clinic captain. As the next level up from the CO in the correctional hierarchy, captains are easily recognizable by their white shirts.

The captain who oversaw the clinic was a hefty woman with thin brown hair pulled back into a tight little bun. With a cigarette usually dangling from an unsmiling mouth, Captain Murphy had a reputation for doing things "by the book!" But I wasn't worried. I expected my request to be nothing more than a formality, as small parties for the mentally ill were considered part of their therapy. There was always a line outside the captain's office, and when it was my turn, I laid out the party plans. She dragged hard on her cigarette, mulling it over. "Come back tomorrow! I'll let you know then."

I was a little surprised. But I didn't protest—after all, we were "guests in their house," something that, I noticed, DOC never passed up an opportunity to remind us of.

The following day, I reported to her office, and she was ready with her decision. "You're cleared to bring in the tapes."

"Oh, thank you, Captain!"

"But you may not bring in the tape recorder."

"What?"

"Department regulations!"

"But what good are the tapes without the recorder?"

Ignoring me, she motioned to the person behind me in line. "Next!"

I stormed back to the conference room, fuming to my comrades, "These people are crazy!" Overhearing my ranting, Overton popped his head in. "You want to know why you can't bring in a tape deck? You see the signs around the island? No cameras, no recording devices allowed. It's because of that. A tape deck plays tapes—but it also *records*."

"Aahh!" I ran back to Murphy's office, jumping the line. "Captain, if I can find a tape deck without a recording feature, would that be okay?"

"Yes, but I'd have to see it first," she snapped.

I was now on a mission, checking tape players at home and enlisting the aid of friends and family. Everyone was on the hunt. But no luck.

A week before the festivities, it looked like our MO party would be a quiet affair.

In the meantime, we suspended the last nursery session before our winter break for a party. When Allison and I arrived, the silver tree was lit up and Bing Crosby was crooning "White Christmas." Curious about the music, I traced it to a boom box that I inspected closely. Sure enough, the word RECORD was right on it. Ha! According to DOC's own rules, this device should never have been in the jail—but I wasn't going to point it out. Instead, I would walk it down the hall for the MO party later in the week, and return it afterward.

With my problem solved, I returned to the festivities, joining Allison in setting out plates of donuts with red and green sprinkles. In the living room, Marisol and baby Teresita were enjoying the tree. On the couch, Lucy held little Michael, giggling with him, playing peekaboo, smothering the laughing baby with kisses. It was nice to see Lucy laughing, as she ordinarily had an intensity about her, a determination that was exhausting.

Yet despite the tree and the music, the party was a bittersweet affair, as only a few of the mothers came. The others tended to chores or retreated to their cells. When I noticed tear-stained faces, I pulled Addie aside and asked her why she wasn't joining us. Choking back tears, she said, "There's no Christmas in here—when I get out, then it'll be Christmas again." Separated from family, cut off from the world, incarceration during the holidays is especially painful for detainees, and many simply wanted to get it over with.

A few days later, there was an entirely different mood on the MO. The Mental Health staff set aside their paperwork and walked over to the protective unit where the mentally ill inmates were already gathered, eager for their party and relishing the unusual show of attention. Staff members dragged chairs into a widening circle, and Rose Singer's Mental Health chief stood up and said a few words of goodwill, and, as always, pushed the women to take their medication. "Make that your New Year's resolution!"

Wendy and Allison passed out the goody bags while I popped a tape into the borrowed nursery boom box. With the festive tunes playing, these fragile people, whose lives knew far too little joy, delighted in their treats, laughing and popping chocolates into their mouths. A good-natured psychiatrist, best known to them for looking over the brim of his glasses as he queried them about medication, donned a Santa Claus cap, which drew howls of laughter. When "Jingle Bells" began to play, everyone joined in on the familiar tune—*"o'er the fields we go, laughing all the way, HEY!"* Even the officers tapped their feet and sang along, and in the bubble,

Officer Timlinson was peering through the big picture window and smiling. As the women laughed and the singing continued, for a few blessed moments it felt like we were all transported out of the cheerless Mental Observation Unit, far away from courts, handcuffs, medication, and jail. When the singing slowly wound down, patients and staff sat for a moment in satisfied silence. The silence was broken by the little woman with the mismatched eyes who'd told me she'd seen the Easter Rabbit. "This is the best party I've ever been to—in my whole life."

A few days later, the rosy hue of the party still lingered as I worked on my charts. I was humming Christmas carols when agonizing cries suddenly pierced the clinic. "Hey! Hey! Hey!" Overton was yelling. Staff members rushed out of their offices toward Overton, who was pulling a sobbing inmate down from one of the seats. Above her was the string of lights he'd brought in, and stuck in her wrists and forearms were bits of broken colored glass. "Kill me— just kill me!" I recognized her as one of the women who frequented Sister Marion's office and had been on Rikers for a good year before we'd arrived. Always demure and polite, she was familiar to us as one of the women from South America who'd been arrested at a city airport for carrying drugs. I'd often noticed her in the nun's office, deep in prayer—praying for mercy, praying for compassion, praying for a miracle. But earlier in the week, her case had finally resolved. There had been no miracle, no last-minute reprieve, no dream team to swoop in and save the day. Her sentence for the nonviolent first offense of smuggling a small amount of drugs: twenty-five years in prison.

As she was rushed over to the medical side of the clinic, propped up by the unit chief on one side and a psychiatrist on the other, her shrieks grew louder—"*Mis niños, mis niños!* My children, my children!" The rest of us stood by, dazed, save for Overton, who was sweeping up the glass, muttering, "You try to do something nice, brighten things up for the holidays . . ."

I retreated to the conference room and clamped my hands over my ears, trying to block out the heart-wrenching cries. So, this was the War on Drugs—up close and personal, the side that no one ever sees: a newly sentenced human life coming apart. How could these cruel sentences be the answer to the drug problem? Why was the solution to complicated social and psychological problems always a bigger hammer? Brutally punishing this woman meant nothing to the powerful drug trade. But for children waiting for their mother, it was everything. The thought of little children in some far corner of the world waiting for a mother who would never come home was one that would haunt me long after my internship was over.

* * *

As the semester wound down to the last few days, we kept up the vigil in our "anti-TB room," quietly finishing term papers and wrapping up chart work, toiling away in a room that was now ice cold. To keep my hands warm but still manage a pen, I'd cut the tips off a pair of old gloves. Every time we considered shutting the windows, a new rumor would surface that someone else on the island had tested positive for TB. And with each new report, our supervisors told us to "think positive, work hard, get good rest, and you'll be fine."

And with that, the first semester ended.

9

THE WINTER RECESS BROUGHT A TWO-WEEK HIATUS from school, and I enjoyed the break from classes and the weary trek out to Rikers. I got to see a lot more of my family over the break, and by now I had much more to tell them about the women at Rose Singer and life "on the inside." Mostly, I was struck by the unevenness of life, how these women had had to survive fragmented, impoverished families when so many of us are blessed with comfortable, intact ones. One of my brothers, Charlie, a New York City firefighter, was stationed in a busy firehouse in a rough section of Brooklyn, and he well understood. He told us about the neighborhood children who showed up at the firehouse doors, dragging in old bicycles with flat tires. "We fill them up with the pumps we use on the rigs, and we pull out tools and just try to get their bikes working. I feel so bad for them. They're just trying to have little-kid fun—not easy because they're growing up in a hellhole. When I'm doing my overnights, the neighborhood turns into a war zone—all night long, pop-pop, pop-pop! Guns! Unbelievable! I lay there and think, *My God!* Where the hell am I?"

My brother's report of gunfire came as a jolt. Oddly enough, despite working in a jail, I was far removed from the violence he described. Life at Rose Singer was orderly and controlled, although I was well aware that it was only one of the ten jails on Rikers, and that the other nine housed men. I also knew that, for the most part, the men were charged with more serious crimes.

I tucked away my brother's comments, and by early January I was back at school with fresh enthusiasm for the second semester. At the end of December, Wendy and I had been asked to start a support group for adolescent inmates between sixteen and nineteen years old. The "girls" were notorious for fighting, often sporting black eyes. Our challenge was to see if a therapeutic group might defuse some of the violence.

Since the girls attended school during the day, the plan was that Wendy and I would each run an evening group in their house, which was divided into two sides. For our first session, we walked through unfamiliar corridors until we reached the house, located in a remote section of the jail. We explained our mission to an amused housing officer. "Good luck! These girls, they're just gonna play you." Nonetheless, we signed in to the logbook and split up, with Wendy going to work on the A side while I took the B side.

Inside the cellblock, twenty-five cell doors bordered a common space where a bunch of girls—one of them hugging a blanket and sucking her thumb—was crowded in front of a TV that was blasting a bawdy sitcom. Everyone else was running around, shrieking and laughing with youthful energy. No one seemed to notice me as I plunked down my papers on a round plastic table. I wasn't exactly sure what to do next, so a little self-consciously, I stepped to the center of the room and said in as loud a voice as I could muster, "I'm Miss Buser from the Mental Health Department, and I'm starting a support group in this house."

There was no reaction. Either they didn't hear me or they chose to ignore me. I opened the box of donuts I'd brought along and placed it on the table. I'd learned the value of bait.

Just then, the officer stormed out of the bubble. "Get over here, ya ungrateful bitches! Can't you see this lady's trying to do something nice for you?!"

For a moment the silliness and roughhousing came to a stop and all eyes were on me. This was exactly what I did not want. I wanted them to come of their own accord, and I understood that this might take time.

"It's okay," I said to the officer. "I appreciate what you're trying to do, but it's okay."

"Well, I was just trying to help!"

"Yes, I know—and I appreciate that."

"Whatever!" she sniffed, and retreated to the bubble.

An awkward silence followed; the girls looked at me and then resumed their horseplay. But two of them, a lithe Black girl and her shorter Hispanic friend, meandered over. The tall girl spoke first. "Hi. I'm Ebony, and this is Diana. Mind if we sit down?"

"Please do," I said, offering the donuts, which they happily dove into.

"So you're from Mental Health," started Ebony. "Well, we have a problem," she said, glancing at the giggling Diana. "Do you do—what do you call it—couples therapy?"

"Are you two a couple?"

"Sort of . . . the problem here is that I know how I feel about Diana, but I think that when she gets out of here, she's going to flip back—and run straight back to her boyfriend."

"I am not!" Diana protested. "You keep on saying that, but it isn't true!"

Flipping was the jailhouse term for heterosexual women who were in relationships with other female inmates. Although most refrained from sexual dalliances, the sight of couples walking down the halls with arms interlocked was not uncommon.

As Ebony and Diana bickered, I simply listened and did a little mediating, aware that others were strolling by. One of them asked if she could have a donut. I told her she could, as long as she sat down with us while she ate it, my only requirement. She pulled up a seat and said her name was Crystal.

As soon as Crystal joined us, Ebony and Diana changed the subject. I could tell Ebony was disappointed, but she made an effort to switch gears, and the four of us chatted about nothing in particular.

When the hour was through, they asked me if I was coming back the following week.

"I'll be coming every week," I said.

The three of them seemed a little proud that they'd befriended me and insisted on walking me the short distance to the bubble. As the officer buzzed me out, a stray shout came from the rear of the cellblock: "Good night, Mental Health!"

On the walk back, Wendy and I compared notes. Her experience had been similar to mine, and we were both excited about our first session. Although most had ignored us, a few were interested. "A good start," we agreed. Definitely! We then discussed the problem of the well-meaning officer, who'd also yelled at the girls on Wendy's side. We decided it would be best if we chatted with her a little before things got started. Everything in jail works better if the officers feel included, an interesting lesson we were catching on to.

On a stretch of dim and lonely corridor, a couple of unfamiliar COs were walking toward us; with them, telltale IDs clipped to their shirts, were three male inmates. This was my first encounter with incarcerated men, but I remembered at some point being told that our jail and one of the men's jails were connected; this particular corridor was apparently a common hall. As they got closer, the inmates nodded to us. "Evening, ladies," said the officers. We nodded back and kept moving. When we reached Rose Singer's brighter, more familiar halls, I felt mildly relieved.

Since it was evening, the jail was quiet, save for the STEP rehab regiment, which was in full swing. *"Hup! Hup!"* the women chanted. At the rear of the line was Tiffany Glover, a skinny little figure in an oversized uniform. Every time I ran into the STEP troops, Tiffany was struggling to keep up, the runt of the litter. I waved to her as they passed by, and she managed a weak little smile. Despite her high hopes, this STEP venture didn't seem to be going well, although she'd never let on in our sessions that she was unhappy. But a couple of days after this evening encounter, her misery spilled over. "I can't do it," she said. "All they do is yell and curse at you, and half the time I'm just crying."

Squirming in her seat, she said, "Miss B, do you think it would be terrible if I quit?"

"No, I don't."

Her face lit up. "You don't?"

"No. Not everything we try is going to work out. What's important is that you tried."

"Oh, thank you, Miss Buser! I just don't want people to be disappointed in me."

"I'm not disappointed in you. I think you made a good effort here, and that's what counts."

"Would you mind telling that to my mother?" she said, grabbing the desk phone and placing it in front of me. "Here—I'll dial."

"Now wait a minute, Tiffany! Hold on! This is a call that you've got to make."

Tiffany bit her lip, and with trembling hands retrieved the phone. I stepped away to give her some privacy, just catching the words, "Hello, Mommy. How you feeling today?"

* * *

The weekend after Tiffany Glover's decision to quit STEP, the city was hit with its first major snowstorm of the year, and the island was blanketed in downy whiteness. For a brief moment, the cold collection of jails could have been mistaken for a serene picture postcard. But the winter wonderland was thawing fast, and it wasn't long before the barbed wire was poking through the snow, glinting in the winter sun. The following Monday, as I trekked through a distant corridor, droplets of melting ice were pinging on the tin roof. My destination was the infirmary, always referred to as "way, way over at the other end of the jail." A long walk.

I hoped to make this a brief visit. Just before the semester break, Janet had assigned a new case to me—a woman named Daisy Wilson. In the late stages of AIDS, Daisy was waiting on her "Compassionate Release," a court-issued edict that would allow her to go home to die. Although I'd worked with several women who were HIV positive, Daisy was the first who was so gravely ill. I'd already met with her twice, and in those two sessions she'd made an impression on me—an unsettling one. With a moon-shaped face and wide roving eyes, Daisy Wilson was pretty—save for a missing front tooth. In our first session, it was through a thick Haitian accent that she told me she'd contracted HIV through a dirty needle and didn't know how to tell her family that she had AIDS. She also said she wanted to make peace with God before she died. This would have been a rich starting point for our work together, but then she abruptly abandoned the topic to boast about her burglary skills!

I was a little taken aback, but I went along with it for the moment, finding myself easily drawn into her stories. If nothing else, Daisy Wilson was a skilled storyteller. I was especially taken with the rather amazing circumstances that had landed her at Rikers. "It happened while I was robbing a house in Brooklyn," she stated quite matter-of-factly. "After I filled my shopping bags, I got hungry and fixed myself a little something to eat. Then I noticed these cute little stuffed dogs. They weren't worth anything, but I liked them and wanted them for me, so I packed them up. Then I sat down and smoked some crack, and that's when everything got crazy. Those little dogs, they jumped up out of the bags and started barking at me! I ran up the stairs, but they were right behind me—barking and barking! So I ran back down, but they had me up against the wall. I was scared! I panicked! So, what do you do when you're in trouble? Think about it."

I shook my head faintly.

"You call 911."

"*What?*"

"Yup—I called 911. Not too smart, huh?"

As I tried to comprehend this crazy scenario, she moved right along. "Next thing I know, cops are at the door. I'm coming down from the smoke now and realize I just made a *big mistake!* So I opened the door . . . prob'ly shouldn't have. But anyway, I did. I told those officers, real polite, that I didn't know anything about any problem—that I was just the domestic, and that maybe they had the wrong address. They were just about to leave when one of them pokes his head in and sees my pipe on the kitchen table. *Shit!* So I say to them, 'Look, I feel terrible telling you this . . . but these people who live here—they're drug addicts.' And you know—they *almost* bought it. I was *this* close!" she grinned, holding up thumb to forefinger. "But then they called up the homeowners at work to check out my story, and, well, here I am."

When the session ended, I felt like I'd been on some kind of a wild ride. But I just assumed that the next time we met, we could set all this aside and focus on her illness.

But the next meeting was a repeat of the first. This time I tried to cut her off and get us on some kind of therapeutic track. But she simply ignored me, and off we went. After that, I didn't see her for a couple of weeks, although I regularly summoned her to the clinic. When someone repeatedly failed to show up, we assumed they weren't interested in therapy, had them sign a refusal form, and closed the case.

Tucked under my arm was one of these forms. When it came to Daisy Wilson, I had an uneasy feeling. There was something very different about this woman, and as much as I hated to admit it, I didn't like her. I felt guilty about this, as I had just assumed that there would be no one about whom I couldn't find *something* to like. But rather than trying to sort out my feelings, I figured it made better sense to just close the case. I certainly wasn't helping her to make peace with her death, and besides, she was leaving soon and would probably be relieved to sign the form.

"Comin' in, miss?" An officer's voice stirred me from my thoughts. He held the door open and I stepped into the infirmary, thoroughly unprepared for a grim site: long rows of cots with white sheets covering listless women who were coughing, moaning, quietly staring. Wheelchairs and canes cluttered the aisles. The eeriest part was that they appeared young—most suffering from AIDS, I surmised. In the center aisle, a veritable skeleton with hair was shuffling along with the aid of a cane. She stopped to look at me, the round brown eyes of her hollowed-out face seeking me out as if there was something she wanted to say. As we gazed at each other,

I realized that she wasn't more than thirty years old. *This was terrible*. Through the small windows was the river, and just across from it the city, bursting with vibrancy and promise, impervious to this death house in its midst. In the distance, nurses were quibbling about a coffeepot. The skeletal woman never said anything, but planted her cane and resumed her lifeless trudge.

I'd never seen anything like this before. I had to get out of here. I grabbed the refusal form and scanned the beds for Daisy. "Hi, Mental Health!" she waved.

The manner in which she addressed me was irksome, and I disliked her all over again, but I managed a professional smile. "Daisy, I haven't seen you in a while."

"I know," she said, using her arms to hoist her legs over the edge of the cot. "I know you've been calling me, but I've been too sick to make that walk to the clinic. And now you came all the way down here to see me. I wanted to talk to you so bad—for my therapy. There's some chairs in the dayroom. Let's go." She stood up slowly, steadying her small frame.

I felt a pang of guilt and folded up the refusal form.

"By the way," she announced, as we sat down, "my name's not really Daisy Wilson. I have an aunt by that name who told my family not to let me in the house 'cause I was stealing stuff. On account of her, I wasn't allowed in my own mother's house. You believe that? But I got her back, all right—I took her name, so when the police are looking for me, they try and arrest her!"

Great!

After she recovered from a coughing fit, she waved her hand at the women in the cots. "These girls are disgusting. You really shouldn't talk to them—they're prostitutes," she hissed. "They'd do anything for drug money. Trash! That's what they are."

"But Daisy," I pointed out gently, "you were addicted to drugs yourself."

"True. But in all those years, I never, ever prostituted myself. I wasn't raised like that! What I did was—you know the parking lot behind Sears in Brooklyn?"

"No."

"I'd go to the corner there, get into a car with an old man and let him think he was gonna get a blowjob."

"Daisy! We need to talk about your illness and—"

"Oh, we'll get to that. So then, I'd tell him to go into the parking lot—this was at night, see, so there weren't any cars around. Then we'd park and he'd lean over to undo his fly, and I'd pull out my handy rock and *POW*—bash him in the head with it! I was good at it—one shot usually knocked 'em right out. Then I'd go through their pockets."

"Daisy!"

"But it's very important that it's an old man," she mused. "That's the trick."

"Do you see anything wrong with this?" I asked, my anger growing.

"I'm just explaining to you that I was never a prostitute. I pretended to be, but I always stayed pure."

"*Pure?!* You hurt people!"

"Afterwards I would take a cab home," she said, ignoring me. "I always made the cabbie drive by the parking lot, and sometimes I'd see—you know, the flashing lights."

"You may have killed someone."

She said nothing but gave me an almost smile, and we both knew that she had.

When the session ended, I marched straight to Janet's office. When it came to Daisy Wilson, I was at a complete loss. She wasn't like anyone else I'd met. All of the others tried to justify or explain their criminal behavior, insisting that it didn't jibe with who they really were. But not Daisy. This is exactly who she was—and proud of it!

As I described Daisy and her boastful tales, Janet calmly sipped her tea. "You know what you have here, don't you? A remorseless conniver? No conscience?"

I hadn't yet put the pieces together, but in that moment I did. "A sociopath?"

"Yup. And you're right. She's not like the others—and never will be."

With the revelation that I had a full-blown sociopath on my caseload, I naturally assumed Janet would deem me too inexperienced and relieve me of Daisy Wilson, forthwith. So I was stunned by what she said next: "This is good for you, Mary—a lot to learn here."

A lot to learn! "But Janet," I said carefully, "I'm not sure I can handle this. I'm not helping her. I feel like she's in charge and I'm being dragged along for the ride."

"Then take charge. Part of the reason you're having trouble is because you're expecting her to be something she's not. Stop being outraged. Get past it. Yes, she's a bad person, but look at it this way: she's the one sitting on Rikers Island dying of AIDS, and that's what you need to tap into. You're doing fine."

I wasn't doing fine, not by a long shot. But I knew better than to argue with this stern taskmaster. Janet was a stickler about everything. If I wrote "Patient depressed" in a chart note, she handed the chart right back to me. "No, no, full sentences—'Patient *presents* as depressed.'" The charts had to be as polished as Janet's carefully chosen suits. It was all becoming way too much.

But I wasn't completely without hope. My secret wish was that Daisy Wilson's Compassionate Release would come through and that she would just go home.

10

IF MY RELATIONSHIP WITH DAISY WILSON WAS GOING
nowhere, my little adolescent group was picking up steam. Maybe
it was to escape boredom, or maybe it was to enjoy a donut, but
whatever the reason, when I arrived each week more of the girls
were pulling chairs up to the group table. And as I became a familiar weekly figure, they took to calling me "Miss Mary." That,
however, is where the civility ended. As soon as I placed the donuts
on the table, a mad lunge followed. *"Hey, that was my donut!"*
"Fuck you!" Rather than getting upset, I repeated calming words:
"There is always enough for everyone in our group. There is always enough." When the scuffle ended, they sat back with squished
donuts and scowled. Although the behavior was primitive I didn't
mind. All I cared about was that they were coming—and even better, after the treats were gone, they were staying.

Coincidentally, I was taking a class on group therapy where I
was learning more about group dynamics. The group is a powerful
unit; its inherent draw is that it offers a sense of belonging, a universal human need—which explains much of the allure of gangs.
Between my formal training and my own natural instincts, I approached this adolescent challenge with relish. In the early going,
the mood of the group was light as the girls chatted, giggled, and
talked about nothing in particular. I listened carefully, mindful of
who was talking and who was silent. If someone was being over-
shadowed, I made sure she had her moment. I gave each speaker

my undivided attention and managed to offer relevant feedback so they knew they'd been heard. And as I focused on one person at a time, I noticed that the others started to keep quiet. I can't say they were actually listening, but they at least remained silent when someone else was speaking. I was surprised at how quickly this restraint developed, but I suspect it was because they realized that with this method they, too, could have their golden moment—their moment to be heard. And as I knew so well, *everyone needs to be heard*.

These little rudiments of socialization were not only a beginning, but a necessity. If these girls were going to get anywhere in this world, they needed to develop a little basic courtesy—which was not part of their repertoire. Streetwise and battle-scarred, the crew around this table were products of the worst of foster care and group homes. Ebony grew up with a foster family who kept not only the refrigerator locked, but the entire house locked until midnight. Cast out to the streets, Ebony survived by working as a lookout for drug dealers. Peering around street corners and hovering on rooftops, her job was to watch for approaching police. A modern-day Artful Dodger, Ebony lived by her wits and intuition. The others did the same, struggling to survive, growing up way too fast. But behind their tough bravado, in many ways they were still children.

Over the next few weeks, we continued our pattern of gathering together and simply taking turns speaking. And then a new bud developed—they began offering bits of feedback to the speaker, glancing at me for approval, which I happily provided.

Of course, things were going just a little too smoothly. One evening, a girl named Carly announced her arrival by pounding her fist on the table and accusing a bewildered-looking Tonisha of the great jailhouse insult: calling Carly's mother a crackhead. In any other setting, I would have laughed off such nonsense, but not in here. If they had the means, these girls were fully capable of pulling a knife to avenge this perceived slight. In the neighborhoods where they grew up, people were stabbed for less—for failing to say "excuse me" or for accidentally stepping on a sneaker. Among these girls, an accusation like this was serious business. As Carly got louder, chairs scudded back from the table. Anticipating a scuffle, the officer ran out of the bubble, radio in hand. Despite the mounting tension, I was determined to stay calm and use our new tools to handle this. Projecting a composure that I did not feel, I said, "Carly, you seem to be very upset about this."

"Oh, I am! You don't say that about somebody's mother—you just don't."

"But I didn't say it!" Tonisha protested.

The girls looked a little bewildered, not sure whether to rumble or weigh in with their thoughts on the matter.

"So, Tonisha," I continued, "you feel you're not getting a fair shake?"

"That's right—I'm not!"

And then Veronica, a quiet girl with long braids, pulled back up to the table and said, "I think everybody needs to just calm down."

"Yeah—no point doin' something stupid, Carly," added a sweet-faced girl nicknamed Polite. "You don't know for sure Tonisha even said it!"

With the scales tipping toward discussion, they all quietly pulled back up to the table.

Carly sat with folded arms. "Oh, she said it all right!" But the steam was gone.

"Besides," added Ebony, "wouldn't it be nice to have five minutes of peace in here? Just five minutes. Wow! Amazing!"

When the hour ended, Carly and Tonisha refused to look at one another but left the table in peace, and the others quietly dispersed. The fight never happened. At the bubble, the shocked officer shook her head. "Could you come here every night? *Please!*"

It was a triumphant walk back to the clinic.

After that pivotal session, a new trend developed whereby the girls saved up the slights and insults they'd suffered during the week and brought them to the table for arbitration, knowing that the group offered a safe forum for feelings to be expressed and hurts to be acknowledged. A breakthrough had occurred, and every girl around that table knew it. And as the group evolved, there were other changes. For one thing, the mad grab for donuts ended. Instead, they took to passing the box around with exaggerated British accents: "Aftah you, dahling," "Ewh no, but I insist!" It was hard for me to keep a straight face and they knew it, very much enjoying entertaining me.

These were happy moments, but the best news of all came when Janet called me into her office and told me it was official, that DOC had reported a dramatic reduction in violence on the problematic unit.

"Isn't that something?" Janet beamed. "They're growing, Mary! And here's the proof!"

I was thrilled. People don't really want to fight. They just need a way to handle their differences without losing face.

* * *

In every way, the adolescent group was a joy. I only wished the same for the nursery, but the babies never stopped crying and the mothers were perpetually exhausted, so we muddled through as best we could. But one blustery afternoon, a terrible shock awaited when Allison and I arrived to find everyone gathered in the living room, weeping.

"Miss B," Addie cried, "it's Millie—Millie's dead!"

"What! Millie Gittens? What do you mean she's dead?"

"Apparently," said a slack-faced Camille Baxter, "Millie never made it to that program. They picked up the baby, all right—but somehow Millie wound up right back on the streets. We got word this morning from one of the nurses that she died in a crack house. The nurse knows her people and said they found her body yesterday afternoon. She overdosed."

My eyes were stinging and my mind was whirling. Millie Gittens was dead! I wanted to sit down and cry with everyone else, but I had to hold it together. The mothers needed this group, and with an intensity I'd never seen before, they talked, cried, and even smiled, recalling the good and bad about poor Millie.

"And here we thought Millie was so lucky to be getting out of here," Addie mused. "Turns out jail was the best place for her to be."

"Maybe not the worst place for us, either," whispered Marisol.

"Better than dying in some crack house," voiced another.

As they rocked and clung to subdued babies, each one knew that Millie's fate could just as easily have been her own.

Back at the conference room, my own tears started flowing, and Wendy and Allison comforted me. Inevitably, I wondered if I'd given up on her too soon. "No, Mary, you did everything you could," said Wendy. "You went above and beyond for her," said Allison. From our car-ride conversations, Wendy and Allison knew all too well about my "Millie struggle," and I appreciated their words. In my heart I knew they were right. All I could do now was say a prayer for Calvin, who would go into foster care in preparation for adoption. I just hoped the sweet little boy would fall into loving hands.

In the days following the news of Millie's death, I took new stock of my relationships with these women and stepped up my efforts to help them. There was so much at stake, and this window of intervention into chaotic lives had to be maximized. I was especially concerned with Rhonda Reynolds, who was unraveling. Gone were the pigtails, fuzzy headgear, and waiting room hijinks. "The police lied to me!" she cried. "They said all I had to do was tell the truth and everything would be okay. And I did—I told the truth about that girl jumping on me, and now I'm going to prison! They lied! I'm so stressed—and these nightmares aren't going away. I need sleeping pills!"

"Rhonda, isn't it time you gave up on the pills? Whatever it is that happened to you," I said softly, "I'd like to help you with it."

She looked up at me, beads of sweat trickling through her scalp.

"You come here every week, faithfully," I said, "for a reason. I think you know me well enough by now that you can trust me."

"You want me to tell you about the nightmares? You really want me to tell you?"

"Yes, I do, Rhonda. It's time. Let me help you."

"I wanted to tell someone when it happened, but nobody listened to me. Nobody cared!"

"Someone is listening now."

"All right," she quivered. "All right then! I'll tell you . . . I'll tell you. The blood I dream about—it was my blood. Something happened. Something bad—real bad."

With a faraway look, Rhonda finally began. "It happened a couple of years ago. I was gettin' high a lot, you know, smokin' weed, whatnot, and this one afternoon in the summer I see this guy comin' down the street. I'd seen him around the neighborhood, and I ask him if he wants to party. So he comes in and we smoke weed, and then he pulls out some cocaine—crack—and we smoke that too. We were pretty high, everything goin' fine. And when it's over, I go to the door to let him out, and he jumps on my back, and I'm like, *What?* Then he pulls me down to the floor and starts punching me, punching me hard—hard! In my face, in my stomach, everywhere. *Oh, God.* I didn't know what was happening. And then he tore off my clothes—and raped me. *He raped me!* And then . . . he just got up and walked out the door like nothing—*like absolutely nothing.* And when I tried to get up, I couldn't. My legs, my arms, they were just sliding around in blood. When my daughter came in, I was naked, laying in my own blood. It was horrible for her to see me like that. She was only six.

"I told her to throw a sheet over me and call 911. When the police came it got worse. There was three or four cops, and at first they didn't even want to call an ambulance. They just stood around drinking coffee and telling jokes. They were laughing at me— *laughing!* They told me to get up, that I was faking it. They said I wasn't even worth the paperwork, that I was just a piece of . . . of garbage. When they finally called the ambulance and I got to the hospital, I was on a gurney that got pushed into a corner—like a shopping cart. The cops were joking around with the nurses, like I wasn't even there. Everyone just ignored me."

As Rhonda's horrible ordeal poured out, my own eyes were stinging.

She glanced up at me and saw the tears. "Heh," she whispered, fixing her gaze at the floor. "Just another nigger."

"Oh, Rhonda! No! Oh, no! You are a human being, and *nothing less!* The guy who did this to you—and the police and the nurses—they're the ones who should be ashamed, not you!"

She looked up at me for a moment, a glimmer of hope in her tear-filled eyes. "But that's just it, Miss Buser—it was my fault. *I let him in!*"

"You let him in to party with you—not to attack you!"

She thought about it for a moment and shrugged. "I was in the hospital—in rehab—for five months, just learning to walk again."

"My God, Rhonda. You've been through hell. I can't believe you haven't told anyone about this."

"I didn't think anyone would care."

Out in the clinic, Overton was announcing the start of the afternoon count. I went out to his desk and asked that Rhonda be included on the clinic count so she wouldn't have to leave just then. I returned and sat with her, just the two of us. When she was finally cried out, she let out a deep breath and sighed. "Well, you wanted to know."

"I know it wasn't easy for you to relive this, Rhonda," I said softly, "but it needed to come out."

"Yeah," she sniffled. "Yeah, I know. I think I'd like to go lay down now."

After she left, I returned to the session booth and sat for a while, barely able to comprehend the horror of what Rhonda had endured. The inhumanity of it—not only from the rapist, but from the police and hospital staff—was incomprehensible. To the police, Rhonda was a skel, not quite a real person, undeserving of any human compassion. And it wasn't lost on me that if I or any of my friends had been so brutally assaulted, the police response would have been entirely different. And Rhonda Reynolds's agony was no less simply because she was poor, Black, and a drug addict.

11

BY THE MIDDLE OF THE SECOND SEMESTER, TERM PAPERS
were due; for one class, I had to write about my most difficult case
and explore strategies for improving it. I had no trouble identifying
the case: Daisy Wilson, of course. Although I was regularly making
the trek to the infirmary, supposedly to help this woman come to
terms with her imminent death, our sessions remained an unending
litany of her criminal escapades. When I protested, reminding her of
more pressing issues, she would brush me off, saying, "Oh, we'll get
to that"—and off she went. Afterward, I was angry and repulsed. I
dreaded my sessions with Daisy, hated going to the infirmary, and
kept wondering what was holding up the Compassionate Release.

Perhaps writing about her would help, although I didn't quite
see how. Nonetheless, I gathered detailed information on sociopathy, thumbing through articles on its causes, diagnosis, and
treatment. One article stressed that therapeutic relationships can
be tricky, as the therapist can easily be seduced by the sociopath's
charm and guile. That certainly resonated. Daisy was most charm-
ing—never rude or unpleasant—and when it came to her tales, "seduced" was exactly how I felt, drawn in to listen. Another article
stated that criminals do things to others that the rest of us might
actually enjoy doing had these impulses not been socialized out of
us; yet hearing about these deeds can be tantalizing, which explains
the wild appeal of crime-based books, movies, and TV shows. All
of this was very interesting, but I didn't connect it to me—yet. It

was while I was at home on a rainy weekend, doing dishes of all things, that Daisy's tales seeped into my thoughts. Her wild stories were better than any TV show, that was for sure. And then something started clicking. Was it possible that I was more intrigued with her stories than I realized—and that she was entertaining me? It was a crazy thought. After all, I was trying to help this dying woman. Besides, I didn't like her stories. Every time she started up, I protested. *But then I listened.* I put down the dish towel and grabbed a notebook. As I put thoughts to paper, I knew I was on to something, something I'd never anticipated, something that was highlighting my own fallibility. I hated to even consider the possibility that I was an enabler here, but instead of fighting it, I allowed the idea to take hold. And as it did, everything started coming into focus. As I sat down and let it all sink in, all the anger was gone. In its place was determination. I wanted another crack at this relationship. I wanted a chance to get it right. Though I had yearned for the Compassionate Release to come through, now I needed it to be delayed just a little longer.

On Monday, I marched to the infirmary with an authority I'd never felt before, and it was a very different Daisy who greeted me. Funny how things are sensed. Wobbling along in an aqua-colored shift, she led me to the dayroom, her exposed legs covered with dark lesions, a distinct mark of AIDS. She was not doing well. No sooner had we sat down than she began to cry. "Do you know what it's like when your own mother won't let you in the house 'cause she's afraid you're going to steal something?"

"No," I said. "Tell me."

And she did. We met two more times, and I helped her to break the news of her illness to her family, who opened their hearts and their home. Shortly afterward, the release was approved and Daisy Wilson went home to die.

Afterward, I went over everything with Janet. "Aren't you glad you saw this through?" Janet chided. "Looks like there was a lot to learn here—not only about sociopaths, but about ourselves. Therapists don't work with hammers, nails, or computers, Mary—our tool is ourselves. You need to always be honest with yourself, and be very clear about your own feelings. Otherwise you're going to have problems."

"Yes, so I see."

"Good work, Mary Mac," she said, using her newly minted nickname for me. "And here you thought I was being so mean."

"No, I didn't!"

"Oh, yes you did," she laughed.

"Well, maybe a little," I admitted. I was so lucky to have been paired up with Janet. What an ace—no question about it!

* * *

Daisy Wilson was my first encounter with someone who might be considered evil, but contrary to the perception that jails are filled with "bad people," I found few at Daisy's level of sociopathy. Most are somewhere in the middle, ordinary people who are drug-addicted and may have committed a crime while under the influence of drugs or alcohol, those who've made errors in judgment or who've acted impulsively or out of desperation. With a little guidance and support, so many in that middle range had the potential to find their way and move on.

A prime example of someone who was finding her way was Lucy Lopez. After much finagling with the Bureau of Child Welfare, Lucy finally won approval for a visit with Junior, her four-year-old. Lucy was ecstatic and talked of little else. When the "big day" arrived, she raced to the visiting room for a reunion with the child she hadn't seen in over a year. Her worst fear was that Junior wouldn't remember her, but as soon as Junior spotted Lucy he cried out, "Mama!"

"It was beautiful," Lucy told me later. "I held him, talked to him, rocked him on my lap. I never wanted it to end."

"The only hard part," she said, "was being nice to *that* woman." "That woman" was the foster mother who'd brought Junior to the visit, and who Lucy suspected was the prospective adoptive parent. In preparation for her encounter with the foster mother, Lucy and I had carefully reviewed what she would say. I reminded her that she still had legal recourse to keep her son, but that any angry outburst, while momentarily satisfying, would only work against her in the long run. "Miss Buser," she said, "you don't know how bad I wanted to say to her, *He's my baby, not yours!*" Lucy stopped and took a deep breath. "But I didn't, Miss Buser, I didn't. I just said to her, 'Thank you for taking such good care of my child.' It took everything in me to get those words out—everything. But I did it."

The two of us sat back and smiled. Both the visit and Lucy's comportment throughout the hour were a huge victory for her. "You handled it all very well," I said, "very well!"

But a setback was looming. A few days later, Lucy got into a spat with Swanday, one of the instigators in the original Millie Gittens incident. When Swanday told Lucy she'd never see Junior again, Lucy slapped Swanday across the face, knocking her to the floor. In one moment, all of Lucy's growth seemed to evaporate. She regretted it instantly, but the damage was done. An infraction ticket was issued—a ticket that carried ten days in isolation.

"I can't believe I lost it like that!" she sobbed in the emergency session that followed. "I've gotten through worse than this—much worse! I don't know what happened to me. And now I'm going into solitary—*solitary*. I'll be alone in some dark cell . . . *Oh, God!* And I won't see Michael for almost *two weeks*."

But the assault on Swanday had further implications. It meant possible expulsion from the nursery, with baby Michael sent out to foster care. A meeting was held to determine whether Lucy could remain, but Camille Baxter, noting Lucy's hard-fought progress, chalked it up to an unfortunate but isolated incident. "Lucy and Michael aren't going anywhere," she said. During Lucy's absence, the nursery staff would pitch in to care for the baby.

A grateful Lucy said this reprieve would enable her to endure her punishment. A few days later, a captain and a couple of officers arrived to escort her to solitary housing. In a parting embrace with

Michael, Lucy was biting back the tears. But while she steeled herself, the baby didn't understand. "Mama, Mama!" he cried.

"All right now," Camille Baxter said, prying the terrified child from his mother. Lucy grabbed her plastic bag of clothes, and as the baby shrieked, she was led out.

It was a heart-wrenching scene. Slapping Swanday was unacceptable, of course, but solitary confinement seemed like a horrible punishment—not only for Lucy, but for her innocent baby. I thought that something else could surely have been devised that would have taught Lucy a lesson without harming the baby. But this was the one and only jailhouse punishment, a punishment that was meted out every day, in every jail on the island.

Ugly hallway scenes with a crying, pleading woman being dragged along the floor by officers, en route to the solitary unit, were common. Jailhouse protocol dictated that everyone simply step aside as they passed by. It was an awful sight. But Janet told me that punishment for the women was mild compared to the men. "They get much longer sentences," she said, "and they don't serve it in their own jails. They get bused over to the Central Punitive Segregation Unit—they call it the 'Bing.' Sounds happy and upbeat—it's anything but. The place is huge, 500 cells."

As Janet described this grim facility, I felt relieved to be working with women and well insulated from such misery, with no inkling that in time I would become well acquainted with the notorious "jail within jail."

*   *   *

Lucy's ten days in isolation came and went, and by now it was early spring, though it hardly felt like it. As the days grew longer, the cold only seemed to grow stronger, but the added daylight encouraged some to venture outside. One late afternoon, through the frozen windowpane, I recognized a bundled-up Tiffany Glover sitting by herself, listening to her Walkman in the courtyard. The wind blew her hair around as she swayed to the music, alone with her thoughts. Although quitting STEP had been a big defeat, she no longer seemed as lost, and I also noticed she wasn't as thin, which meant she was finally eating. Apparently, Tiffany had been doing a lot of thinking, as she arrived for our next session with a surprising announcement: "I want to join STEP again—I wasn't ready before, but this time I can do it. I *know* I can!"

And so Tiffany Glover reenlisted in the STEP program, but this time things were different. She was moving up in the hallway line. No longer greeting me with a weak little smile, she boomed, "Hello, Miss B!" And then Tiffany was right up front, leading the troops through the Rose Singer jail. "Miss B!" she would yell, "look, I'm gettin' fat!" Reaching into her uniform, she grabbed her midriff to show off a little roll of fat. "Ha, ha!" she laughed. Sure enough, she was actually getting heavy. Like the rest of us, Tiffany would now have to watch her weight. But at least she was in a new realm, having finally broken loose from the grips of addiction, a far cry from the sad person I'd first met in the receiving room. Like Janet had said in the beginning, "You will see these people change." It was a delight to witness.

Tiffany was like a new person, bursting with pride at her success in her second go-round. "I knew I could do it, I knew I could!" And then there was news about her case. "I'm taking the one-to-three," she said, "which means I'll be locked up for one year, and then I'll be on parole for two more. So it means I get to stay here to serve the one year. I'm not going to prison! 'Course, if I mess up when I get out, I could be remanded to serve the other two, but that won't happen! No way! In less than a year, I'll be home, Miss Buser—home! I talk to my mother and my baby every night. We tell the baby I'm in the hospital. And when I get out of here, I'm taking care of my son—every day. That's my *new* rule," she beamed. "Every single day! I'm going to be such a good mother. I can't wait! I just can't wait!"

Things were certainly looking up for Tiffany. The one-year sentence did mean that she could stay at Rose Singer, as sentences of a year or less were permitted to be served at Rikers. But just when it seemed that nothing could sully this ever-brightening picture, it did. And it happened in a surprising twist that I never saw coming. During our sessions, Tiffany was speaking more and more about one of the officers who'd taken an interest in her.

"You seem very fond of him," I remarked.

"He's helped me so much," she said. "Right after I quit the first time, he kept coming up to me in the halls, telling me to try again."

"So, he's been like a coach?"

"Yeah, he really has," she said, twirling her ponytail. "And maybe a little more."

"What do you mean?"

She said nothing, but stared at the floor and blushed.

"Tiffany . . . what's going on here? Has he tried to kiss you or something?"

"Kiss me?" she laughed. "We've been having sex!"

"*What!*"

"Sure. Outside in the back, there's these trailers—"

"Tiffany!"

"Don't worry, he's very responsible. He always uses condoms—always."

"Oh, I'm sure he does! He'd have a tough time explaining your pregnancy!"

Tiffany's sunny smile was gone, replaced by concern. "You can't tell anybody, Miss Buser. You told me when we first started meeting that everything we talked about was confidential. You can't tell!"

"Tell" was exactly what I wanted to do. I wanted to go straight to the warden and report this predator. The idea that this guy would abuse his authority like this was sickening.

Tiffany's eyes bored into mine. I had to get hold of my anger. She'd raised an important issue, and it was one that I could not ignore: confidentiality. A therapeutic relationship is a privileged relationship in the eyes of the law, meaning that all conversations are confidential unless the client has a plan to kill himself, to kill another, or is involved in any type of child abuse. We were required to disclose this clause at the outset of therapy, a disclosure Tiffany had well remembered. Having sex with a correction officer did not remotely fit into the criteria of killing oneself, killing another, or engaging in child abuse. I was bound to keep this bombshell to myself.

Reluctantly, I said, "No, I will not repeat this."

"'Cause that wouldn't be right," she said. "After all, I've been talking to you freely. I always thought I could trust you."

"Yes, I know. And you can," I said, with a little more conviction. "You can. But this is still a big problem."

"He's a good guy," she protested. "He's helping me. We have plans."

"Tiffany, this isn't a good way to start a relationship. You're not on equal footing, and he's taking advantage of that. My concern is for you."

But she could see none of it. From her perspective, she'd found a way to get special treatment in jail—no small feat. But from my standpoint, her relationship with this guy was a replication of her affairs with drug dealers in the streets. There, it was sex for drugs; here, it was sex for priority treatment.

But her jaw was set. She was on top on the world, and I was bringing her down. Although I tried to get us back on a more familiar track, the session ended awkwardly. The following week she missed her appointment, and she never showed up again. I can't say I was surprised, but I still had a hard time believing the relationship was over. Out in the halls, I tried to get her attention, but she stared straight ahead. No more yelling out to me, no more big smiles. Looking back, I realized that I'd broken the cardinal rule of refraining from judgment. If I'd been a more experienced therapist, maybe I wouldn't have reacted as strongly. But as I was forced to accept that it was over, I took comfort in knowing that through our work together, Tiffany Glover had still come a long way.

12

WITH STARS SPLASHED ACROSS AN EARLY APRIL SKY, IN-
side a dreary Rose Singer housing unit the adolescent group started
out quietly. To add a bit of structure to the group, I'd started bringing in coloring books, and the girls were happily coloring. As they
shaded in outlines of bunnies and tulips, much of their "tough girl"
facades vanished. The coloring seemed to bind up their energy, and
I noticed they were a little more thoughtful and contemplative with
this added bit of structure.

"Maria," I said casually, "your hair looks a little different today. Are you wearing it in a new style?"

"Yes, but I won't leave it like this for long. I'll change it back."

"Can't keep razors in a style like that one," chided Ebony.

"Shut up, Ebony."

As Maria colored, she cleared her throat. "When I'm out on the
street, Miss Mary, I keep razor blades in my hair."

"Why?"

"Protection! The streets are dangerous."

"Yeah," chimed in Polite. "Just before I got locked up, I was out
late and I hear, pop-pop! pop-pop! Next thing you know this kid
comes crawling around the corner. He was on his hands and knees
and he crawled right up to me, and there was blood pouring out of
his ears, and he says, 'Help me, help me,' and then he just kind of
fell on his stomach and didn't say nothin' else."

"Was he dead?" asked Michelle.

"Dead as a doornail!"

They all laughed.

"Well, get this," said Diana, "I was at this club one night and a guy asks this girl to dance. And when she says no, he pulls out a gun and shoots her in the face. Party over!"

"Yeah," said Ebony, "and I saw a guy get shot up on the roof—the force of the bullet knocked him clean off the building. Splat!"

They all laughed again.

"Miss Mary," said Carly. "Haven't you ever seen somebody die in front of you?"

I shook my head. "I can't say I have. How many of you have seen someone die?"

Every hand shot up. I was stunned. Not only by the violence, but their numbness to it.

"Hey, life in the big city," said Crystal. "No big deal."

There were knowing nods as they fell into a terse silence, grinding the crayons into the bunnies and tulips. Despite the grim dialogue, the hour ended on a mellow note, and in what had become a closing ritual they walked me to the bubble, their parting words a key part of the ritual. Ebony cleared her throat and began: "Be careful of the bushes when you're walking home tonight, Miss Mary, and if anybody jumps out, then you tell them"—and here she would cue the others with an invisible baton—"that—you—got—friends—on—Ri–kers Island!" And we all laughed.

On our way back, Wendy and I talked about the violence. "Can you imagine?" I said. "The thing is, we're not in some third world country here. All this shooting and killing happens right here—upper Manhattan, Queens, Bed-Stuy, the South Bronx. It's a whole other world, right under our noses—a world that the rest of us don't even know exists."

"I know," Wendy agreed. "Same with the girls on my side. It's unbelievable."

On the stretch of corridor common to the men's jail, our conversation was interrupted by angry shouts. To our left were long rows of bars, and on the other side empty patches of darkened space. Behind the bars, four or five COs were surrounding a male inmate. "No, man! I didn't do nothin'!'" shouted the inmate.

"Shut the fuck up!"

They were pushing the young man into a corner where a set of bars intersected. All we could see of him were his jeans and sneakers as his legs were being spread apart—*"Nooh!"* he shouted. Just then, a white-shirted captain coming down the hall spotted us. "Move along!" he ordered. No smile, no "good evening" nod. We hesitated momentarily. "Keep moving!" We did just that. As we neared the end of the corridor, Wendy said, "They're going to beat the crap out of him."

As much as I tried to think up another explanation, I knew she was right. I felt dazed. The next day, I told Janet about it. She just shook her head, and for the first time my wise mentor didn't have a ready answer. "Some bad things do happen in here, Mary—there's no denying it. We do the best we can," she sighed. "We do the best we can."

After a couple of days of dwelling on what I had seen and heard, I decided to let it go. I didn't know his name. I didn't even know for sure if he'd been beaten. Obsessing about it was only keeping me upset while doing nothing for him. I just hoped he was okay and that this was an isolated incident. Years later I would learn otherwise. But then, I simply said a little prayer for him and tucked it all away.

* * *

There was always some sort of drama in the jail, and the three of us were constantly jumping up from our table to investigate. One afternoon, Overton was leaning out the doorway, checking out some hallway commotion. We jumped up just in time to see a gurney flying by with a shrieking woman on board. "I told them the baby was coming! I told them!" Overton shut the door and scrambled over to the inner door leading to the medical side of the clinic. He unlocked it and we plowed through, joining a growing mob of nurses, pharmacy techs, clerks, and officers, along with a crowd of inmates who'd abandoned their waiting room seats. "Sit the fuck down!" the officers ordered the inmates. But no one budged and the orders became halfhearted, and then they stopped. For a moment, duties were ignored and hierarchies dissolved, as everyone was pulled toward something much larger.

"Ambulance on the way!" shouted a nurse.

"Too late!" yelled the chief physician, stepping out from behind a wall of white curtains. Pulling on a long gown and fastening on an elastic face mask, he ducked back in. The crowd waited, held back by a three-foot-high cement partition. The doctor barked, "Push harder! One more time—push harder—harder! One more! There we go!" And then the dingy clinic was filled with the sweet sounds of an infant's first cries. Everyone was beaming, from high-ranking correctional personnel all the way down to the lowly inmates, many with hands over their hearts. Even the mirthless Captain Murphy looked a little misty. After a few moments, the doctor stepped out from the curtains and raised his arm high up overhead. In the palm of his large hand he held the tiny new life for all to behold.

13

THE AIR WAS FINALLY WARMING, AND PURPLE AND WHITE crocuses were pushing up from the thawing earth, and the Canada geese had returned. Bus drivers were slamming on their brakes to avoid the fluffy goslings meandering along the island's roadways.

"Spring is here," said Allison, pulling out her trusty calendar. "And that means we'll be out of here soon."

Wendy and Allison were counting down the days, but I was in no hurry for the year to end. Regardless, the weeks were, indeed, winding down; we were no longer assigned new cases, but rather called upon for quick referrals only. Janet started pushing me to discuss my impending departure with the patients on my shrinking caseload, particularly Rhonda Reynolds, whom I suspected had forgotten I was a student. "She's come a long way with you, Mary, and this is going to be tough on her. She needs time to process this."

After Rhonda had finally revealed the source of her nightmares, she talked of nothing else, needing to express every aspect of the brutal attack that she'd barely survived. As we talked it through, I helped her to understand that although she was a drug addict and needed to address this, she bore no blame for the assault. Slowly, she began to view things differently, shifting the blame to where it belonged. She never stopped pushing for sleep meds, but her requests were halfhearted. "Hey, I gotta try!" she smiled. And as she spoke more freely, initial reports of an idyllic childhood gave way to uglier memories—beatings with extension cords, a stepfather's drunken tirades, of growing up in constant fear. Her eyes glazed over as she talked, but she was on a determined path to releasing so much pain, to getting it all out.

And then on an ordinary morning, her demeanor was strangely different when she arrived for her session. She was looking at me, but somehow seemed far away.

"Are you okay, Rhonda?" I asked.

Gazing into the distance, she softly whispered, "I didn't mean for her to die."

"What, Rhonda? What did you say?"

And then, louder, "I didn't mean for her to die. I never thought she'd *die*. I just made up my mind that no one would ever hurt me again—no one was ever going to jump on me. *But I never meant for that girl to die.*"

"I know you didn't."

"But she's dead."

"Yes."

"And I killed her." Rhonda dropped her face into her hands. *"Oh! God! Oh! God forgive me! God forgive me! Oh! . . ."*

It was a moment of profound sadness. Sadness for a young woman who never could have known that innocent horseplay would cost her her life, and sadness for Rhonda, who was now headed to prison for an act that was borne not of malice, but of perceived self-protection.

When she slowly lifted her tearstained face, she said, "My lawyer's trying to get the charge reduced from murder to manslaughter, but even so, it'll be ten, fifteen years. Why did this happen to me, Miss Buser? Why? How can so many bad things happen to one person? I thought the rape was the worst thing ever—but this? Why?"

I shook my head. There were no ready answers to her questions. It seemed to me that the hard in life, such as Rhonda's miserable childhood, ought to be balanced out by good things later on. It only seemed fair. But more often than not, it's the opposite. Without intervention, the bad just keeps snowballing. I kept thinking that if only Rhonda had received help following the rape, this stabbing might not have occurred. But a thousand "if onlys" would change nothing. A woman was dead, and Rhonda was going to prison for a long time.

When our session ended, it was on a somber but peaceful note. Afterward, I caught up with Janet and told her. "I never thought she was going to be able to face it," I said.

"You've done very good work with her, Mary Mac," Janet smiled.

I muttered a thank-you, knowing Janet wasn't one for gratuitous praise.

"Now, have you reminded her you're leaving? What about the others—have you brought it up?"

"No . . . not yet."

Janet looked at me sharply. "You have to begin this conversation. It's not fair to them, Mary—they've put their trust in you, and that's not easy for these women to do."

I knew she was right, but saying good-bye is just so hard. Recognizing the difficulty in terminating these relationships, a professor at school suggested a method of softening the news. He said that after discussing our upcoming departure, we might then "step out of character." He gave an example of perhaps meeting a client for a cup of coffee as therapy neared its conclusion. I thought it was an intriguing idea, although in my case the local coffee shop wasn't an option. Nonetheless, I tucked the idea in the back of my mind.

In the meantime, I was in for a shock one morning when I was walking to the MO and a nurse pulled me aside in the crowded hall. "Get this," she said. "I was just down in the receiving room and guess who just arrived? Millie—Millie Gittens."

"*What!* There must be some mistake," I said. "Millie Gittens is dead."

"Well, looks like she's back from the dead. It's her all right. Oh, and another thing—she's pregnant. Baxter's down there now."

I was stunned. I didn't know what to do. Reflexively, I started toward the receiving room, unsure whether I wanted to hug Millie or throttle her for the needless grief we'd all been put through.

But then I stopped. What was the point? I had never been able to reach Millie. Maybe the next therapist would. I hoped so. I turned around and continued on my way.

* * *

I began my farewells with my short-term cases. Regardless of whether these women were to be released or were destined for prison, I encouraged everyone to continue seeking guidance and support, and above all else, to never ever give up on themselves.

Next came the nursery. Ever distracted by demanding babies and their own fatigue, the mothers took the news in stride. And I wasn't worried about Lucy either. She would be departing for prison at about the same time I would be leaving. Lucy had been sentenced to two-to-four—two years in prison, two more on parole. Since she'd already been at Rikers close to a year, she only had a little over a year to serve upstate, as the time spent in detention was credited toward the sentence.

After the slapping incident, Lucy had gotten herself right back on track. Her efforts extended beyond the jail's walls as she wrote letters to the family who'd long ago given up on her. "I had to swallow my pride," she said. "They said some pretty nasty things about me—calling me a useless crackhead."

Her letters initially went unanswered, but then an elderly aunt who'd always had a soft spot for Lucy wrote back. The letters led to phone calls, and then—a big break—the aunt offered to take in baby Michael while Lucy was upstate. And when Lucy was released from prison, the aunt agreed to take Lucy in, provided, of course, that she remained drug-free.

"It's a miracle, Miss B—a miracle! God answered my prayers! I'll never touch drugs again—never! Never! I'm done. Done! I still don't know about my little Junior. I have to get my little guy back. But I'm just going to keep praying and working on it, same as I've been doing all along. That's all I can do, Miss B—do the best I can, and leave the rest in God's hands."

Lucy was due to go upstate at any time, and not knowing exactly when she'd be leaving, we said our good-byes. "Oh, Miss B," she cried in a parting embrace. "Thank you for believing in a useless crackhead."

"Oh, Lucy!" I bit back my own tears, recalling just how far she had come—from a lost soul lying on a subway platform to a poised woman with purpose.

A couple of days later, Lucy Lopez was gone, having boarded an early morning bus for Bedford Hills Prison. Somehow, the jail wasn't the same without Lucy tearing around the corners clutching stacks of legal papers on one of her many missions. I already missed her.

The tougher good-byes were still ahead, and with little more than a few weeks remaining, I began the dreaded conversation with Rhonda Reynolds. "Do you remember when we first met back in the fall—that Miss Waters told you I was a student?"

"No."

"Well, I am—and what that means is that in another month, I'm going to be leaving."

"*What!*"

This was going to be bad.

"You're kidding me," she said, with a hopeful little smile.

"No, Rhonda. I'm sorry, but I was assigned to work here for the school year."

"So, that's it? Your school year's over, and now it's—'*see ya!*'"

"Rhonda—this isn't easy for me either, but I thought it would be better to remind you in advance so we still have time to talk . . . time to say good-bye."

Her hand was over her mouth, her eyes welling up with tears. "I trusted you. Can't you tell them you want to stay?" she asked, alternating between anger and hope.

"It doesn't work like that, Rhonda. It has nothing to do with you or the importance of our relationship."

She was sobbing now. "I want to go back to my house."

"Oh, Rhonda." But she was on her feet and out the door.

When Overton called for her the following week, she was a no-show. "Don't worry," Janet said. "Not unusual. If you're going to leave her, she's going to leave you—at least for now."

For the first time, I wondered if it was worth it. Was it really worth getting so close to these women, just to break their hearts?

But Janet viewed it differently. "Would she have revealed the rape, Mary? Would she have faced it that she killed someone? Some very important things happened here. It's sad that it's ending, but it's far more important that this relationship happened. She'll be back."

I prayed Janet was right. In the meantime, I broke the news to the adolescents, who did not take it well either. "So you'll be back in September?" asked Ebony.

"No—I won't."

"You're just going to leave us?" said Veronica.

"I'm not *leaving you*. My internship is ending."

"What's the difference?" said Maria.

"The difference is that this group—all of you—you mean a lot to me. The reason I'm leaving has nothing to do with any of you."

Crystal got up and walked away, followed by Carly.

But Ebony wasn't ready to give up. "Can't you tell them you want to stay—you know, sometimes you have to push things a little, Miss Mary."

Looking at this group of expectant faces was breaking my heart. "Listen," I said, "most of *you* are leaving Rikers pretty soon too. Ebony, you're going to be released for time served—and the same with you two," I said to Maria and Veronica. "And the rest of you will be leaving also—Rikers isn't permanent. You know that."

"That doesn't matter," said Ebony.

And in their eyes, it didn't. To them, I was just one more person letting them down. When the hour was up, I made the trip to the bubble alone, where a concerned officer let me out. It was a depressing walk back.

Time was dwindling down, and Allison and I visited the nursery for the last time. Many of the faces had changed from that first day when Janet had introduced me to the mothers. Lucy was gone, as were Addie and Marisol. Now there were new faces, new mothers trying to make a go of it with their babies.

In recognition of our final gathering, Camille Baxter brought in a cake that read "Good Luck, Mary and Allison," and she handed us each a small box. Inside was a simple silver bracelet. "This is from all of us," she said.

"Yeah," said Tasha, "we all went to Macy's and picked it out—the warden said we could go, as long as we promised to come back."

"And here we are!" said another. "Who says we can't be trusted?"

We laughed, ate cake, and showed off our bracelets.

The little farewell party was actually fun. For a few blessed moments, not one of the babies was crying, and for the first time, I rocked one of the infants in my arms. Always wishing to maintain a professional demeanor, I had enjoyed the babies from a distance but had never actually held them. But now it was time to "step out of character." It felt nice.

When it was all over and time to go, Camille Baxter, mothers, and babies walked us to the door, and with a final wave from the whole gang, the door with the Mickey Mouse decal closed behind us for the last time. I wiped away the tears on the walk back.

The only remaining business was Rhonda Reynolds and the adolescent group. I called Rhonda a third time, and this time, to my great relief, she came. "I've missed you," I said.

"I was going to hang up," she said, using the jailhouse term for committing suicide.

"Oh, Rhonda."

"It's just that any time something good happens, God pulls the rug right out from under me. You've been something good, and now you're going away."

"Yes, I'm leaving, but the thing is, Rhonda, the work we did together—the changes you made, which have been very big—those are yours to keep. Our work together will never, *ever* go away. It's in your heart, Rhonda. It's yours—forever."

She looked at me with a flicker of hope. I laid my arm across the desk and reached out my hand. She took it.

Later on, I got an idea that had to do with my professor's suggestion, and I ran it by Janet. "What would you think if Rhonda and I had lunch together for our last session?" Janet scratched her head. "I don't see the harm in it, but you've got to clear it with DOC."

I went directly to Overton's desk, hoping to get the okay from him, bypassing another Captain Murphy tape recorder fiasco.

"You wanna *what?*" the beleaguered officer said.

"I want to know if it would be all right if, instead of our session, Rhonda Reynolds and I could have lunch together?"

"Whaddya think this is—the Russian Tea Room? This is Rikers Island!"

"I'll bring in the food and we'll sit at our usual desk."

"She's goin' up the river, you know."

"Yes, thank you for that. Any objections?"

"Hey, you want to waste your money—feel free."

"Thank you, Officer Overton, thank you very much! After I'm gone, I'll always have such fond memories of you!"

"Baahhh!"

Just as Rhonda had rebounded from my departure news, so did the adolescents. When I next met with them, I pointed out their changes, reminding them of how they used to lunge for the donuts and of their new strategies for handling anger. In the same way I told Rhonda that her changes were for keeps, I told them that they had matured, and that that could never be undone. Although they weren't happy, they were a resilient bunch, and, skilled listeners that they'd become, they heard me out. And then there was giggling and impish looks. They had a secret, and when they could contain it no longer, Ebony pulled a big pink homemade card out from under the table.

"Read it! Read it!"

On the cover was a carefully traced rose, and inside were the words: "If this was a perfect world, and if dreams really did come true, then our dream would be that you would stay with the group." It was signed by each of them.

I wanted to cry. Instead, I looked up at their beaming faces. "Thank you," I said. "I can see that a lot of thought went into this—and it means so much to me."

"You really like it?"

"I love it!"

The hour went by quickly, and just like old times, they walked me to the bubble for a final "You—got—friends—on—Ri–kers Is-land!" And then this bunch that had become so dear to me gathered in front of the bubble window, waving. I walked backward, waving back, holding up my big pink card. It wasn't till I turned a corner that I let the tears flow.

After obtaining Officer Overton's grudging approval for lunch with Rhonda Reynolds, I told her about it in our second-to-last session.

"We're going to have lunch together—you and me?"

"Yes, I thought it would be a nice thing for the two of us to do."

She looked a little suspicious but said, "Okay."

We decided on pizza, soda, and cupcakes for dessert.

On the appointed day, I poured soda and nuked the pizza.

"I haven't had soda or pizza in over a year," she said.

"How does it taste?"

"Delicious," she smiled.

After months of intimate conversation, all of a sudden we were a bit like strangers. "Hey," I said, "remember the first time I met you, when you came down in that fuzzy blue headband?"

"Sure do!" she laughed. "I loaned it to someone. Reminds me, I need to get it back!"

As always, time sped by and our little luncheon was over. She started to cry again, but this time just a little. We stood up and hugged. "I'm so glad I got to know you, Rhonda. You'll be in my thoughts and prayers."

"Good-bye, Miss Buser," she said. "Thank you."

As Overton unlocked the clinic door, she turned back one more time and waved, and then Rhonda Reynolds was gone.

* * *

On our last day at Rose Singer, the three of us were packing up our papers from our anti-TB room, leaving early since our supervisors were taking us out to lunch. We had toyed with the idea of closing the windows in April. After having made it safely to spring, we figured we were home free. But then Wendy said, "Wouldn't it be something if we got through winter, let our guard down now—and got TB?" That did it. The windows stayed open. But now, on our last day, we shut them, stood back, and clapped. We made it!

"Yeah, sure," said Overton, who'd poked his head in, "now that it's warm out—time to *open* the windows—you decide to *shut* them. Thanks a lot!"

"Oh, Overton!" said Janet. "Say good-bye to the students. To-day's their last day."

"Yeah, and in September there'll be three more to ruin my life. Least I'll have the summer in peace." But as he walked us to the door and unlocked it for the final time, he gave up a smile. "Baahhh—good-bye, already!"

Out in the lobby, I gazed up at the portrait of Rose Singer, re-calling her wish that this jail be a place of hope and renewal. For many of the women in here, it had been just that. Change comes slowly, and while it remained to be seen just how these women would fare once released, those who had sought support were cer-tainly better positioned for managing life on the outside. For my part, I was thrilled to have been part of their growth and, of equal importance, to have given something of value to the most beaten-down among us. I knew I'd found my niche, and as we stepped out of the gritty jail and into the sunshine of the day, I also knew that I would be back.

14

AS A REWARD FOR TREKKING OUT TO RIKERS ISLAND, ALL
the Rikers students were handed plum assignments for our second
and final year of fieldwork. For me, this meant a family services
agency in Midtown Manhattan, just a few doors down from Car-
negie Hall. From this smart new address, I continued to hone my
therapy skills, branching out to work with troubled families and
children. But much as I appreciated the pleasant surroundings, my
mind always drifted back to Rikers.

In the spring of 1993 I received my master's degree. To celebrate, my mother hosted a backyard party, and friends and family
stopped by to offer congratulations. This degree was a long time
coming—four years, in fact, including night classes for two years
prior to the Rikers placement. To support myself while attending
school, I'd worked for a Manhattan investment bank, first as a late-
night word processor and then as an evening receptionist.

After graduation, I considered job possibilities, with Rikers at
the top of my list. Since I'd left Rose Singer, Janet and I had stayed
in touch, and we'd been discussing my return—not if, but when.
"But this time around," said Janet, "we'll be working side by side.
How does that sound?"

As much as I loved the idea, the memory of my rich experiences
at Rose Singer was starting to fade, and I was growing ambivalent
about an immediate return. As a full-timer, things would be different: three days would become five, and nine cases would balloon to

over thirty. And then there was the practical matter of getting to Rikers. As a student I was lucky to have been in a carpool. But without a car and on my own, accessing the island would be a two-hour ordeal by train and bus. But something else was bothering me. Although family and friends had been supportive of my jailhouse internship, a return was another matter. While my mother was enthused, my father and others echoed Wendy's first-day-at-Rikers sentiments—that it was one thing to work in jail as a student, but to *choose it—no!*

Between practical considerations and this unexpected wave of anxiety, I thought I might try something else for a while, maybe work with a similar population, but just in a different setting. Janet understood, adding that the island was in the midst of staffing changes and that it made sense to hold off anyway until the right position opened up. This sealed it for me, and with a decision made, my interest turned toward drug addiction. If nothing else, my year at Rikers had shown me that our jail and prison populations are driven by addiction, and I wanted to learn more about this modern-day scourge. With this in mind, for the next couple of years I worked with parolees at a South Bronx–based drug rehab facility called El Rio, followed by a stint in the alcoholism unit of a Manhattan outpatient clinic. My immersion in the world of drug and alcohol recovery was a rich and valuable experience, but two years later, my interest in returning to Rikers had not waned. During this time, Janet and I had continued to stay in touch, and she'd kept me up to date on the doings at Rikers. By now, the staffing changes were complete, and with this came the bombshell news that Janet was no longer at Rose Singer: she had been transferred to a men's jail. As always, Janet took it in stride. "It's working out very nicely," she said. "I actually think I like working with men better—they're quieter. Not so much drama."

In the spring of 1995, Janet alerted me to an opening in her new jail. "This is it, Mary Mac. You ready?"

Although this was the moment I'd been waiting for, now I wasn't so sure. I hadn't expected to be working with men, who were likely charged with more serious crimes.

"It doesn't matter what they're charged with," Janet said. "It's the exact same work. Believe me, you'd adjust easily. Besides, we have a first-rate team here, a lot of support. You'd learn a lot, and you'd fit in very well."

Sometimes we have to take things on faith. Regardless of whether it was men or women, I sensed that the time had come. I told Janet I'd see her soon.

15

ON A SUNNY JUNE MORNING, I DROVE ACROSS THE RIK-
ers Island bridge, no longer a student but a neophyte professional.
Although several years had passed since I'd left Rose Singer, things
still felt familiar—the seagulls, the roaring jets, the barbed-wire
compound unfolding as you got closer. Not only did it feel familiar,
it felt right. By now, my family and friends had more or less accepted
that this was what I wanted. But even better, I had met someone
special who was solidly behind me. Alex was a psychiatrist whom
I'd met through one of my jobs. Originally from Ecuador, he had
a limited license to practice medicine in New York State. Although
fully licensed in his native country, he was studying to pass stringent exams in order to become fully licensed in the United States.
As I encouraged him in his studies, he supported me in my unusual
aspiration to work with the incarcerated, even helping me to find a
reliable secondhand car. The night before my return, we'd gone out
to dinner to celebrate.

But now, as I shifted gears in my little car, I felt tension in the
briny air. Frenzied black sedans with flashing blue lights whipped
back and forth across the bridge. And along the riverbank, a beefed-
up fleet of security jeeps patrolled the island's edges. Most ominous
of all were two gray tanks creeping down the main roadway, ready
to squash any uprising. In the time I'd been gone, there'd been a
surge in the inmate population, and the island was on high alert.

The city had a new mayor, Rudolph Giuliani, whose trademark was an emphasis on crime reduction. Suddenly, even minor transgressions such as trespassing and jumping turnstiles at the subway were being aggressively policed, resulting in unprecedented numbers of arrests. The jails were now packed to capacity, with barges ferried in to house the overflow. On this 415-acre island, a record 24,000 detainees awaited their fate. Considering that entire prisons typically house about 2,000 inmates in total, the numbers here were staggering.

At the bus depot, I boarded a different bus than the one I'd taken to Rose Singer. As it rumbled down the road, we passed a dump truck, its bed filled with male inmates in olive drab uniforms on some sort of work detail. Unlike the detainees, who were the mainstay of the Rikers population, these were actual prisoners, those who'd been sentenced to a year or less and were permitted to serve it on Rikers itself. The jail they resided in was technically a prison. With cases behind them, and sentences of less than a year, they were often referred to as the "lucky ones."

The bus made a quick unfamiliar turn and pulled up in front of an imposing, boxlike building, the George Motchan Detention Center, my new workplace. One of Rikers Island's largest jails, GMDC housed 2,200 men. A bronze plaque commemorated the jail's namesake, George Motchan, an officer killed trying to thwart an inmate escape from a city hospital.

The lobby was crowded with correction officers and civilian workers in the midst of a shift change. Framed photographs lined the walls: photos of a smiling Mayor Giuliani, of the correction commissioner, and of George Motchan. Although I saw nothing comparable to the Rose Singer portrait, just above the entryway bars someone had scrolled the famous Dostoevsky quote: "A society can be judged by the condition of its jails." I wondered what life at GMDC would say about us.

After navigating security windows and magnetometers, I waited as the entryway gate inched open. A throng of navy blue–uniformed officers spilled out, and behind them was Janet, waving to me. Though her hair was longer, she still wore her trademark suit and in every other way remained her stately self. "Hey there, you," she said, giving me a big hug. "Finally!"

Beside Janet was a short, pretty woman in her mid-forties, whom I recognized from my interviews as GMDC's Mental Health chief, Pat Ballard. "We're glad you're here!" the chief smiled, shaking my hand. "We're so glad you decided to come on board!"

"Come on," said Janet, "everyone's waiting to meet you." We hustled back through the open gate and past an inner security window. But once inside the jail, we stopped short and stood back along the wall. Officers in riot gear were streaming down the hall, shedding helmets, face shields, and chest padding. "They're returning from a housing search," Janet whispered. "They look for weapons." Two big German shepherds, held in check by an officer in a DOC baseball cap, were wending through the commotion. "Part of the K-9 unit," Pat said. "They take dogs into the houses to sniff out drugs. Believe it or not, Mary, there's plenty of drugs right here in the jail."

I'd seen neither search teams nor dogs at Rose Singer, and I knew in that moment that working in a men's jail was going to be very different. But with the escalating inmate population, I also knew life behind bars was simply becoming more violent, for men and women alike. A 1994 cover of *New York* magazine asked, "Is Rikers About to Explode?" Mayor Giuliani boldly brushed it off while quietly mandating that order be maintained; I assumed these search teams were part of that effort.

When the coast was clear, we crossed over to a stairwell and ambled up to the second floor. Halfway down the corridor was a set of double doors. "Home base!" said Pat.

Inside were office cubicles, bulletin boards, and a small conference room where coffee and bagels had been set out. Charley Simms, the assistant chief, a tall strapping man with a big toothy smile, was rounding up the troops. "Come on, everyone—let's welcome Mary!"

We all sat around the table, and Pat introduced me to the crew: Robert Goodwin and Victor Alfaro, two psychiatrists; Richard

Delgado, a psychologist; and therapists Ellie, Chuck, Frederick, and Connie. Later, I would meet the evening staff.

"So, Mary," said Dr. Delgado, a twinkle in his eye, "you ready for the big leagues?" A squat, fiftyish man with salt-and-pepper hair, Delgado was the unit's clinical supervisor.

"Of course she's ready," said Janet, with feigned indignation.

"After all," he winked, "I heard that Rose Singer's like working in Mickey Mouse land."

"Oh, go on!" Janet laughed.

"Well," said Charley, "with nine men's jails to one women's house, you can see who the real criminals are—although you'll find the men are quieter."

"But then again," said Ellie, "the men will quietly cut your throat."

"Whoops! She's going to quit before lunch!" joked Dr. Goodwin. The psychiatrist, speaking in a soft Haitian accent, wasn't going to miss out on the fun.

"No, she's not," Janet asserted. "Mary knows that for these inmates, we're the good guys. They know we're trying to help them. The violence in here is pretty much inmate on inmate."

"Sad, but true," said Pat.

As we chatted, I felt immediately at home with my new colleagues and fortunate to be joining this highly regarded team. With a combined total of close to twenty years on Rikers, Pat and Charley had an island-wide reputation for strong, competent leadership. And based on what I was learning, their leadership, and the support of this team, would come in very handy in the days ahead.

"Count just cleared!" somebody yelled. Out in the corridor, a rush of noise and activity interrupted our little gathering, and the crew scrambled up from the table, tossing Styrofoam cups into trash pails. Armed with piles of charts, they headed down to the clinic to meet with the morning's patients.

When all was quiet, Pat showed me around, pointing out a bulletin board that listed GMDC's mentally ill inmates—one hundred in total—who were housed on not one but two MOs. We leafed through various logbooks, and she showed me the all-important basket of referral slips. Just as at Rose Singer, the basket was overflowing. "Tomorrow," she said, "you'll start evaluating some of these—anybody who needs follow-up will go onto your caseload."

While Pat took a phone call, I flipped through the pile of referrals and swallowed hard. The referrals read: *"Wants to die," "Says he'll kill himself if he blows trial," "Can't hold on much longer," "Says he's innocent and no one will listen," "Mother just died—distraught," "First incarceration—can't stop crying."* I put them back in the basket. The stakes here were much higher than at Rose Singer. But it was okay, I told myself. I'd do what I'd always done—listen to these men, connect with their humanity, and learn from this veteran team.

Pat then suggested a tour of the clinic, just a short walk down the hall from our office. At the clinic entryway, a female officer was seated at a small desk. The nameplate pinned to her uniform read "Edwards." "Mary," said Pat, "I'd like you to meet Miss Edwards. She's our Mental Health officer and we'd be lost without her." I reached out my hand to a petite Black woman. "Hello," she said, tersely. After the dour Officer Overton, I wasn't surprised by her tepid welcome, and Pat gave me a little wink as we stepped past her desk.

The Mental Health area was long and narrow, divided in half lengthwise by a Plexiglas wall. A door at the end connected the two sides. The right side was a waiting area with a long row of colored plastic chairs pushed up against the cinder-block wall. On the other side were semiprivate session booths; toward the back was an open space for group therapy.

The waiting room chairs were empty, the morning session almost over. But in one of the booths, an inmate who was little more than a teenager quietly wept; in another, a scruffy older man in a torn flannel shirt struggled to answer Dr. Goodwin's queries as to where he was and the time of day.

Pat directed me to an empty booth. "This one will be yours."

With a little desk and two chairs, it was small but adequate.

A sharp yell came from Officer Edwards: "That's it, folks!" For emphasis, she beat the plastic window with her small fist. "That's it!" she shouted. "Feedings are starting—time for inmates to clear out!"

I looked at my watch. Although it was only 10:15, lunchtime at Rikers is at 10:30.

After the remaining inmates had left, Pat resumed my orientation, pointing to a small button on the wall behind my desk. "That button," she said, "will sound an alarm if you ever feel you're in danger. If you push it, the squad will come running."

"Do these buttons get pushed often?"

"No, but good to have them—just in case."

With the clinic tour complete, we were about to leave when Pat stopped short in the doorway. "Too late!" snapped Officer Edwards. "Houses are moving!"

Out in the corridor, long silent lines of inmates now filled the halls, each line representing an entire fifty-inmate house. With green plastic cups in hand, the houses were headed to the mess hall. Unlike in the women's jail, where the women noisily meandered to the cafeteria, talking here was prohibited.

A few yards away, one of these lines had halted in front of a strip of duct tape affixed to the floor that served as a traffic marking. The men were dark-skinned, heavily tattooed, and mostly young. With ID badges clipped to their T-shirts, they shifted from one leg to the other, eyes darting about. Although their jeans, T-shirts, and sneakers were the garb of the detainee, they bore the subdued look of prisoners.

An angry officer marched back and forth, inspecting the line. "*I said*—shut—the fuck—up!"

A youth caught my eye and gave me a sad little smile.

"*Take—the bodies—down!*" came a command from around the corner. "*Take it down!*"

The house started moving. With sneakers squeaking against the floor, the line silently rounded the bend, while the next house was coming forward.

"Come on," said Pat. "Let's go!"

The two of us darted out and ducked into our office just as the new line approached.

16

THE NEXT MORNING, I WAS READY TO BEGIN. WITH A couple of referrals in hand, I settled in at my session booth and took a deep breath. The first referral simply said "Anxious," and the second one read "First incarceration—evaluate for depression."

There was little time for first-day jitters as Miss Edwards shouted, "Miss Buser! *YOU GOT ONE!*"

I stepped out to the waiting area where Hector Rodriquez, the "anxious" inmate, was pacing the floor. "Sit down, Mr. Rodriquez—sit down!" yelled Edwards. I introduced myself, and he stood still long enough to shake my hand, but as soon as we were seated, his legs jiggled wildly. "Can you get me out of here, miss? Can you get me back to the Brooklyn House? They brought me out here to Rikers last night. I don't know why. My mother's very sick—she'll never be able to make the trip out here. We don't have a car. She could die! My bail's only a few hundred bucks, but we don't have it. At least let me see my family. *Please, miss! Please! Can you help me?*"

Overhearing him, Janet, who was engrossed in paperwork nearby, leaned out and beckoned me, and I excused myself briefly. "You're going to see a lot of this," she whispered. "Most of the boroughs have their own jailhouse, but because of the huge numbers of people arrested, most are held here on Rikers. The thing is, the smaller jails are closer to home, easier for family visits. They all want to go back, and you can't blame them, but this is a DOC matter. Don't get pulled into this. You have to tell him there's nothing Mental Health can do. We can help him with the anxiety, but not a transfer."

I returned to Rodriquez and repeated what Janet had told me. "I'm so sorry," I said. "Maybe you could speak to a captain or someone in DOC."

"Yeah, I should do that," he said, with a glimmer of hope. "Maybe this is just temporary. I'll talk to a captain—yeah, that's what I'll do! Maybe they'll send me back."

He declined any further mental health support, and as he stood trembling at Edwards's desk, waiting for a hall pass, I wished I could have done more. But more than that, I was confused. Hector Rodriquez had been arrested and charged with a crime that he may or may not have committed. He had yet to have his day in court. But in the interim, because he couldn't make bail—for lack of a few hundred dollars—not only could he not remain at home with his family, he was remanded to an inaccessible island. His pretrial incarceration was not a question of guilt or innocence—it was a question of money!

But I couldn't dwell on it. My next referral was already signing the logbook. I walked him to my booth, noticing that the lanky Antwan Williams was fighting back tears. As soon as we were seated, he doubled over and began rocking, *"Oh, God, miss! They want to give me twenty years! Jesus Christ! They got me on a drug sale."*

Putting my intake questionnaire aside, I listened as the thirty-year-old Williams told me what had happened. "It started out like nothing," he whispered. "I'm not a bad guy—I was just desperate. That's why I did it." He explained that he was the center of an immigrant family from Jamaica, a hard-working clan that had scraped and borrowed to open a small bodega in Brooklyn. But despite their best efforts, the store struggled. Antwan had a younger brother, Tariq, a twenty-two-year-old with no interest in shopkeeping. Instead, Tariq sold drugs. But Tariq's life in the fast lane came to a violent end when rival drug dealers shot him dead on a street corner. "It was horrible," Antwan whispered. "After Tariq was killed, everything changed. Things were going bad at the bodega to begin with, but after that, it went downhill fast and I was borrowing money everywhere I could. And then Tariq's friends came by and told me Tariq was owed a lot of money, and they thought it should go to his family. I didn't ask questions—I just said, 'Give it to me!' But they said if I wanted it, there was a few things I had to do. I was desperate, and out of my mind over my brother's murder. Everyone was looking to me for answers—it was too much. So I said okay, and I started carrying duffel bags to different drop-offs. Small stuff—and these guys gave me a *lot* of money for doing practically nothing. It was so easy. *Just so easy.* And my wife was saying, 'What are you doing?—look what happened to Tariq!' I told her I was only going to do it a few more times—just enough to recover from the store and get out."

But it was too late. While parked in his car one afternoon, Antwan Williams was surrounded by police. "They put a gun to my head and told me to get out. Then they put me in handcuffs, took me to a precinct, and played back a tape—one of the guys I was dealing with was wired. *They had me red-handed!* I've never been in jail before—I can't eat, I can't sleep, I can't think. I swear to God, miss, if it wasn't for my kids, I'd string up a sheet and end it—I swear to God I would!"

"Okay," I said, feeling slightly overwhelmed. "Okay, now. I know this is all a terrible shock, but we're going to help you get through this, okay?"

He bit his lip and nodded.

Given his reference to suicide, I wanted to transfer him to the MO. But when I proposed it, he gripped the edge of the desk. "*No! Please!* I can't take any more changes. Don't move me! I'm not gonna do anything—I wouldn't do anything to hurt my kids! I swear!"

As desperate as he was, I believed him. I set the MO aside for the moment. But I did want him to meet with a psychiatrist for medication. Although a pill couldn't undo the damage, at least it would help calm him down, and to this he agreed. "But can I talk to you again?" he asked. "You've been very nice to me. You can't trust anyone in here, and I really need someone to talk to."

I pulled out my calendar, and we scheduled our next appointment.

"Thank you," he whispered.

When Miss Edwards announced that the morning session was over, Antwan Williams, my first case, got up and returned to the cement cell that was part of his new and horrible world.

After he was gone, my thoughts were racing. Antwan Williams seemed like a decent person who'd made a terrible error in judgment, yet the price for it could be twenty years—a huge number in a human lifespan. My mind flashed back to Sister Marion and the mules at Rose Singer who faced fifteen- and twenty-five-year sentences for similar transgressions. Once again, I didn't understand how a nonviolent drug sale could be placed on par with murder. If Williams got the maximum, this father of three would leave prison in his early fifties. His children would be grown and the prime of his life over.

17

AS THE DAYS PROGRESSED, I GREW ACCUSTOMED TO THE rhythm of the men's jail—the quieter halls, the long silent lines headed to chow. At mealtimes, white-shirted captains stood at the mess hall entryway and scrutinized the arriving lines, watching as the inmates removed their belts and passed through metal detectors. After refastening them, the men were hustled in to eat—and just as quickly hustled back out. With an allotted "feeding" time of five to seven minutes, there wasn't a moment to spare.

I began each day with a stack of referrals and a morning of assessment interviews. Through these interviews, I found that the male inmates shared the same sad profile as the women: poor, minority, drug-addicted, products of foster care or group homes. Most were high school dropouts, with tenth grade seemingly the universal dropout grade. Many were illiterate; many more had spent their early school years in "special ed." Whenever I asked what took place in special ed, the answer was always "Nothing."

But when it came to criminal charges, men and women differed radically. No longer was I sitting across from people charged with drug possession, prostitution, and shoplifting—now it was drug sales, rape, assault, arson, and murder. Although these men were detainees and innocent until proven guilty, I knew very well that many were guilty as charged. But just as I had done all along, I resolved to leave judgments to the courts and keep my focus on their mental status.

Despite the more serious charges, the work itself, as Janet had promised, was the same. I settled into a comfortable groove, transferring the mentally ill onto a Mental Observation Unit and scheduling clinic-based follow-ups for everyone else. I was just starting to feel confident in my ability to work with male inmates when I began making mistakes. The first occurred during the evaluation of a forty-year-old referred for possible mental retardation. When I questioned him, he was mute and appeared lost and disoriented. I decided it best to transfer him to the MO for his own protection and further evaluation. My next referral was a twenty-three-year-old brought to the clinic by two officers who'd spotted him fashioning a noose out of bedsheets. I wasn't going to take any chances here and immediately transferred him to the MO.

On the face of it, these two situations seemed straightforward and my response to them appropriate. In both cases I'd been duped. The "suicidal" inmate began extorting the mentally ill, and within days of his arrival on the unit, the "mentally retarded" inmate was hailed as the house chess champ! Both were promptly discharged back to population, and I landed in Pat's office, feeling a little chagrined.

"Don't worry," said the chief. "It happens to all the rookies."

"Happens to the veterans too!" Charley piped in. "These guys are good, Mary—they know exactly how to play us. Welcome to the wonderful world of malingerers!"

Malingerer, I learned, is the psychiatric word for a faker, and a big buzzword behind bars.

Charley and Pat explained that, for a variety of reasons, the island's Mental Observation Units are coveted houses. Terrified first-timers in jail often fudged mental illness because they figured that with the Mental Health staff's regular presence on the unit, the MO was a safer haven. Others thought it might help their legal case. Unfortunately, others viewed the mentally ill as perfect prey for extortion. But the biggest motivation for feigning mental illness and exacting a transfer to the MO was a key policy clause: "Any inmate housed on a Mental Observation Unit is considered too fragile for solitary confinement." What this meant was that someone who'd been issued a "ticket" was apt to appear at our door prior to his transport to the Bing. If he could convince us that he was suicidal or mentally ill, he'd be transferred to the protected house, safe from harsh punishment.

"The two guys you put on the MO, Mary, they'd both been issued Bing tickets the night before," Charley said.

Now it all made sense.

"You can't blame them for trying," Pat said. "They're scared to death of solitary—but on the other hand, we can't allow our units to become havens for Bing beaters."

Armed with this new information, I conducted my evaluations with a little more savvy. As a gatekeeper for our Mental Observation Units, I needed to protect the mentally ill. If someone told me he felt like killing himself, I didn't automatically believe it. I assessed his energy level and body language. Did it add up? Or was he joking around in the waiting area just prior to telling me about his death plan? When I asked myself these questions, many claims did not pan out. If I still had doubts, I checked with DOC to see if there was an outstanding Bing ticket at play. In many cases, the answer was yes.

With a little more experience, I began recognizing ruses and staged maladies. Some were quite sophisticated and convincing, while others were so obvious they were almost comical. One young man, outfitted in designer jeans and gold chains, who'd been holding court in the waiting area, claimed to be hearing voices. "When did you start hearing these voices?" I asked.

"The other day—just like that!"

"And how often do you hear them?"

"All the time!" he insisted. "All the time . . . you better transfer me to the MO."

"And what do these voices talk to you about?"

He thought about it for a moment before making his fatal mistake—"Sports!"

I tried not to burst out laughing, but I did smile, and when he realized it wasn't going to work, so did he.

While frustrating, situations like these actually provided a little levity, and in some ways they were a welcome diversion from the more complicated decisions that I was starting to face. Although many would take a broad brush to malingerers, attributing their chicanery to the "criminal mentality," I was finding that most jail-house malingering was driven by sheer terror.

It was through Curtis Bellows, one of my earliest cases, that I came face-to-face with the dire straits the detainee is up against. A thoughtful thirty-three-year-old, Bellows was battling drug addiction and depression. In and out of jail most of his adult life, he'd endured a horrific childhood at the hands of a sadistic foster mother. Belt-buckle beatings and near drownings at bath time made for a man who functioned with great difficulty. But he and I were forming a solid therapeutic alliance, and I wanted to help him find some peace in his life. Although he'd be going upstate for a few years, we were working on a postprison game plan. But one afternoon he arrived for his session with eyes downcast and lower lip quivering. He told me he was in grave danger. Apparently, he'd borrowed a pack of cigarettes from a housemate through the jailhouse practice of "juggling." The repayment terms were steep: twice the amount loaned is due back on an agreed-upon date. For each day it isn't repaid, the owed quantity doubles. Curtis had juggled the cigarettes with the promise of payback later in the week when he received money from his sister. But things took a bad turn when his sister, usually faithful about sending him ten bucks a month, was unable to do so. With the owed cigarettes rapidly multiplying, he'd never be able to pay off his "creditors."

Janet told me that DOC would not make housing transfers based on these everyday squabbles, and that an inmate who owes money to a housemate is a sitting duck for violent retribution.

In one case that occurred before I arrived, a young man's desperation led to ultimate tragedy. My cube mate, Ellie, told me how he'd juggled cigarettes and candy, knowing his grandmother would be visiting and bringing the money he'd use for payback. But when she wasn't up to making the trip out to Rikers that week, he panicked. Instead of pretending to be suicidal or psychotic, and possibly being pegged by us as a malingerer, he devised a risky plan for getting out of his house. The idea was to step into a bedsheet noose while a pal of his, who "happened to be walking by," would then yell out for a CO. With such a dramatic act, he'd be a shoo-in for the MO. However, the plan went awry when the timing of the rescue was off. By the time the COs arrived, he'd already hanged for too long. Although an ambulance was quickly summoned, this twenty-one-year-old was dead on arrival at the hospital.

Curtis Bellows's situation was similar, and I tried to help him figure some way out of it. "Maybe you could call your sister again— explain things to her."

"No," he said. "She has her own health issues and barely has enough money for herself. If she had it, she'd have sent it."

We were quiet for a moment before he shook his head, tears rolling down his cheeks. "I hate fighting, but I'm gonna to have to. I don't know when I'm going to get jumped . . . at night . . . in the showers . . . I just don't know. But they're coming for me."

I was half-tempted to give him the money, to put it in his commissary account and end the whole thing. But to do so was taboo, both from a therapy standpoint and because giving *anything* to an inmate was strictly prohibited. Theoretically, I wasn't supposed to get pulled into these situations. As a therapist, it was my job to stick to mental health concerns. But I had to do something. And what I had in mind was a transfer out of his house and onto one of our Mental Observation Units. The only problem was that he wasn't mentally ill. A move like this would require Pat's approval. "Wait here," I told Curtis.

I went back to the office where I hashed it over with the chief. Her response was exactly what I'd hoped for. "Get him out of that house. Go ahead and put him on the MO. We're always trying to make sure we don't get played that sometimes we lose our hearts. He's in emotional distress—I think that qualifies him for the MO, don't you? You don't ever want to lose your heart, Mary," she winked.

In that moment I felt a stab of love for Pat. While it would have been much easier for her to default to a bureaucratic template, Pat hadn't lost her own heart, and even if I were duped by a malingerer here or there, I wasn't going to lose mine either!

I practically skipped back to the clinic to deliver the good news. Bellows was ecstatic. "Thank God! Oh, thank God! Thank you, Miss B, thank you!"

I filled out the transfer form and within hours, Curtis Bellows was packed up, escorted out, and spared the trauma of certain violence.

18

BY SUMMER'S END, I'D BEEN BACK AT RIKERS FOR THREE months. My plate was full, with a caseload that had swelled to thirty people as well as handling the accompanying paperwork demands. The inmates I met with suffered primarily from depression, anxiety, and often a combination of both. There was little time for the in-depth work I'd enjoyed as a student, but with each person I met, I listened wholeheartedly, tried to nurture maturation, and instill reasonable hope. When I packed up to go home at night, it was with the quiet sense that I was doing something important.

And in my outside life, there was cause for celebration. Alex had passed his exams and was now a full-fledged American doctor. With his long struggle over, a world of opportunities was opening up for him. And as he began exploring new possibilities, I became more deeply immersed in my work with the men at GMDC, a population of little concern to the outside world.

But if the public was disinterested in the Rikers detainees, one accused criminal *had* captivated the entire nation—O. J. Simpson. By the fall of 1995, his trial was under way and the case was discussed endlessly in newspapers, on TV, in the home and workplace. The fervor was felt no less on Rikers, where officers, civilians, and inmates alike offered passionate opinions as to whether Simpson was guilty of the grisly double murder. By early October, the trial was finally wrapping up, and on a bright autumn morning, word spread that the jury had reached a decision. Officers and civilians crammed into a clinic lounge while inmates gathered around their house TVs for the verdict. When the words "not guilty" were uttered, a massive roar rose up over Rikers Island. The inmates were ecstatic—dancing in their houses, cheering in the clinic. The dour faces on the mess hall lines were replaced with broad smiles and pumped fists. None of my sessions was complete without a quick sidebar on the verdict. "Finally," they said, "White justice for a Black man!"

But as the O. J. euphoria died down, and the inmates realized that his victory meant nothing for their own cases, the jail returned to its usual somber state.

At GMDC, I found a profound sense of sadness that I had not felt at Rose Singer. Not that Rose Singer was "Mickey Mouse land" by any means, but the difference, it seemed to me, was hope—hope for a better life after jail. Numerous programs prepared the women for better things after release. But at GMDC, programs were scarce, and the idea of something like the meditation group that Lucy Lopez had attended seemed laughable. And perhaps my biggest shock: for all of the Mental Health Department's efforts in denying women sleep medication, no such policy existed here. In fact, it was the opposite. Here, sleep meds were doled out freely—even encouraged—as though there was an unspoken understanding of the men as a lost cause and a desire to anesthetize their pain as best we could. I suppose with more serious charges, and the heavier sentences that waited, there was little point in focusing on life afterward.

As part of my evaluations, I asked about physical injuries, and the men whipped up T-shirts to display scars from gunshots and stabbings, the result of gang warfare and stray bullets. Before GMDC I'd never even seen a bullet wound, but now the sight of scarred and puckered abdomens was routine. Many had also suffered blows to the head, usually through accidents or fights. In one grief counseling situation, I worked with twenty-four-year-old Alex Mora, who'd just learned that his younger brother had been killed by a stray bullet. He sobbed uncontrollably, grieving for the "good one" in the family, wishing it had been him. And it could just as easily have been. Alex had already survived seven gunshots to his back and now walked with a limp. Post-traumatic stress disorder was almost as common a diagnosis as drug addiction, but here, the walking wounded weren't soldiers returning from any war, they were victims of the violence that comes with being part of New York City's rough-and-tumble underclass.

Not surprisingly, drugs were at the heart of most men's charges. Whether it was sales, working as a lookout, "steering" customers to dealers, robbing to get money to buy drugs, or committing a violent crime while under the influence, all roads led back to drugs.

But as I got to know these men, I discovered that they viewed drug dealing as their salvation. It was not only lucrative, but within their impoverished subculture it carried prestige. As Alonzo Gomez, a soft-spoken twenty-year-old referred for attempted suicide, put it, "I had real money in my pockets, and for the first time in my life, I was a somebody!" In their insular world, drug dealers command respect. Many are viewed as neighborhood "godfathers," doling out cash for groceries, Pampers, and other necessities. In the larger society, these men are uneducated, unskilled nobodies, but through drug dealing, they've found a shortcut to the American dream of big money, power, and respect.

But the dream is short-lived, and the downside—violence, death, prison—is horrific, as Antwan Williams was discovering. Since our initial session, I'd been meeting with Antwan regularly, and as the shock of his arrest wore off, he knew his life would never be the same—nor would the lives of his family. By the fall, his three boys, aged ten, eight, and five, were returning to school and becoming more upset that Daddy wasn't home. "I used to walk them to school every morning," said Antwan. "That's where I should be now—taking my kids to school."

Initially, Antwan's wife tried to shield the children from the truth, but when it became apparent that he wasn't coming home any time soon, she started bringing them on visits. "It's terrible for them to see me in here like this. My youngest, he just hugs me and cries, 'Papi, come home!' I can't take it, Miss B! The whole reason I did this was to help my family. I wasn't looking to buy fancy cars. It was to take care of them—and now look at the pain I've caused!"

Although medication provided Antwan with considerable relief, he still lived in a state of high anxiety, especially as he contemplated his future. Not only was he facing serious drug charges, but he was also being implicated as part of a larger operation. "They're saying I'm part of some big drug gang that I never even heard of! I wasn't in any gang. I just ran duffle bags around for a few weeks!"

Antwan was determined to take his case to trial and reject any plea bargain. "These charges aren't fair!" he protested. But after several court hearings, he was reconsidering. His judge was a woman who'd carved out a citywide reputation for the heavy sentences she imposed on drug dealers—she'd been hailed in the press and lauded by Mayor Giuliani for being tough on crime. "Just my luck," lamented Antwan.

But there was some hope. After his arrest, his family rallied to come up with money for a lawyer and succeeded in amassing $5,000. With this precious bankroll, Antwan could hire private counsel and was hopeful of at least getting his case switched to another judge. At Rikers, a private lawyer is a rare luxury; virtually all the detainees are represented by court-appointed attorneys. Although $5,000 was a fortune for Antwan's family, sadly, it was eaten up in the earliest stages of the case and the private lawyer was gone. His spirits plummeted as he faced the same judge, but now with a Legal Aid lawyer. Although still inclined to go to trial, his apprehension about this judge was further heightened when court officers warned him against it. "These guys rush up and whisper, 'Don't go to trial with her—nobody *ever* wins in here! *Don't do it!*' I want to go to trial, Miss Buser—I want to fight these charges, but I'm so scared of this judge. I don't know what to do. I mean, it's not like it's coming from the guy in the next cell—*it's the officers in her own courtroom!*"

As Antwan agonized over his case, he also faced day-to-day survival behind bars. "It's scary in here. Guys get jumped, beaten.

I can understand why so many of them join gangs—nobody messes with you. But that's not all," he whispered, glancing out at Miss Edwards. "It's the officers too. We had a search this morning, and it was bad. All these COs showed up in helmets and face shields, and they made us strip and line up with our hands against the wall. Then they started flipping mattresses and throwing our stuff all over—pictures, shoes—and laughing while they're doing it. My muscles are shaking, and I'm just saying, '*Oh God—please get this over with!*' And the one in charge is yelling, 'Don't move, don't anybody turn around.' And this one kid, he's kind of stupid, you know, and he must have turned around 'cause next thing you know, he starts screaming, and they're dragging him off to a corner and beating him. All the while, they're saying to us, 'Don't turn around!' *Jesus!* It's like they were hoping for someone to move so they could beat the shit out of him. Then they threw some clothes on him and dragged him out. I don't know where they took him . . . maybe to the clinic or to another house . . . I just don't know."

After our session ended and Antwan left, my mind was swirling. I don't know what troubled me more: the judge or the housing search. I thought judges were supposed to be the impartial referees of the legal system. Instilling terror in the courtroom was not our legal system as I understood it. And when it came to the search, I just hoped Antwan was exaggerating. It couldn't have been that bad.

At least, I hoped not.

19

BY THE SPRING OF 1996, NEW YORK CITY WAS IN THE throes of a budget crisis. In a cost-cutting move, the city drastically reduced inmate support programs, with the deepest cuts in Social Services. Responsible for handling veterans affairs, social security issues, and funeral leaves, the Social Services Department provided critical personal support to the detainees. At GMDC, these services were whittled down to one person handling the needs of 2,200 inmates. The only thing that was remotely possible was notifying the men of outside family deaths.

The gutting of Social Services stoked anxiety among the Rikers health-care staff—medical, mental health, and pharmacy workers, all of us employees of Montefiore Hospital. Montefiore had assumed the Rikers contract back in 1973, when the city was desperate to comply with a court order to provide a minimum standard of care to detained inmates, and no other hospital would do it. The contract was quietly renewed at three-year intervals for the next twenty years. The white lab coats with the Montefiore patch, worn by close to a thousand jail-based hospital workers, seemed as permanent as the jails themselves. But things were changing. The new profit-driven approach to health care was making its way to the gates of jails and prisons. Valued at hundreds of millions of dollars, the Rikers contract was now being eyed as a moneymaker. For the first time, the city was in a position to choose among an array of vendors.

Anticipating competition, Montefiore sought to demonstrate its ability at capping costs. For us, this resulted in the creation of the "Mental Health Center." A step up from the standard Mental Observation Unit, this 350-bed facility was designed to provide a higher level of care to the most severely mentally ill. In the past, inmates who couldn't be stabilized were transferred to the prison wards of local hospitals at great cost. Now, all such referrals would be to the on-island Mental Health Center instead. If a hospital transfer was still necessary, it was done sparingly and at the sole discretion of the new facility. The opening of the Mental Health Center was greeted with fanfare as the largest jail-based psychiatric facility in the country.

But while everyone was buzzing about it, I paid little attention, keeping my head low and focusing on a demanding caseload. Roughly two-thirds of my cases were from GP, with the remaining eight or nine from our Mental Observation Units. Our mission with the mentally ill was to get them stabilized and, hopefully, discharged back to population. Since medication could not be forced, the initial challenge was to persuade someone in the throes of psychosis to start taking it, which could be quite a daunting task. This is what I faced with a twenty-one-year-old schizophrenic named Michael Tucker. When I first approached Michael, he was sitting in the corner of the dayroom, disheveled and mumbling to himself. I was only able to make the faintest of eye contact with him. Conversation about anything, much less medication, was hopeless. About all I could do was get his mother's phone number from his chart and hope she might have some ideas.

When I was at Rose Singer, Janet had advised me to call the families of the mentally ill for background and treatment history. These calls were often heartbreaking. On the other end of the line were families who at their wits' end in caring for their mentally ill child. While upset that their loved one was in jail, they were also grateful to know they were safe and being cared for.

When I reached Helen Tucker, Michael's mother, she reacted with a familiar gratitude and relief: "Thank you—oh, thank you for calling me."

After I assured her Michael was safe, she filled me in on the disheveled young man seated in our dayroom. She said he'd been the apple of her eye, an A student, a former altar boy. His schizophrenia had emerged in his late teens, when he'd become inexplicably withdrawn, neglected to bathe, and began muttering to himself, responding to a strange world within. He was started on medication, but she said the medication gave him terrible side effects, so he'd stop taking the pills and get sick again. Instead of going to school, he started wandering the streets, getting into trouble. "We kept trying to get him back on track, but we couldn't watch him every second of the day—we had to go to work!"

Like most families in this situation, the Tuckers tried to get Michael into a program where he'd be supervised, but found there were none. "He couldn't be left alone, but there was no place for him to go. They shut down all the hospitals because they were snake pits. Okay, fine! But what did they replace them with? A few programs here and there, yeah—but not *nearly* enough for everyone who needs one. It's simple math! What were we supposed to do? We had to go to work, but we couldn't just leave him with a babysitter—people don't understand."

At a loss to secure help, Helen Tucker went traipsing out at all hours of the night, into the streets and local parks, in search of her wandering son. "Some nights I'd be on the subways at twelve, one o'clock in the morning looking for him till I found him all filthy dirty—talking away to absolutely no one. Oh, Miss Buser," she whispered, "do you know what it's like when the bum on the train is *your* child? My sister says, 'You can't always be running after him, you have the rest of your family to think of,' but he's still my son. How'm I going to sleep not knowing where he is with all the danger out there? How? I'm his mother! I can't just turn my back on my child—*I can't!*"

But many families of the mentally ill do just that. After years of chasing after a loved one, trying to procure help that doesn't exist, their energy and resources exhausted, they simply give up and leave their child to fate. For every Michael Tucker that I worked with, there were ten more whose families were no longer in the picture.

"It's terrible that he's in jail," she whispered, her voice quivering. "But at least I can sleep at night knowing where he is."

Fortunately, with joint coaxing from his mother and from me, Michael began taking his meds. With each passing day, his eye contact improved, and the muttering lessened. One morning, I arrived at the MO to be greeted by a freshly showered young man who was combing his hair. "Hello," he said, shyly. "Well, hello," I smiled. "Welcome back."

Getting to know Michael Tucker was a delight. Underneath the psychosis was someone intelligent and artistically gifted. He began drawing sketches for me and Dr. Goodwin, his psychiatrist, and we pinned his artwork over our desks. Goodwin also gave him meds to soften the side effects of the powerful antipsychotic drugs that he needed. As Michael and I talked about his illness and the challenges he'd face once released, he bore little resemblance to the psychotic soul he'd been just a few weeks earlier. With clean clothes and his hair neatly braided, Michael Tucker now bore the youthful promise of any other twenty-one-year-old.

His mother was overjoyed.

Being a part of Michael's amazing transformation, as well as offering emotional support to his beleaguered mother, were wonderful moments for me, filling me with a deep sense that this is exactly where I was meant to be.

But at the same time, my joy was tempered by disturbing discoveries I was making about other aspects of life behind bars. For one thing, despite my hopes otherwise, Antwan Williams's account of the housing searches was neither exaggerated nor isolated. Within the privacy of our sessions, one inmate after the next repeated Antwan's story—of the ransacking, the beatings. With terror in their eyes, they described the banging of batons on the gates at all hours of the day and night, signaling the start of another terrifying, humiliating search.

By all official accounts, the Giuliani administration's mission of violence reduction was working and publicly hailed as a great success. But the fact that these searches were, in and of themselves, becoming a whole new source of terror never quite made it to the public square.

But the brutality extended beyond the searches. Carlos Rosario, referred for post-traumatic stress disorder, told me that just the sound of jangling keys and the sight of navy uniforms set his pulse quickening and his palms sweating. His symptoms were the result of a "beat-down" in a GMDC corridor. "I was in the wrong place at the wrong time," he said. Returning to his house from the law library one afternoon, Carlos ran into a swarm of livid officers. Apparently, someone had thrown urine at a female CO. "It was open season on the inmates," he said. "Any inmate would do. I kept trying to tell them I didn't do anything, that I was just coming back from the library, but it didn't matter. They shoved me into a corner, cursing and yelling—they had me on the floor and they kept kicking me, stomping my groin. The women were the worst—they were trying to kill me. I lost control of my bowels and my bladder. I shit all over myself," he whispered. "Nobody stopped them—nobody helped me. All I could do was yell, 'God sees you! God knows what you're doing!'" Carlos stopped to wipe away the tears. "God is the only one who knows what happens in here. The planes fly over us, and the rest of the world's going about its business, never thinking about what's going on at Rikers Island."

As his story unfolded, every muscle in my body tensed up. I was horrified. "My God, Carlos, have you reported this?"

"No! I wouldn't dare!"

"Well, what if I—"

"No! Next time they'll kill me. Don't say a word—please!"

"No, of course not," I said. "Of course not."

Carlos Rosario's wishes placed me in a quandary that would become all too familiar: detainees confiding the abuse they'd suffered but imploring me to say nothing. As much as I wanted to do something, it wasn't a simple matter. First and foremost, I was bound by the rules of confidentiality, but even if I wasn't, by reporting instances of brutality I would be potentially placing someone in even greater danger for retribution. One inmate told me about someone who'd been transferred to his house, his arm in a sling. The new arrival told the others that his arm had been broken by officers in another jail. That night, a band of unfamiliar COs showed up, asking which inmate had filed a complaint against COs in the other jail. When they spotted the sling, they attacked the screaming inmate, beating him to the floor and stomping his arm, yelling to each other, "Did you get the pins—are they all out?" When they were done, they tossed a pack of cigarettes to a few other inmates and ordered them to rough him up a little more, so as to mask their own actions. Pointing a finger at one's captors can be a dangerous business.

So far, I had not witnessed brutality firsthand. DOC was circumspect in delivering their punishment, whisking the civilians behind doors, shielding them from disciplinary measures. But one morning they let their guard down. I was headed downstairs to our Mental Observation Units when an officer instructed me and a couple of nurses to hold up inside the ground-floor stairwell. He locked the door, but it had a small window and we peered through it, just in time to glimpse an inmate, white plastic handcuffs binding his hands behind his back, being marched down the hall toward the receiving room by officers in riot gear. I was already hearing rumors that harsh punishment was often meted out in the receiving room. A few minutes later, the stairwell door opened abruptly, and we jumped back as this same handcuffed inmate, now bloodied and moaning, was propped up by two COs, one on either side of him, still in their riot gear. As they clambered up the stairs to the clinic, I froze against the wall, watching in horror as the young man's limp legs dragged and bounced off the steps.

As soon as they were out of sight, I charged back up the stairs and told Pat and Charley what I had just witnessed. Their reaction felt like a flashback to Rose Singer, when I'd told Janet about the beating in the darkened corridor. Charley shook his head somberly. "Yeah, Mary, things like this do happen in here. There's no getting around it. Unfortunately, there's not much we can do—we walk a fine line in here. You make a little too much noise and you find your tires slashed. We rely on these COs to open doors, and all of sudden the door you need to get through isn't being unlocked, or they get around to it very slowly."

I understood what Charley was saying. One physician's assistant who'd arrived at GMDC after being bumped from another jail told me that after reporting his frank impressions of an inmate's devastating injuries at the hands of DOC, a deputy warden informed him that he should no longer feel safe in that jail, prompting his transfer out.

"But what's important to keep in mind," Charley continued, "is that just our presence, just the civilian presence in here, reduces the overall violence."

"Yes," Pat agreed. "I think it would be a lot worse if we weren't in here. And don't forget, Mary, that they're being watched." Pat was referring to the jail's oversight agency, the Board of Correction, which reviewed inmate injury reports and regularly visited the jails. "There'll probably be a report on this guy, and hopefully they'll investigate."

This reminder that someone official was watching reassured me, and when I discussed it with Alex, he urged me to stay focused on my work. "Let the oversight agency do its job, and you do yours," he said.

After these conversations with my superiors and with Alex, I breathed a little easier and resumed my work with my mind at relative ease, a necessity if I was to be psychologically available to those in dire emotional distress.

* * *

Perhaps nowhere did I need to be more attentive than with the dying. Behind bars, the HIV infection rate is roughly ten times greater than in the outside community, and all of us worked with HIV-stricken inmates. One of my cases, the likeable Kirby Evans, was gravely ill. Unlike the unforgettable Daisy Wilson, Kirby Evans wasn't interested in the Compassionate Release and was not looking to go home. Knowing he was terminally ill, he'd deliberately placed himself in a position to be arrested. In a halting Jamaican accent he told me, "I tried so hard to stop using drugs on my own, and to start taking care of myself with this disease, but I couldn't—I just couldn't do it. I didn't want to die in the gutter, miss—and that's what would've happened. I needed help. Coming to jail was the only way I knew that two things would happen: one, I'd be cut off from drugs, and two, I would get medical treatment. Crazy, huh?"

"Maybe not."

A bright man, Kirby Evans had worked as a bookkeeper before he made the mistake of dabbling with cocaine. His descent into the abyss of addiction left him alienated from family and friends, and now he was sick and alone. Still, he refused to view things tragically. Instead, he focused on his newly found drug-free existence. When his health deteriorated to the point that he was eligible for a transfer to the island-wide men's infirmary, Kirby declined, unwilling to give up his relationship with me and with the physician's assistant who was treating him. Meaningful relationships in jail are rare, and I understood this. His PA and I were dedicated workers, as were most of the hospital staff. But sadly, some in white uniforms were not. One night, Kirby became violently ill and his housing officers summoned a captain. The captain brought him up the stairs to the clinic, and, as Kirby told me the next day, the trek was horrific. "I could barely stand up—I don't know how I was able to walk."

At the clinic, an overnight nurse sized up Kirby, who was slumped over on a wooden bench, and requested a particular form from the captain—something he didn't have. She said without that piece of paper, Kirby could not be treated. As the outraged captain told it the next day, he argued that Kirby was obviously very sick and that due to the late hour, he was unable to access the form. He assured her he would bring it the next day. Incredulously, she refused to budge, saying they should bring Kirby back the next day—with the form. In the captain's log entry he wrote that he had no choice but to take Kirby back to the dorm, and that he and a couple of COs essentially carried him down the stairs.

The following morning, Kirby was rushed up to the clinic on a gurney, his condition so grave that an ambulance was already on its way. His PA and I sat with him during the wait. Though sweating profusely, he told us everything that had happened, including a surprising twist when he'd returned to the dorm. In a crude but caring way, his fellow inmates had taken over. Instinctively, they carried him into the showers and held his feverish body under the cool water. When chills set in, they carried him back out to his cot where they wrapped him in sheets until the fever shot back up. Again, they held him under the shower. According to the housing officers, this went on all night. Barely an inmate slept as this house of crooks, drug addicts, and thieves, in a moving display of humanity, nursed Kirby in a way that he'd been so cruelly denied.

When the ambulance arrived, I said good-bye to him, certain I'd never see him again. I tried to contact his family to let them know where he was, but I was only able to reach an elderly aunt and uncle, who were saddened to hear of his plight but were angered by his drug use and too saddled with their own health problems to visit him. Through phone calls with his lawyer, who did visit Kirby at the hospital, I learned that despite his critical condition, he remained upbeat and cheerful, joking with her and the officers who guarded him. I wasn't surprised. Kirby had always found a way to make me smile. A week later he slipped into a coma, and when doctors pronounced that death was imminent, the handcuffs shackling him to his bed were removed. Half an hour later he was dead.

Kirby's death hit me harder than I expected, and it was in a teary sit-down with Pat that she suggested I remember Kirby by starting a support group for HIV-positive inmates. Although the afflicted were treated medically, little was offered by way of emotional support. Many learned of their diagnosis in jail; after that a referral to Mental Health was mandatory. Some agreed to follow-up supportive therapy, but most declined, usually out of fear of being identified as having "the monster," the jailhouse term for AIDS. For this reason, I was skeptical about stricken inmates coming together as a group. Although the group forum would offer relief from isolation, there was always the risk that someone would violate confidentiality and disclose names to the larger jail population. It was a risk most were unwilling to take. But to my surprise, when the group was offered, I was given a list of interested inmates. For confidentiality reasons, I could not call it the HIV Support Group; instead, I came up with the title Healthy Lifestyles. Although no one but the members would know the group's real purpose, I thought it prudent to let the gruff Miss Edwards in on it. Although I expected little more than a perfunctory nod, I was surprised by her reaction. "Healthy Lifestyles . . . I like it."

"You do?"

"Yeah, that's good. It could be a drug recovery group, for all anybody would know."

And so, with the unexpected support of our Mental Health officer, the group got under way with seven inmates showing up for the first session.

20

AS MY ONE-YEAR ANNIVERSARY APPROACHED, I'D MET with hundreds of detainees who'd been charged with crimes that ranged from trespassing to murder and never once had cause to push the emergency button behind my desk. The people on my caseload became a blur of faces that came and went quickly. A few were bailed out, and others died of AIDS. But the vast majority departed Rikers for an upstate prison. Sadly, Antwan Williams, my first case, simply disappeared one day from GMDC's census. Even though I was theoretically prepared for people vanishing from my caseload for one reason or another, the abruptness of it was still jarring. I just hoped that wherever Antwan was, he would continue to receive emotional support and that his case was resolving fairly.

Despite days that were long and draining, my decision to return to Rikers Island had been a good one. A big factor in my contentment was our mental health team. Pat, Charley, Janet, Dr. Delgado, and the rest of the crew were a special group. When we were meeting with the inmates, we were serious and professional, but behind closed doors we laughed, joked, and forged friendships that enabled us to go out into the jail to listen to, and care about, the woes of society's most disdained. Every Tuesday morning, we gathered in the conference room for breakfast. Huddled around that rickety table, breaking bread with jail-sanctioned plastic knives, I often felt like I was in some remote outpost—certainly not within the midst of New York City.

In the beginning, it felt a little odd to walk past Janet's desk to meet with Delgado, my new clinical supervisor. Janet and I were equals now, although she was still quite senior to me—something she liked to rib me about: "Remember, Mary Mac, I'm way ahead of you!"

"Yes," I said, "but I'm catching up fast!"

"That you are," she laughed.

Although Delgado was a consummate professional, challenging me to become an ever better therapist, he was also a bit of a mother hen, always fretting about germs. He was forever cautioning us to avoid the medical waiting room, where sick inmates coughed and shivered. His fears weren't entirely unfounded. Although the TB crisis had died down, AIDS, hepatitis, and various other maladies were still a concern. During that first year back, I found myself chronically fatigued, relying on endless cups of coffee to make it through the day. A visit to the doctor ruled out anything serious, but when I described my workplace and all of its ills, the doctor explained that my immune system was being battered. Janet told me it was two years before her immune system adjusted. I just hoped it wouldn't take me that long to feel better.

The only sad note was that by the end of that first year, Alex and I had gone our separate ways. He'd started a demanding new job, I was absorbed in mine, and we simply drifted apart. But I still had a circle of good friends, the camaraderie of my work family, and the support of my real family, although at family gatherings I found myself a little quieter at the dinner table, prompting my mother to ask, "Don't you enjoy your work anymore, honey?"

I told her that I did, and that in some respects I considered my mission with these inmates to be sacred work. But things were a little different now. I was becoming aware of a larger picture. Once, the world had faded away when I sat down with someone and sunk into my session. But now I had one ear out for a shriek or a stray cry. If I heard it, I flinched. Was someone being beaten?

What should I do? Often, nothing followed but innocent laughter, and I exhaled.

But I wasn't only troubled by brutality. I was becoming more attuned to the criminal justice system's treatment of the poor. I had not forgotten my first-day encounter with Hector Rodriquez, who desperately wanted to return to a jail closer to home. He turned out to be just the first in a parade of detainees who flocked to the clinic, hoping we could influence a transfer back to a borough jail. Nothing had come of Rodriquez's efforts to return to the Brooklyn house, and I had since learned that no one is returned to a borough jail once they've been bused to Rikers to await trial. The traffic is one-way only. But sadly, Hector Rodriquez's worst fear was realized when his sickly mother died. The distraught man was brought to the clinic, where one of my colleagues tried to console him. Although I was in a session with someone else, I could still overhear him: "I didn't get to see her again—I didn't even get to see her. I'm here on some bullshit charge, and we just didn't have the bail money. *Oh, God—my mother is dead!*"

As I listened to his sobs, I felt terrible for him. If only Hector Rodriquez had had the few hundred dollars he needed for bail, he could have paid it and remained at home while his case was being resolved. He could have visited his mother in the hospital, held her hand, said good-bye. And yet he'd been denied these final moments because he was poor.

But banishment to Rikers Island during the pretrial period was just the opening volley for the poor. Incarceration means fighting legal charges from behind bars—a far different scenario than fighting from home. Whereas those who can afford bail simply take themselves to court for their hearings, the impoverished detainee is "produced" by the Department of Correction. The inmates described a miserable court day drill, of being roused at four in the morning, fed breakfast, and held in a bullpen until eight o'clock, then handcuffed to another inmate, loaded onto a bus, and shuttled to court to wait in more bullpens before appearing before a judge. A few narrow wooden benches line the bullpen walls, rarely enough to seat everyone. The only other furnishings are a semiprivate urinal and a water fountain. The pens are dangerous, as fights and slashings are common among tense groups confined in small spaces. After being brought before a judge, which in the early stages of the case takes about five minutes—whereupon the case is adjourned for another month—they are brought back to the bullpen, cuffed, and returned to Rikers. If they're lucky, they'll catch the midday bus back, but most don't return till much later on, with many arriving back at the jails as late as ten and eleven at night. Court days were always characterized as grueling and dreaded.

But the bail fallout didn't end there. It continued in the unlikely area of clothing, something I learned about when I met Keith Bargeman. Referred for teariness and agitation, Bargeman told me he'd rejected a plea bargain offer and had already been on Rikers for two years, doggedly holding out for trial. As frequently happens during a lengthy pretrial incarceration, he'd been shuffled around the island from jail to jail. With each move, he packed up his "court suit." Whether rightly or wrongly, appearances matter—especially in a courtroom, the epicenter of judgment. For those out on bail, clothing is a mere footnote to larger legal concerns. But if a detainee is lucky enough to even own a suit, he must fiercely protect it. Each inmate has a locker by his cot, but since they don't actually lock, securing the suit requires constant vigilance. Going out to rec, to the clinic, or the law library can be risky. Many refuse necessary medication if a side effect is drowsiness, as this makes them vulnerable to theft.

But earlier in the week, after a hearing where he hadn't needed his suit, he'd returned to Rikers to find it gone. When I sat down with him, the teary Bargeman twisted in his seat. "I need that suit for my trial, miss—I need it! Please help me with this! I've already waited two years! *Please! Please!*"

I felt awful for him, but his problem fell into the huge category of detainee heartaches that we couldn't fix, and I gently told him so. But I did walk him out to Miss Edwards, hoping she might lend a hand, which she did. She picked up the phone and called various captains and housing units. But each time she hung up, she shook her head. "No—nothing."

It was more than he could bear. Out in the corridor, he became loud and agitated, and when officers told him to check himself, he didn't—or couldn't. A captain pulled out an infraction pad, and not only was his precious suit a lost cause, but because of the outburst, Keith Bargeman would now spend ten days in solitary.

I watched the whole hallway ruckus from Miss Edwards's desk, and as he was escorted down the hall, I felt sick. Had he been able to make bail, he never would have had to contend with any of this. His suit would have hung in a closet, ready for court.

With or without the suit, Keith Bargeman was one of the brave few who would actually make it to trial. I hadn't forgotten my first day at Rose Singer when Janet had surprised me by saying that most detainees never go to trial. I didn't understand it then, but I was starting to get the picture now. Though I'd sat with many an inmate who protested his innocence, vowing to see his day in court, I was learning that the odds of holding out till trial are poor. Before I came to Rikers, I, like most Americans, believed in the ideals of our criminal justice system and was shocked to discover that many of these ideals play out poorly in real life. Despite the Sixth Amendment's heralded guarantee of a speedy trial, trial is often years away. This would be a long wait for anyone, but for the impoverished detainee, the pretrial years must be spent behind bars. The only alternative would be the expedient plea bargain, frequently offered by the district attorney: If the accused foregoes trial and accepts some measure of guilt, he will typically receive a lighter sentence than what would have been handed down had he gone to trial and lost. But what it also means is that detainees will agree to it, not necessarily because they're guilty, but because the pathway to trial is just too daunting.

When I met an inmate named Chris Barnett, I was drawn into this issue more deeply. Chris hobbled into the clinic on crutches, and his referral read, "Just came from hospital—evaluate for depression." A slight young man, the twenty-three-year-old carefully eased himself into the seat across from me and tearfully told me that two weeks earlier, he'd been out for a carefree motorcycle ride when a teenager darted out from behind a bus. "It was like he fell out of the sky and was on top of my bike. Before I knew what happened, it was over."

Chris sustained a broken hip, broken collarbone, and internal injuries, but the teenager was dead. Chris denied he'd been drinking, and a Breathalyzer confirmed it. He also said he hadn't been speeding, which was borne out by eyewitnesses as well as a police test on the tire marks. Though Chris had been neither drinking nor speeding, he still was arrested for vehicular homicide, which perplexed me, as this seemed like a clear-cut accident. But I assumed there had to be more to this. After all, I only heard the inmates' version of things.

In the sessions that followed, I learned that Chris, like most at Rikers, had been raised in a poor neighborhood, had dropped out of high school, and was involved in minor skirmishes with the law. But after a couple of misdemeanor charges, he went back to school, earned a GED, and was thrilled to have landed an entry-level position on Wall Street. The pay was low, but the future was promising, and Chris was smart enough to see the possibilities.

"They're still holding my job for me," he said, proudly.

Chris's father was out of the picture, and his mother was not well. His family lacked the resources to pay his bail, but he did have a steady girlfriend who promised to see him through the ordeal.

Considering his life circumstances, Chris had done remarkably well. And on a personal level I liked him and felt for him and the predicament he was in. An accident like this could have happened to anyone. And based on his continued impressive behavior, I was convinced that this was, indeed, an accident. But what especially intrigued me about Chris was that he didn't have a prior felony. A lifelong black mark, the felony forever casts suspicion and serves as a permanent barrier to job opportunities, regardless of positive changes made as an individual matures. Virtually all the inmates had at least one felony, mostly for nonviolent offenses. Many had ruefully told me it had been their dream to become a fireman, or even a policeman, only to realize—too late—that because of the felony, this could never be and that they were now permanently exiled to a fringe-type existence. This one difference set Chris Barnett apart from thousands of others.

The district attorney was offering Chris a plea bargain of two to four years. If he accepted it, he would serve two years in prison and remain on probation for the remaining two. But as part of the offer, he would also have to accept the felony. If he insisted on a trial and lost, his sentence could be in the range of eight to ten years. There was a lot at stake here. More than anything, Chris wanted to hold on to his job and the life he was creating. But if he accepted the felony, he could say good-bye to Wall Street, and frankly most other job opportunities, forever.

As Chris hashed it over with me, he became angry. "I'm sorry this kid is dead—but I didn't do anything wrong. He ran out from behind a bus. I wasn't drinking and I wasn't speeding. It was an accident! I'm not accepting this offer! Doesn't he have any responsibility for what happened? I got hurt too! I'll take my chances at trial."

I was delighted by his decision. Although I knew that difficult days lay ahead for Chris, I vowed to provide the moral support he would need to see his day in court. "You're not alone in this," I told him. "I'll help you in any way I can. If an issue comes up between our sessions, have your housing officer call me. I'm only a phone call away. Remember, you're not alone in here."

We stood up and shook hands, and a determined Chris Barnett positioned himself on his crutches and was on his way.

21

BY THE FALL OF 1996, MY HEALTHY LIFESTYLES GROUP was doing well. Despite the risk of being publicly identified as having "the monster," eight to twelve HIV-infected inmates regularly attended. With an emphasis on emotional support and medical education, the weekly hour sped by as the group members voiced their anxieties, fears, and even their hopes. In listening to these men, I was always struck by their range of coping skills. While a few quivered in terror every time they sneezed, fearing imminent death, there were also a surprising number for whom the disease prompted personal growth and a long-elusive feeling of peace.

The constitution of the group was Black and Hispanic, a microcosm of the larger jail. Unlike the larger jail, however, where there was chronic tension between the two ethnic factions, in our group harmony reigned. Distanced from the judgments of their peers and bound together against a deadly foe, the support group served as an oasis of goodwill, and I only wished that more of the sick took advantage of it. Once a month I brought in a medical specialist to discuss treatment and answer questions. For one presentation, I was able to get the doctor on the island who specialized in AIDS to explain the latest advances in treatment. By the late 1990s, HIV was being treated with a cocktail of drugs, and although it was exorbitantly expensive, New York City still provided this level of treatment to stricken detainees.

Following up on her initial interest in this group, Miss Edwards lent further support. If a group member failed to show up, she was quick to pick up the phone and investigate. I often overheard her yelling at the housing officers, "Where's so and so? Give him a pass and get him up here! Do your damn job!"

She spoke to her fellow officers in a way that I would never dare, and her efforts paid off nicely as the no-shows appeared within minutes of her calls. After the sessions ended and the inmates had left, Miss Edwards would share her thoughts, telling me who she thought looked well and who did not.

Based on our mutual interest in the group, Miss Edwards and I began to chat. When things quieted down for the count, she'd light up a cigarette and tell me about her life as a CO. "This is a good post," she said. "You're not in the houses—it's better. The post I hated most was the visiting room. That was the worst, 'cause of the kids. When I had to announce that time was up, that visiting hours were over, those children would start crying. They didn't understand that Daddy was a drug dealer. To them, he was just Daddy. Sometimes I'd let the time go a little longer. I wasn't supposed to . . . and a few times, those little kids would run right after their father, and we'd have to tear after them. That's when it really gets to you."

Miss Edwards's reflections on the visiting room and the wrenching scenes with the children were a reminder that jail doesn't only punish the incarcerated—it punishes their families too. I never forgot the tragic plight of the mules at Rose Singer, and the poor children who waited for them. And I thought of the babies in the Rose Singer nursery, whose mothers would simply vanish from their fragile new lives when their mothers went to prison, and of how baby Michael had panicked when Lucy was sent out to serve ten days in solitary. And of Antwan Williams's sons, who sobbed so during visits, and of another patient who told me his eight-year-old stole candy from the corner store in the hopes of being arrested and sent to jail where he imagined he could be with Daddy. Another inmate charged with robbery recounted a childhood of waiting for his imprisoned father, who was serving a lengthy sentence on a drug charge, to come home. "Me and my brothers waited and waited for the day when we could be a family again. We were just kids and didn't understand how long it was going to be. By the time he was released it didn't matter anymore."

Although these parents had committed a wrong, wasn't there also a wrong in tearing families apart? Obviously, in cases of violent or more serious crimes, society needed to be protected, regardless. But for otherwise nonviolent offenses, the criminal justice system demonstrated not only a lack of compassion, but a lack of foresight. Children raised in such heart-wrenching circumstances are far more likely to do poorly in school, often turning to drugs and increasing their own chances for arrest and incarceration. I wondered why alternatives to incarceration couldn't be utilized in an effort to protect children, keep families intact, and break the cycle of misery.

* * *

The arrival of the holidays in 1996 brought the usual air of festiveness to New York City: the tree lighting at Rockefeller Center, the gaily decorated department store windows, and the hordes of tourists who flock to the city to enjoy the season's beauty. But the cheer was not felt on Rikers Island. Unlike the Christmas party at Rose Singer, there were no festivities for the mentally ill at GMDC. With little fanfare the holidays came and went, but not without a surprise New Year's Day visit from Mayor Rudy Giuliani. Since Giuliani had taken charge, the city was enjoying an unprecedented drop in crime. Even Charlie, my fireman brother, saw the changes. "There's no more gunfire at night, nothing! He did it—Giuliani did it!"

Along with Correction Commissioner Michael Jacobson and Deputy Commissioner Bernard Kerik, the mayor came out to Rikers to personally commend the Department of Correction for its role in the city's crime reduction. Making the rounds and shaking hands with the rank-and-file, he stopped off at various jails, paid a visit to the Central Punitive Segregation Unit, and met with the Emergency Services Response Unit. The two-hour visit was capped off with a message to the troops: "As we begin the new year, the city's crime rate is at its lowest level since the 1960s. Hundreds of thousands of New Yorkers have not been victimized and are living healthier and happier lives because of the fine work by you and your co-workers in the Police Department, the courts, and prosecutors' offices."

But while the city celebrated and police and prosecutors congratulated themselves, I had mixed feelings. While it was hard to argue with my brother's enthusiasm, and harder still to argue against safer streets, I believed that the same results could have been achieved without traumatizing society's most vulnerable citizens and loading up the jails with people whose needs could have been humanely addressed on the outside. Giuliani's policy of aggressive policing cast a wide net, picking up not only dangerous criminals, but trespassers, loiterers, the homeless, the hapless, and the mentally ill. Hardly the villains that most people imagine. Most Americans believe the incarcerated are all the heinous demons sensationalized on newspaper covers, getting exactly what they deserve. Most would be surprised to learn that the multitudes are low-level, nonviolent offenders. And even for serious offenders, it is assumed that the punishment, while harsh, is still humane. The public might be surprised to know that life behind bars is a grim exercise in psychological survival, and shocked to discover that many inmates must literally fight for their lives.

This I learned through Alex Lugo. He was newly diagnosed with HIV, and my immediate impression of Lugo was that he was a *real* criminal. In his early thirties, he was strongly built, with a tough, carefree swagger. An elaborate crown, identifying him as a high-ranking member of the Latin Kings gang, decorated his right forearm. But this tattoo was less striking than the three inked teardrops that streamed down from his right eye. Supposedly, a solid teardrop represents a body—a murder—whereas a hollow or empty teardrop is more benign, symbolizing grief.

All three of Alex's teardrops were solid, and the moment we shook hands, I knew he had killed.

"So—what am I being called to Mental Health for?" he demanded.

"According to this referral, you've just been diagnosed with HIV."

He propped his heavy boots on the trash pail, folded his arms, and looked at me squarely. "So what?"

"So what? This is a life-threatening illness."

"Hey, we all gotta go sometime. What's the big deal? Listen, why don't I just sign the refusal. I never talked to anyone in Mental Health before and I'm not gonna start now."

On my desk was a stack of refusal forms. I could have handed him one, but for some reason I didn't. "Maybe you never had a reason before, but talking about this might help you."

He thought about it, pulled his legs down, and said, "What can I say? How did I get HIV? Is that what you want to know? A dirty needle, probably."

"You're a heroin user?"

"You bet! If I could stay high till the day I died, I'd be the happiest guy in the world."

"No wish to recover from your addiction?"

"None whatsoever."

This guy was a tough customer, and I wasn't quite sure what to say next. But, like most people, when Alex was offered an opportunity to be heard, he took it. "I dealt heroin for so long before I tried it; I guess I wondered what was so great about it. I sold a ton of the shit."

"So, you were also a drug dealer."

"Yes, ma'am! Made a lot of money. Of course I got locked up a lot, but hey, you take the bad with the good. I've lived in the fast lane, as they say, but I got no regrets."

"None at all?"

"Well—maybe one. I have twin girls. They're only four. I really love those little kids, and I never expected that. I don't care much about anybody, but them, well, that's when I think maybe I could have done things differently—you know, been a father and stuff. I haven't seen them in a year. I have to admit that I'd love to see them, but not in here."

"Where are they?"

"Florida. With their mother."

Since Alex seemed more inclined to talk than he realized, I used the remainder of the session to complete my evaluation. When I asked how many times he'd been arrested, he said he'd lost count. When I asked him to estimate, he shrugged and grinned. "Forty, fifty times. Who keeps track?"

We talked about his earlier life. One of six children, he grew up in Florida, where his mother worked double shifts at a convenience store. "She worked so hard to make this little nothing money. Made me sick!"

When our session ended, he said he felt comfortable talking to me. "Maybe I'll come back next week and we can talk more about this HIV thing."

The following week he arrived promptly. Apparently, our meeting had churned some things up in him. Although he started off talking about his illness, the conversation quickly turned to more troubling matters. He spoke about his life as a drug dealer. "It's a tough business. I ran a couple of crews. Keeping people in line is a lot harder than sellin' the shit."

"How so?"

"You know—you have to enforce things. You gotta be able to send out a message when somebody fucks up."

"Did the messages have anything to do with the tears on your face?"

He looked at me for a moment, then nodded. "Yeah—two of them. Hey, it's business, you know. It's not like you're hurting some innocent person. Everybody knows what they're in for when they get into drugs. It's rough, but no worse than the so-called straight life."

"What do you mean?"

"Just that. I'm no worse than this system is. This criminal justice system—what a fuckin' joke! Do you know that for the fifty or whatever times I've been arrested—and this has been on the East Coast, West Coast, you name it—not one of those lawyers, not even one, ever said to me, *Did you do it?* And that's paid lawyers *and* court lawyers. It's all a game. All they ever say to you is, 'Take the cop-out!' It sure ain't what everybody watches on TV, these trials that get at the truth . . . that's all a crock. And then they put you in these cesspool jails where you're supposed to learn your lesson and go out and be a productive member of society. Gimme a break! I've been in a lot of jails, and I've seen a lot, but the California prisons, they're the worst. The guards out there, they're in gangs themselves. They have gang tattoos on the inside of their wrists and what they do is, they take their wristwatches and turn them in so that the watch part covers the tattoo." He twisted his own watch around to demonstrate. "Gangs are very big out there, and these guards, they got their entertainment from us . . . I want to get this third tear scraped off," he said, tapping his finger to his face.

"Why?"

"The others, they were business, but this one . . . no. In that California prison, we were human pit bulls. That's how the guards got their kicks. They made us fight each other—to the end. And this one day, they picked me and this other guy to fight. I had nothing against this guy—he was just another mate trying to survive. But I had no choice. So when we get out to the yard, I'm scared, scared to death, and I can see that the other guy's scared to death too. I had nothing against him," he repeated softly. "Nothing at all. He wasn't a bad guy."

Alex stopped talking and ran his hands through his short hair. "And the thing is that—*oh, Jesus*—the thing is that . . . he . . . this other guy, he thought it was gonna be a fair fight, you know. He actually believed we were gonna fight fair. And then when he saw my shank—I'll never forget the look on that kid's face. I'll never forget . . . As soon as he saw it, he knew it was over. I was scared,

I was so scared, and the guards were all around us, yelling 'Go, go, go!' I was never so scared in my whole life."

Alex put his face in his hands, before slowly raising his head, real tears flowing over the tattooed drops. "And then I killed him."

I never saw Alex Lugo after that second session. On the day we were scheduled to meet again, I didn't make it to work due to a snowstorm. When I returned, he was gone, having been extradited to another state.

His story was chilling, but I believed every word of it. Coincidentally, in 1997 televised news stories reported that in certain California prisons inmates were being forced into fights to the death, with guards sometimes wagering on the outcome. But even if I hadn't seen this, I still would have believed him. Very little surprised me anymore.

22

CHRIS BARNETT, THE HAPLESS MOTORCYCLIST, WAS
slowly recovering from his injuries. He no longer needed crutches,
and his limp became less pronounced each day. I'd often run into
him in the halls, where he was on his way to the law library, always working on his case. Though small in stature, he was big in
"can-do" spirit. "Miss B," he kidded, "I'm spending so much time
in the law library that I think I'll forget Wall Street and become a
lawyer!"

"You're doing it, Chris, you're doing it! Keep hanging in there."

"You bet!" he said, flashing a smile and a thumbs-up.

Chris was a rare bright spot on my caseload, and seeing him
through to his trial had become a personal mission of mine. But
even for those with less promising prospects, I tried to find value in
the moment, believing that maybe in some larger sense their growth
and maturation still mattered. Within the sanctity of my sessions, I
continued to find purpose and fulfillment.

But outside my session booth, it was a different story. I was
growing frustrated and often felt powerless in my surroundings.
Sometimes I spotted officers reading the inmate charts. They knew
their medical and mental health information was confidential, yet
they flipped through the pages as nonchalantly as if they were reading the newspaper. I didn't dare say anything to them directly. Making waves was risky. But I did report it to Pat and Charley, and
Charley would go down to the clinic for a little chat. The rebukes

were not appreciated, and probably did nothing to stop the behavior beyond the moment, but I admired Charley for speaking up. If I ever became an administrator, I hoped to be as courageous as he and Pat. In the interim, I grew extra vigilant about my chart notes, keeping my documented conversations with the inmates general and vague.

The message that was drilled into me before I'd ever set foot on Rikers Island—you are a "guest in their house"—still very much applied. And nowhere did I feel like more of a guest—albeit a poorly treated one—than when it came to the inefficient route buses that we depended upon to get us from the parking lot to the jails. Even though it would have been about a three-minute walk from the bus depot to GMDC, walking anywhere on the island was strictly prohibited, and we had the feeling that if we tried it, we'd be thrown into handcuffs ourselves. With no schedule available, the wait for a bus ranged from thirty seconds to what felt like forever. One morning, having stood in the depot for half an hour, a group of us were getting angry. In any normal situation, we could complain to someone in charge. But just who was in charge of these buses was one of Rikers Island's biggest mysteries, one that I doubt even the CIA could have unearthed.

However, there was a mysterious little office in the main Control building that we all suspected was related to the buses. That morning, I'd had enough. It was time to assert myself! I told my colleagues I was going inside to check out this little office. When I asked if anyone wanted to join me, they all shook their heads.

So I went in alone, and when I reached the door, I hesitated and then rapped on it.

"Whaddya want?" a woman barked.

Turning the knob, I entered tentatively. Three COs, one woman and two men, sat around a small desk enjoying morning cigarettes, coffee, and a box of Munchkins donuts.

"Excuse me," I said to the woman, "but we've been waiting half an hour for the GMDC bus. Do you know if it's running today?"

She pushed the donut box aside and took a drag on her cigarette. Exhaling a cloud of angry smoke, she snuffed out the butt, all the while glaring up at me. The men pushed away from the table, smiling at the floor. I was about to get it with both barrels. And then she was on her feet. "Don't you tell me there ain't no fuckin' bus! I've been sitting here all morning and I've seen it half a dozen times!"

"Oh, really," I said, trying to collect myself, "well you haven't seen it in the last half hour."

"You trying to tell me what I see, and what I don't see? You better not be! You hear her? She's trying to tell me what I see and what I don't . . . meantime the bus is probably out there right now while she's in here running her mouth."

My blood was boiling. Short of punching her in the nose, I didn't know how to deal with someone like this. I said nothing and walked out. But this wasn't over—not by a long shot! I would get her. Just that week, Mayor Giuliani had announced a highly publicized crackdown on surly civil servants. Boy, did I have a whopper for him! I would have no peace until I'd composed my letter to city hall detailing this outrage. When Giuliani read my letter, he'd be all over this. Maybe he'd come out here to deal with her personally! Yes, when all was said and done, she'd be one sorry civil servant.

My buddies at the depot were waiting. "Well?" they smiled.

"Well, nothing," I said. "The bus is coming."

Eventually it did come, and as it rumbled down to GMDC and the day got going, my great letter idea faded away.

But my feelings of powerlessness were giving way to anger. Every morning when I came in and glanced up at the Dostoevsky quote over the entryway gate, I shook my head. "A society can be judged by the condition of its jails." If I'd wondered what life at GMDC would say about us, I had my answer, and it wasn't good. By now I knew that inmate abuse was chronic and systemic, and that neither the Board of Correction nor the civilian presence in the jails was enough to meaningfully deter it. I was especially frustrated that there was no safe mechanism for me to report it. Not that such a mechanism wasn't possible. As a social worker, I was legally mandated to report suspected incidents of abuse of innocent children. In a jail setting this issue rarely came up, but what we were faced with was a procession of inmates who'd been brutalized, yet no laws required us to report abuse of the "presumed innocent."

I never wished for a mandatory reporting mechanism more than in the aftermath of a housing search that went badly wrong. We were in the middle of our sessions on a late summer afternoon when an alarm went off and the entire jail was abruptly placed on lockdown. The sessions stopped, and the inmates were hurried back to their houses.

As we learned afterward, the inmates were lined up against the wall, where an older man with arthritic, gnarled hands was unable to flatten his palms. The search team circled him, yelling, "Open your fuckin' hands!" A younger inmate came to his defense, blurting out that the older man had arthritis. Outraged by the audacity of his outburst, the team attacked the young protector. But as he was being punched and kicked, the other inmates were coming off the wall; the situation was destabilizing. Recognizing the growing danger, the squad pulled the inmate to his feet, ordered the others back to their cots, and left. But they had been challenged, and this would not go unaddressed. They returned, this time with the Emergency Response Services Unit in tow. Easily identifiable by their gargantuan proportions, the ERSU is an elite unit available on a moment's notice to assist with searches, squelch uprisings, and generally provide physical intimidation and force. Frequently seen patrolling the jails' hallways, they're often called the "Ninja Turtles" because of their heavily padded gear. They had another nickname, though: the Goon Squad.

The dorm was quickly overrun with security squads and elite units. As the afternoon dragged on, tension was mounting. In the clinic, we joined the medical staff in wait. The big clinic usually operated at a frenzied pace, but now the waiting area sat empty. Everyone nervously chatted, but beneath the small talk were the unspoken questions: "How bad is it?" and "When will it end?"

Shortly, a few COs straggled in, holding up injured fingers. After they were examined, it was paperwork time. On every spare desk, they spread out their forms. The chief physician, a short wiry man from the Philippines, paced the clinic. "Where are the inmates?"

I walked over to the Mental Health section, where Miss Edwards sat alone.

"So—how bad do you think this is going to be?" I asked.

"Well," she said, lighting up a cigarette, "hopefully not too bad. It's not like it used to be before we got all these regulations. Back in the day, these inmates, they'd wind up with lacerated livers and kidneys. But you don't see too much of that these days—thank God."

If she meant that as a comfort to me, it wasn't.

And then the gurneys started coming up. One after the next. The clinic was suddenly crammed with moaning and dazed inmates.

"Let's clear out," ordered Charley, and we went back to our office.

In the days following the clash, we were desperate to find out what had happened, hoping against hope that maybe the injuries were minor. But rumor had it that an inmate had died. "He was older, had a heart attack," a worried clinic CO whispered to me. "Had a heart condition—anything would have pushed him over the edge."

The thought that someone had died was sickening. But the rumors grew worse, that the dead man had been stomped. "Wouldn't surprise me," said one of the old-timers, a nurse who'd worked at Rikers for a dozen years. "Wouldn't surprise me in the least."

We scanned the papers for news reports but found nothing. And asking the inmates in the dorm for their version of things was not an option. They were gone. After incidents like these, DOC moves quickly, breaking up the house so the inmates are scattered about the island, transferred to different jails. By next morning, fifty new faces filled the dorm. "As though nothing ever happened," said one of the psychiatrists. "And of course," said another, "it makes it almost impossible for them to band together and get a lawyer—DOC has it down pat."

The clinic administrator assured us that calls had been placed to the Board of Correction, and I just prayed that they would get to the bottom of it. But being on-site, we were much closer to these situations than they were. In the days that followed, I was haunted by what might have happened, once again wishing for a reporting mechanism that would have triggered an official investigation.

23

ON A BITTERLY COLD MORNING IN FEBRUARY 1997, I
stood huddled with a group of civilians in the bus depot, waiting
for the good ol' bus. The frozen earth was fringed with snow, the
cold blue sky marbled with trails of white plumes left in the wake
of the LaGuardia jets. When the bus finally pulled in, we piled on,
grateful for the warmth. I grabbed a seat and settled back, taking in
the morning chatter. Above the windshield, someone had slapped
on a bumper sticker that read, "Corrections: Hired in your 20's—
Retired in your 40's—Can't Touch That!"

As the bus nosed through GMDC's parking lot, the talk
abruptly subsided. Affixed to the front of the jail was purple and
black bunting that swayed in the wind. The somber cloth meant
that someone in the DOC ranks was dead. There was immediate
speculation, but with hundreds of officers staffing the big jail, I figured it likely wasn't anyone I knew. The lobby was quiet, and at the
top of the stairwell, an unfamiliar CO unlocked the door. When I
stepped into our office, the first thing I noticed was that everything
was dim—the lights were off and the morning pot of coffee had not
been started. Instead, our quarters were filled with captains and
COs, many weeping. Pat turned to me with a teary face. "It's Miss
Edwards, Mary. Miss Edwards is dead!"

"*What!*"

"Apparently," said an ashen Charley, "she went to the doctor
on Saturday for a routine test where they put you under and put

a camera down your throat. But when they were finished, they couldn't revive her. By the time the ambulance arrived, she was already gone."

Miss Edwards was dead! I'd spoken with her on Friday afternoon just before she left. I could still see her packing up, saying, "See you Monday!" This could not be—it just couldn't. It had to be some kind of a dream. But as more weepy officers filed in, I knew it was true.

That morning began days of tears and profound grief. Because of Miss Edwards's role with the Mental Health Department, our staff and DOC came together in a way that we ordinarily did not. The walls came down, and we mourned as one.

When the HIV group convened, it was the first time it was conducted without Miss Edwards, the quiet ally who'd silently watched over this brood. "She always got me up here," said Pedro, who'd been with the group since its inception. "One time," said Marvin, the youngest at twenty, "when I needed my meds, but it was late 'cause I just came back from court, she helped me. Otherwise, they were telling me to come back tomorrow."

"And here we think we're gonna die any minute, and then BAM! Miss Edwards dies. You don't know—you just don't really ever know, now do you?" uttered Paulie, the group's unspoken leader. As the group members expressed their feelings, I said little, letting their wise words soothe me.

Later in the week, we drove into Manhattan and up to Harlem for the funeral. As happens when someone dies in the prime of life, the church was packed. Family, friends, and coworkers filled the pews. Lines of correctional personnel in dress uniform spilled out the doors as they remembered their comrade, best known to them as "Eddie." Without their workday uniforms, face shields, and helmets, they looked ordinary, if not a tad vulnerable. Like the police, the COs were a loyal and cohesive band. Sadly, what they also shared with the police was an above-average suicide rate and rampant alcoholism. Within the island's massive parking lots, their own despair was evident. Smashed liquor bottles, the remains of after-hours drinking sprees, covered every patch of pavement. Any intact bottles were propped up against the lampposts, a grim greeting to the morning shift. The parking lots were so thoroughly coated in glass that I kept a dust pan and brush in my car to sweep up the shards before pulling into a spot. Periodically, a detail of prisoners was dispatched for a bigger sweep, but within short order, it was right back to its usual depressing state. Jail isn't just hard on the inmates—it's hard on its keepers. Although I was convinced that the more brutish COs were quite simply on the wrong side of the bars, I also had to acknowledge the work of Miss Edwards, and so many more like her, who carried out their duties with honor and integrity. While the NYPD marched proudly down Fifth Avenue for the St. Patrick's Day parade, the unenviable work of the Correction Department—who patrolled New York City's "toughest precinct"—went largely unrecognized.

The minister was at the pulpit, and in front of him was the closed mahogany casket. In the first row, Miss Edwards's bereft sisters sobbed, and a young man I surmised was the son she often spoke about held his head in his hands. And then the minister spoke about the incomprehensibility of death, of how we cannot fathom the ways of God. Throughout his sermon, the congregation joined in, *"Amen, Brother! Amen!"*

There were moments when the whole thing turned surreal. What was I doing here? It was odd to see my coworkers out of place like this. We were all out of place. I was supposed to be back at the clinic, meeting with the daily stream of the depressed, suicidal, and mentally ill. And Miss Edwards was supposed to be at her desk, controlling the whole scene. But one glance at the casket brought me back to this wrenching reality.

Following the minister's remarks, speeches were made by high-ranking correction officials, and on our behalf, Charley stepped up to the podium and lauded Miss Edwards for her diligence as our Mental Health officer.

The service was nearing its conclusion when shouts came from the rear of the church. "Hold up! Bagpipers are here!" In the ultimate clash of two cultures bound by the shared traditions of law enforcement, a quartet of freckle-faced bagpipers in tartan garb bounded into the old Baptist church, muttering apologies for having gotten lost. The bagpipes wailed the bittersweet strains of "Amazing Grace." And then it was over, and in a procession we filed past the casket. I ran my hand over the rich wood and said a silent prayer for the soul of Charlene Edwards.

* * *

As the hard, painful winter thawed into spring, we were once again consumed with a growing concern: the hospital contract, due to expire in less than a year. In previous contract cycles, things would have already been settled, with Montefiore signed on for another three years. But now, with vendors from as far away as Texas in on the bidding, we were operating in a limbo. Nerves were on edge, rumors abounded, and the contract became a major distraction from an increasingly burdensome workload. With the city's budget cuts and the ensuing collapse of the Social Services Department, the Mental Health Department became the catchall for all sorts of problems. The most common request was for long-distance calls, usually to sick family members or to court-appointed lawyers in Westchester or Long Island who didn't accept collect calls. It was Pat's policy that we were to help out as best we could, and we arranged these calls on our phones.

Another unlikely problem pertained to gangs. The predominant gangs were the Bloods, Latin Kings, Nyetas, and, surprisingly, Muslim inmates. Though not a gang per se, within the confines of jail, and because of their large numbers and cohesiveness, Muslim detainees are considered one by DOC.

In jail, the primary appeal of a gang is protection. During the recruitment phase, the gangs downplay their darker agendas and instead espouse loftier ideals. For the Nyetas, their stated purpose is to defend and support Hispanic culture. I'd sat with many a young man who'd enthusiastically talked up the gangs' noble causes before signing up. But after induction, the bloom fades, and the disillusioned found their way back to us, looking for help in getting out—to escape the inevitable violence that comes with the turf. "I don't want to cut anybody—but if I don't, then they're going to cut me" was a familiar refrain.

These inmates hoped we could intervene with DOC to get them transferred to another jail. But other than contacting the Security Department, there was little we could do. A captain would meet with the inmate, but a transfer came at a price: useful information about the gang had to be offered up. This put the inmate in an awful bind; the mere suspicion of talking to DOC warranted a "green light"—death to the inmate. Most tearfully declined the offer and returned to their house to fend for themselves as best they could.

Tragically, jailhouse violence was very real. The time spent in detention is a critical period. It is a time when deals are cut and agonizing legal decisions are made—a period when fates have not yet been carved in stone, and emotions vacillate between soaring hopes for exoneration and plunging despair as grim futures in prison become more likely. Living in tightly restricted quarters with thousands of others consumed with similar pressures, fights and violent outbursts are frequent among the men, and we were often called to duty in the aftermath. This was especially so when it came to the dreaded "lifer scar"—a quick razor attack to the face that leaves an ugly scar extending from the cheekbone down to the corner of the mouth. Charley told me about an incident in the adolescent jail, where a seventeen-year-old was the victim of a particularly vicious assault. After being stitched up and sent back to his house, the bandaged youth fixed a noose out of bedsheets and quietly hanged himself. After that, a new policy mandated that anyone who'd had his face slashed be given a mental health assessment immediately following medical treatment. Consequently, I attended to many of these sad situations: with the telltale gauze across their faces and tears in their eyes, these sessions were sparse on words. Mostly, I would just sit quietly with them, letting them know that someone in this world cared about what had happened to them.

While many would view weapons possession and gang membership as characteristics of criminal behavior, the flip side is that terror would make anyone criminal conduct—take steps to remain safe. Many grappled with the weapons issue in particular, and on one occasion a client of mine arrived for his session and furtively looked about before reaching into his clothing to pull out a hand-made shank, which he handed to me, much like a cat relinquishing a dead bird from its mouth. Startled, I awkwardly held the weapon in my hands. He confessed he'd been filing it against the side of his cot all night, suspecting that the guy in the next bed was plotting to cut him. "I was gonna stab him while he was sleeping, you know, get him before he got me, but I don't know—I kept changing my mind. 'Should I or shouldn't I?' I kept thinking about our session today, and I didn't want you knowing what I'd done."

I poured on the praise for his good judgment, and by the end of the session he was beaming with pride. After he left, I examined the deadly instrument, unsure exactly what to do with it. He'd wrapped a long strip of sheet around the base to allow for a good grip. Out of curiosity, I unwound it and then handed the whole thing over to a surprised captain, who wisely asked no questions.

While most endure incarceration without carrying weapons, jail exacts its toll even from those with solid character who are determined to remain above the fray. Sadly, Chris Barnett could not escape it. "Miss Buser," he said, "my girlfriend came to see me the other day and she got hassled by the officers in the visit house. Now she's not coming out here again."

"I'm sorry, Chris," I said. "A few people bring drugs in, so they make it hard on everyone. But you can't let that get you down. This will all be over after your trial."

"Yes, I know, but I'm starting to wonder if I'm going to make it to trial."

"Of course you will!"

But a week later, Chris was visibly upset when he arrived for his session. "On court days, it's four in the morning when they wake you, and you wanna know how they do it? The CO kicks the cot and yells, 'Get up, asshole!' All I did was drive a motorcycle down the street!"

But things took a decisive turn when his lawyer, who had long supported Chris's plan to go to trial, suggested the plea bargain instead. "I don't understand it!" Chris said. "After I got arrested, he was all gung ho about trial. But the other day in court, he did a complete turnaround. Now he's telling me to take the cop-out. I don't know what to think. He told me to call him and we'd talk, but when I do, I just get his answering machine. Here I am, going to the law library every day, trying to get smart about my case, and now this! I think I need a different attorney. But the guys in the law library tell me that only the judge can assign a different lawyer because the lawyer is court-appointed. And they say judges won't do it 'cause everybody'd want different lawyers."

This was true. The inmates were constantly rejoicing or bemoaning their luck when it came to their court-appointed counsel. With so much riding on the competence of the lawyer, an inmate unhappy with his attorney will go to great lengths to persuade a judge to reassign the case. Most are unsuccessful and need to factor in the quality of the lawyer in any trial decision.

With Chris's resolve eroding, I had the sinking feeling that he'd never see his day in court and would instead accept the plea bargain and the accompanying felony. If this was the case, there would be no return to Wall Street. Far from it, he would be scrambing for employment, forever faced with trying to explain away the felony. Here was a bright young man with a promising future who was involved in what appeared to be an accident. This wasn't right! *This wasn't justice!*

When I left the jail each evening to go home, my goal was to turn off my workday. But more often than not, it was impossible. If my mind wasn't churning with images of another bruised face, then I was angry at a criminal justice system that would never allow detainees like Chris Barnett a fair shake.

But if I was angry, I was also starting to feel lonely and cut off from friends who had little real understanding of my workday world. One summer afternoon I was at a barbeque with friends, and we were chatting about the usual topics of politics and the economy. But when the conversation turned toward crime, I saw my opportunity. Without going into too much gory detail, I told them about the brutality and tried to explain just how the criminal justice system treats people who don't have money for bail. Everyone was listening. Emboldened, I pointed out that Rikers Island was a microcosm of jails and prisons across the country, a nation that led the civilized world in incarcerating its citizens, with a record of more than 2 million behind bars. My little speech was going well until I noticed the husband of one of my friends mouthing the words, "Bleeding heart." "No," I protested, "these aren't liberal or conservative issues. These are human rights issues!" Although everyone nodded politely, the afternoon ended awkwardly and I left the party feeling a little foolish. Penetrating deeply ingrained beliefs about our vaunted system was far more formidable than I had realized.

But there was one person in my life who well understood. Although he'd been unenthused about my Rikers mission from the beginning, I was now speaking regularly to my father, who provided not only comfort, but insights as a lawyer. He patiently listened as I described my efforts to help inmates like Chris to resist the plea bargain and see their day in court. "Good luck," was his dry response. "The system's unfair, Mary. If you don't have bucks, you're out of luck. Simple as that. None of this plea bargaining is law. When I first started out on Wall Street, we were all thrown pro bono cases now and then, and we did a damn good job with them! It was a nice change-up from the usual contracts we did. But now, with everything so overcriminalized, the volume of cases makes it impossible to try them all. Everything gets plea-bargained. It has to. And these prosecutors and defense attorneys that do these deals, they shouldn't call themselves lawyers. This isn't law! And furthermore, I'd like you to get the hell out of there!"

Ignoring those last wishes, I zeroed in on my father's observation about the volume of cases and read a book by a prominent

New York judge that shed an interesting light on the plea bargain process. In *Guilty: The Collapse of Criminal Justice,* Judge Harold Rothwax states that in the mid-nineties, in the borough of Manhattan alone, the annual volume of criminal cases averaged 125,000, but the physical capacity for courtrooms, lawyers, and judges allowed for only 1,350 trials! "Of necessity," he said, "the overwhelming majority of cases must be plea-bargained."

The simple matter of clogged courtrooms explains much of the crushing pressure on the detainee to take the cop-out. I'd sat with many an inmate hysterically telling me of some witness or piece of information that could establish an alibi or affirm his innocence. But the lawyers brushed it aside. Court-appointed lawyers, with neither time nor resources to track leads, pay for expert witnesses, or search for evidence, push the plea bargain. As Alex Lugo, the inmate forced to be a gladiator in a California prison, put it, the mantra of the lawyer is "Take the cop-out!"

Yet the public understands none of this, believing, as I once had, that acceptance of a plea bargain can mean only one thing—guilt. But what the public never sees is an impoverished detainee who doesn't have the luxury of sitting behind bars for a couple of years awaiting trial while a family depends on him. They never see that the court-appointed lawyer is inept, or doesn't want to try the case, and they would never understand that a detainee, terrified in his housing unit, will take the plea as a means of getting on a bus and getting out—to stay alive. The only thing visible is the choice not to go to trial.

* * *

When I next met with Chris Barnett, he was getting closer to the decision I dreaded. "You know, Miss B, I could get through all this Rikers bullshit if I knew I had a good shot at trial. Even if I had to sit here two years, I'd do it, but now with this lawyer, I don't know. I just don't know."

But I did know, and sure enough, less than a week later, his housing officer called and said Chris needed to speak with me. As soon as he arrived, he made his announcement: "I can't take it. I'm taking the cop-out. I have to get out of here. They had a search last night and they beat somebody up bad. I have to get out of this place."

"But Chris," I argued in a last-ditch effort to change his mind, "I'm sure they have searches in prison, and unfortunately, people get beaten up in prison too. Leaving Rikers isn't going to get you away from any of this."

"Yeah, but everyone says upstate is different. You work, they have programs . . . but bottom line, I'll know exactly when I'm getting out. Here, I just sit around all day not knowing what's happening. I can never reach my lawyer. I can't take it anymore. I'm going crazy."

"Yes, I know it's very hard," I said softly. "And I do understand your decision."

"I must have been nuts to think I was going to trial. In the time it takes to sit here and wait for trial, I could serve the same amount of time upstate and go home. It just doesn't make sense. If I had the money for bail, it would be a different story—I could wait it out. But I don't." Hesitating for a moment, he added, "I know I'll have to take the felony, Miss B. But there's nothing I can do about it. I'll lose my job, but I'll get something else. I'll find something."

"I understand, Chris." He was in the terrible position of having to forego his future for the sake of surviving the moment, and I told him so.

"That's right, Miss Buser, that's exactly right," he said tearfully. "I can't take it anymore—I just can't. I have to get on with my life."

He accepted the plea bargain and two weeks later, during the predawn hours, Chris Barnett was whisked away to an upstate prison.

24

BY THE SUMMER OF 1997, THE CITY HAD YET TO DECIDE whether to renew a contract that would expire in six months. Then things finally took a turn—a bad one. In addition to Rikers Island, our employer, Montefiore Hospital, also operated several city hospitals. However, when a dispute arose between the city and Montefiore regarding one of these other contracts, Montefiore threatened to withdraw from all city contracts, Rikers included, if the matter wasn't resolved to their satisfaction. Overnight, we'd become unwitting pawns in a political gambit. Our only hope now was that the city would reconsider its position and Montefiore would remain on the bidding track and win the contract. Still, it was hard to imagine that the pugnacious Mayor Giuliani would back down. He didn't. Shortly afterward, Montefiore Hospital sent a memo to its Rikers-based employees stating that the hospital would be withdrawing from the bidding process and leaving Rikers Island on December 31, 1997.

Dr. Luis Marcos, president of New York City's Health and Hospitals Corporation, paid us a visit shortly thereafter. Marcos, a small, wiry man with bullhorn in hand, reassured us that despite Montefiore's departure, it was business as usual—no need for panic. Prospective bidders were being considered, and a decision would be made quickly.

Regardless of his assurances, no one was convinced that there wouldn't be pay cuts and layoffs. One way or another, change was coming, and our worst fear was that our close-knit team would be affected. But no matter how jittery we got, Pat remained staunch. "Regardless of who takes over," she insisted, "we'll be fine."

It was against this uncertain backdrop that I took on perhaps my most challenging case. In 1976, the Supreme Court reinstated the death penalty. Although over twenty years had transpired since its reinstitution and the State of New York had yet to carry out an execution, there were still those charged with capital murder. In 1996, a Bronx policeman was shot and killed; the alleged gunman, Angel Diaz, was held in a Rikers cell facing possible execution. But before his case went to trial, Diaz hanged himself. After his suicide, mental health support became mandatory for any inmate facing the ultimate punishment.

Although we'd been thus far spared the trauma of a capital case, this changed with the arrival of Jerome Mathis, a twenty-three-year-old charged with a double murder. When Pat assigned the case to me, I was uneasy, unsure whether I could handle a close relationship with someone who might be put to death. But as I prepared to call him to the clinic for the first time, I figured that at the pretrial stage, the possibility of execution was remote. At least I hoped it was.

When Jerome arrived, I thought the housing officers had surely sent the wrong inmate. I don't know what I imagined of some-one facing the death penalty, but I certainly didn't expect a cheery young man waving to me as if he didn't have a care in the world. But there was no mistake. Jerome, wide-eyed and pleasant, af-firmed that he was, indeed, "the one."

"You seem so calm about it all," I commented.

"Miss Buser," he responded in a thick Southern accent, "I put my life into God's hands. God will take care of me."

Then he told me what had happened. After completing his sec-ond year at a community college in Louisiana, he and his younger brother were visiting relatives in a rundown section of Brooklyn. "It was our first time to New York!" he beamed. A couple of days into the visit, Jerome noticed that he and his brother were being eyed by a few guys on a street corner. "This one afternoon," he said, "me and my brother went out for a walk while our cousins were at work. On our way back, my brother stopped off at a bodega, and I went back to the apartment."

Unbeknownst to Jerome, the corner thugs had followed him, and when he unlocked the door, they pushed it in behind him, one of them holding him at gunpoint while the other two ransacked the apartment. "They told me to give up the drugs and the money or they would waste me. But I didn't have any drugs, and the only money I had was a couple of dollars in my wallet. Now I'm scared they're going to shoot me, but what I'm really scared about is that my brother's on his way back—I'm terrified they're going to shoot him. And then I hear him at the door, and the guy with the gun turns around, but the gun gets tangled up in his shirt. He had on one of those fishnet kind of shirts, and I see my chance. I reach for the gun and I've got it, and he's trying to pull it back, and the two others are grabbing my arms, but I'm the one who gets it, and I just start shooting and shooting. It all happened in seconds. I don't even remember pulling the trigger, but all of a sudden it's over and the three of them are laying on the floor, bleeding. And my brother— he's just standing there holding a carton of milk. So I pick up the phone and call 911 and tell them to send an ambulance. But two of those guys—they didn't make it," he said, with a hint of sadness.

The fact that two people had been killed qualified Jerome for capital murder, while his brother was simply arrested. "My brother's here on Rikers in one of the other jails. I don't understand why he's in jail—he didn't do anything! I'm so worried about him, and about my mom. Once a week I talk to her in Louisiana. She can't afford to come up here, she can just afford two collect calls a week—one from me and one from my brother. All she does is cry."

The one person Jerome didn't seem worried about was himself. He showed up for his sessions wearing his white cafeteria scrubs while on break from his job in the kitchen. Instead of dwelling on his nightmarish predicament, he recounted tales of a gentler life along the Louisiana bayou. As he chattered away, images kept cropping up in my head—horrible visions of this young man being strapped to a table and injected with some kind of lethal formula. It was unreal, it was sickening, and it was entirely possible.

But anxious as I was, Jerome remained inexplicably calm. "God will take care of me," he insisted. Never once did he waver in that belief. But I wasn't nearly as confident. If I'd learned nothing else at Rikers, it's that justice is not guaranteed. The implications of this are chilling, especially so when it comes to life and death. With the nationwide resumption of executions, there were more and more accounts of defendants being represented by inexperienced or incompetent lawyers, of innocent people being executed, and of the uneven application of the death penalty resulting in executions of higher numbers of minorities and the poor.

The trial took two weeks, and because Jerome left for court in the early morning hours and returned late at night, I had no chance to talk to him and find out how things were going. But I thought about him constantly and I prayed hard.

When it was over, I called him to the clinic. I was nervous because if he'd been acquitted, he would have been released. But his name remained on the GMDC census.

"Hello, Miss Buser!" Jerome said in his usual cheery fashion.

My stomach was roiling. "Jerome—is it over?"

"Yes, yes it is. Let me tell you how it went. When I took the stand, I told the jury exactly what happened. And that DA, she kept on trying to trick me. She said, 'What's the *real* reason that you *murdered* these two young men?' And I said, 'I didn't *murder* anyone. I grabbed the gun and started shooting because I was afraid me and my brother were going to get killed.' She kept trying to trip me up, but it didn't work. And then she brought in the third guy that got shot—as a witness. At first he was all calm and cool, but when my lawyer asked him if he'd been involved in a murder in Virginia, he said to my lawyer, 'Fuck you!' Just like that, Miss Buser! And when the judge scolded him, he said 'Fuck you!' to the judge, and then he jumps up and starts cursing out the DA and the jury. He went nuts! The court officers had to pull him out. It was a big mess. I don't think that witness worked out too well for that lady DA," Jerome said with a mischievous smile.

"So after that, they call a recess and bring me back to the bullpen. Next thing I know my lawyer comes running down to talk to me, all smiles, telling me he's got great news, that the DA is willing to make a deal. If I cop out to lesser charges, they'll give me fifteen years! *Fifteen years!* Can you believe it? So, I just look at him and say, 'No, thank you.' And then he gets mad and tells me this is a good deal, and that I shouldn't say no so fast. So I say to him, 'How's fifteen years a good deal? I didn't do anything that anybody else wouldn't have done, and the jury's going to see that.' And he says, 'You can't count on that! They might not see it that way at all!' All the while he's sweating and sweating. Next thing I know, he grabs me by the shoulders and starts shaking me. '*Listen to me! Listen to me!* If the jury finds you guilty, the state is going to try to kill you. *Do you understand that?*' And I tell him that yes I understand. Now he's sweating right through his shirt and he says, 'You're only twenty-three years old, you'll still be a young man when you get out! *TAKE THE FIF–TEEN YEARS!*'

"But I say no, that I'll take my chances with the jury.

"So the trial starts up again and a few days later the lawyers are done, and the jury goes out. All the while, I'm feeling so bad for my poor mom. She took the Greyhound bus all the way up from Louisiana and she's sitting there all by herself, just praying and crying, crying and praying. So the jury comes back and we all have to stand up. They start reading the verdicts. First my brother—not guilty on all counts, so he goes free. I'm so happy about that. He didn't do anything, Miss Buser. Why did they have to arrest him? And then me: on the two counts of capital murder: 'Not guilty.' My lawyer, he just collapses in the chair—poor guy. And my mom is crying and hugging me, and then the jurors came up to shake my hand. But there was one catch: they found me guilty of manslaughter. Some of those jurors told me they wanted to acquit me of that too, but they felt they had to give me something because two people were dead. I told them I understood. Looks like I'm going to get five years. I've already been on Rikers for a few years, so I just have to do a little more time upstate."

When he was through explaining, the two of us sat together in peaceful silence. Although it bothered me that he got any time at all for what was clearly self-defense, in light of what the outcome could have been, the relief was huge. In the months that I had worked with Jerome, my anxiety about this case had made for sleepless nights and harrowing dreams.

Finally, it was over.

After the trial, there was no reason for us to continue meeting, but we opted to meet one more time, for old time's sake. Jerome had frequently told me that he liked to write—"poetry mostly"—and was constantly asking me for different words that meant the same thing. For our final session, with the clinic captain's permission, I brought him a little gift, a thesaurus. He wasn't quite sure what it was, but as he leafed through it, a smile crept across his face. "This is exactly what I need! Thank you! This will be just the thing for when I'm upstate and I'm trying to write."

"I thought so," I smiled.

When we stood up to say good-bye, we hugged. "Thank you, Miss Buser. God bless you. Thank you for caring about me."

And then Jerome Mathis was gone, headed back down to his job in the kitchen.

25

ON A SEPTEMBER MORNING, IT BECAME OFFICIAL: THE
city had awarded the contract to St. Barnabas Hospital. Few of us
had even heard of this small Bronx-based outfit. The media immediately pounced on this low bidder, underscoring its glaring lack of
experience in a correctional setting. Regardless, the city was tout-
ing St. Barnabas as efficient and up-and-coming, with a reputation
for being streamlined and aggressive.

Once the contract was finally settled, we were thrown into a
new kind of chaos: the managerial transfer from Montefiore to St.
Barnabas. Since the city was so late in making its decision, St. Barnabas was in a pinch to be up and running for its January 1 take-
over. Setting up camp in a local motel, they frantically interviewed
and hired hundreds of Montefiore staff. Layoffs did not appear to
be imminent. As deals were cut, word spread that St. Barnabas
was giving wild increases and placing unlikely people into key positions. The effect was a sense of giddy uneasiness. Weren't they
supposed to be cutting costs? The terms of the three-year contract
were no secret; they'd been the low bidder for a contract designed
to put money into their pockets for every dollar they didn't spend.
Yet judging by the way things were going, it seemed like the ax was
never going to fall.

But it did.

One afternoon while Charley was at the motel, St. Barnabas
signed him on in his existing position, assistant chief at GMDC,

with a generous raise. Thrilled, Charley raced back and urged Pat to go right over. She grabbed her jacket and they both shot out the door.

But as the afternoon dragged on and Pat and Charley did not return, we became concerned. The following morning we gathered in Pat's office where she announced the unthinkable—she was leaving. Apparently, St. Barnabas's generosity wasn't meant for everyone. Their strategy was to target each jail's second in command by luring them with hefty pay raises to engender their loyalty while snubbing the chiefs themselves, who, it was assumed, were deeply tied to Montefiore.

"My last day will be December 31," Pat said resolutely.

We begged and pleaded with her to talk with them again, but she would have none of it. Shock waves rippled across the island as news of Pat's impending departure spread. Within the week, Charley Simms was bumped up to take over, and Janet Waters was promoted to second in command. In the midst of the commotion, our beloved chief began saying her good-byes.

By late November, with the managerial end of hiring complete, St. Barnabas hurriedly focused on the union. On a cold and blowy afternoon, a group of us trudged down to the river and onto a drab barge that had replaced the motel as St. Barnabas's recruiting base. One by one we sat for brief interviews. Since we were to be paid union scale wages, there was no haggling about salaries. The interviews were nothing more than a formality, and we left the barge in downcast silence, new employees of St. Barnabas Hospital.

On January 1, 1998, riding high on the crest of their improbable victory, St. Barnabas Hospital arrived on Rikers Island. Although this was their first foray into correctional health care, they were already brimming with plans to peddle their services to jails and prisons across the country. Rikers Island was just the beginning.

In the first few months of their tenure, sweeping changes were put on hold while they settled in. Although initially content to coast along with the program they'd inherited, a few changes were implemented, the first being a moratorium on bottled water. The plan was to have the tap water analyzed, and if there was nothing radically wrong with it, then jug water would be a thing of the past. Needless to say, this was poorly received, as was their second change—the installation of time clocks.

In an effort to calm fears and dampen lingering affection for Montefiore, St. Barnabas held a town hall meeting. Regarding the time clocks, they insisted this was normal procedure at their flagship hospital where everyone, from clerks and janitors to surgeons and administrators, not only carried a time card, but were happy to do so! Punching a time clock, they told us, was an integral part of their innovative, no-nonsense philosophy, a philosophy that was landing lucrative contracts and garnering wide acclaim. And as St. Barnabas flourished, so would we all flourish. It was just a matter of "rolling up your sleeves and getting the job done!" They finished up by telling us how lucky we were to be part of the team.

But the crowd, not quite convinced of its good fortune, remained glum. When the forum was opened up for questions, only one was asked: "Why won't you let us have water?"

That was our first and last town hall meeting.

Oblivious to the hospital changeover uproar, the inmates, consumed with their own misery, continued to stream into the clinic, and by early 1998 we were busier than ever. I didn't mind though, as it distracted me from nagging misgivings about our new employer—and, of course, from the aching absence of Pat. Although Charley was a competent leader and Janet was second to none, things just weren't the same without the chief I'd always known. Nonetheless, the drumbeat kept up: we evaluated the referrals, placed the mentally fragile in our Mental Observation Units, transferred those who didn't respond to treatment over to the Mental Health Center, and tried to otherwise stabilize and support everyone else in emotional crisis. Weeks slipped into months, and another harsh winter gave way to spring. We welcomed the warmer months but dreaded summer's heat. Air-conditioning on Rikers was spotty to nonexistent, and with summer's arrival the jails quickly turned into cement saunas.

One morning, at the start of another scorcher, I received a phone call that would lead to one of the most devastating situations I would encounter at Rikers. The caller was an officer from the Mental Observation Unit. "It's Peter Ortiz," she said. "He's asking for you. I think you need to come down now."

She said nothing more than that, and as I made my way down the stairwell I was concerned. Peter Ortiz was a Vietnam veteran suffering from bipolar disorder. When he'd arrived at GMDC, he was initially housed in GP. Preoccupied with religion, he began proselytizing to his fellow inmates, sitting on their cots and cornering them in the showers. He quickly became a glaring problem and was brought to the clinic, with the referral handed to me.

Peter was in his early forties, although his jet black hair and boyish face gave him a more youthful appearance. Pacing the waiting room floor, in the throes of mania, he was crying out to his fellow inmates, "Are you believers?" At my session booth, he was quiet for a moment, politely insisting that I be seated first. But after that, the interview went nowhere. Questions about his history, his charges, and his life were mere cues for his religious diatribe. While he ranted, I flipped through his chart and learned that it was in Vietnam that he'd acquired a heroin addiction; and heroin was undoubtedly related to his arrest. The emergency contact person was his mother, whose address was listed as "California." At this stage of his life I figured he was pretty much on his own. As I filled out the paperwork to transfer him to the MO, Peter rattled off psalms.

Once he was situated on the MO, the challenge was to get him to start taking a mood-stabilizing medication. Because of his nuisance-like behavior, I was concerned for his safety. Of all the forms of mental illness, I found that those in the manic stage of bipolar disorder are the most vulnerable in the jail setting. Because of their inflated behavior, these inmates aren't always properly responsive to DOC's orders. Instead of attributing this behavior to mental illness, it is viewed as an affront to authority, and these inmates become prime targets for abuse.

Thankfully, Peter had begun the medication regime and his mood was starting to even out.

But not fast enough.

When I arrived at the MO, I spotted Peter quietly looking out a window, his back toward me. But when he turned around, I was shocked to see that both of his eyes had been blackened; they were not just purplish, but the color of coal. His nose, now crooked and broken, was pushed to one side of his face. And when he opened his mouth to speak, his front teeth were gone.

"Peter, what happened? Who did this to you?"

"The COs. They did it," he whispered. "They did it. I was coming back from court last night, and when we got back to the jail, a CO was walking me down the hall. When he saw his buddies, he pointed at me and smiled. Then he disappeared and the two of them came over and pushed me in a corner. I didn't know what was happening, and then they just started punching me. They were *laughing*. And you wanna know what they were saying to each other? You wanna know what they were saying while they were beating me?"

I shook my head.

"They said, 'Did you get his nose? Did you hear it snap? Did you get his nose yet?' Other COs walked by, including a captain, but they just kept on going. Nobody helped me, nobody."

Tears were streaming from his blackened eyes, and my own eyes were stinging.

"Oh, my God, Peter, oh, my God!"

"My teeth are gone, Miss Buser—*my teeth are gone*. My nose was broken—and for what? This was a joke to them—*a joke!*"

Looking at this poor man's pulverized face, I wasn't going to stand by any longer. Suddenly I knew exactly what needed to be done. "Peter, listen to me, we're going to do something. We're going to do something here. Let me help you. I'm going to find a way to reach Al Sharpton."

"What? *Nooooohhh!!*"

"But why not, Peter, why not?"

"Don't do anything like that. Please! Don't you see, *they'll kill me.*"

As he stood trembling, I realized that despite my best intentions, I was actually making this poor man worse. I backed off immediately. Once again, I couldn't do a damn thing.

"Promise me you won't say anything," he said. "Promise."

"I promise you, Peter. You have my word."

Back upstairs, I returned to the office and sat at my desk, dazed. Peter Ortiz, a Vietnam veteran, a heroin addict with bipolar disorder, didn't have a mean bone in his body. The ugliness of this might have been a little easier to bear had he been a heinous criminal, but like so many at Rikers, he was simply a lost soul.

I continued meeting with Peter in the weeks that followed, helping him with his meds, and just being someone in his life who cared. About a month after the attack, he told me he'd worked up his nerve and told his lawyer what had happened. I praised him for his courage.

* * *

I would never know how things ultimately turned out for Peter Ortiz. Like so many of my relationships at Rikers, this one would end abruptly. But it was not because Peter was going upstate or being transferred to another jail. This time, I was the one who would be leaving.

By the fall of 1998, I'd been at GMDC for three and a half years. My moments with these inmates were rich and poignant— but never were they easy. I don't think I realized how badly I needed a break from the front lines until I received a call from the unit chief at the Mental Health Center. He had an opening for an assistant chief, and I'd been recommended for the spot. Was I interested?

I was more stunned than anything else. I had not thought of myself as an administrator. Recalling my years at the Samaritans hotline, and my ultimate discontent as a director, my initial reaction was to decline. Yet something had to give. There are no happy stories in jail, and some days I felt like I couldn't bear to hear one more account of childhood beatings, of police and jailhouse brutality, or of courtroom injustice.

Although this promotion would mean that my close personal contact with the inmates would end, I started to consider that a position in management would still enable me to provide our valuable mental health care, but just in a different way. At GMDC I'd come to appreciate strong leaders and recognized that my effectiveness as a clinician was due in large part to the support I'd been afforded. Since I was now a seasoned therapist and also had prior administrative experience, I reasoned that I was in a position to teach and support the newer staff.

I looked to Janet, who had successfully made the transition to management. "I think you should go for it, Mary Mac," she said. "I'm proud of you."

I would miss my mentor and friend, but I sensed that it was time to move on.

While I waited for the necessary interviews to be arranged, I went about my daily routine, and one morning, a nice surprise was in store. Out in the hallway, I bumped into my first case at GMDC, Antwan Williams.

"Antwan—I thought you were gone!"

"Hey, Miss B! They just transferred me back to GMDC. I've been on the island all this time. My case just wrapped up! Can you believe it? Over three years here."

A far different person than the desperate man I'd originally met, he calmly brought me up to date. He'd abandoned hopes for trial and accepted a plea bargain of eight years. "No way I'd go to trial with that woman! I've got five more to do upstate. But at least that's better than twenty!" When I asked about his family, he shook his head. "My wife and I split up a year ago. I told her to move on. I can't take care of them. The most you can make in here is ten bucks a week. What'll that do? It was hard, but it had to be done," he said softly. "My sister still brings the kids for visits. They don't cry anymore. It's all very different. Pretty soon I'm going to tell my oldest why I'm in here. I told him that when he turned twelve, I would tell him why Papi went to jail. I still love my children, Miss Buser. It hurts—it really hurts. They'll be pretty grown up by the time I get out. I never knew how horrible this could be. Never."

"I hope the next five years go by quickly for you," I said.

"You and me both," he smiled. And then we shook hands and Antwan Williams headed down the corridor, a decent man who'd made a horrible mistake.

A few days later I was called to the office of the new deputy director of Mental Health, part of the St. Barnabas regime. A sandy-haired woman with thick glasses and a wide girth, Suzanne Harris took a hard drag on her cigarette as she scanned my resume. While she looked it over, I glanced at her desk, which was covered in Yankee baseball paraphernalia: bobbleheads, bat-shaped pens, and, along the wall, pennants and team pictures. Apparently she was a big fan. She put the resume down and asked a few predictable questions.

A week later I was called back to her office, where I accepted the promotion.

26

IT WAS WITH A RENEWED SENSE OF SPIRIT THAT I AR-
rived at the Mental Health Center, home to the city jail system's
most severely mentally ill inmates. This facility was based in a large
wing of the Anna M. Kross Center (AMKC), Rikers' largest jail.
Though it was only across the road from GMDC, as I sat in my
new boss's office I already felt like I was in another world. Unit
Chief George Davis was a balding, serious man. Joining us was the
chipper Karen Doyle, one of two clinical supervisors. An oversized
bulletin board listed the staff, over two dozen psychiatrists and
clinicians. The place was huge! Karen smiled and pointed to my
name, which she had inked in underneath George's. I felt a flush of
pride at the words: "Assistant Unit Chief."

"We're something of a MASH unit," George explained. "We
treat the sickest of the sick—that's all we do, Mary. Buses pull up
at all hours of the day and night from the other jails, and they come
across the bridge from the borough houses. It's our job to get them
stabilized and returned to their own Mental Observation Units."

"And as quickly as possible," added Karen. "A *big* part of our
job is to make space for incoming patients. We have 350 beds,
which may seem like a lot, but it's never enough."

George suggested a tour, and as Karen resumed her paperwork, we stepped out into the wing that housed most of the Mental Health Center's patients. "We operate a total of seven houses,"

George explained. "Three dorms, four cellblocks. Five houses are in this wing; the other two are in the main jail. We even have our own clinic here, just for our patients."

The clinic, known as Hart's Island, was our first stop. "Believe it or not," said George, "it was named for Hart Island." Located a little farther up the river from Rikers, the mile-long Hart Island serves as New York City's potter's field. "There's a lot of folklore on Rikers, but no one knows who named our little clinic and why it stuck, but it has."

Inside the curiously named clinic was a battered and clouded Plexiglas "waiting room" where a huddle of raggedy patients coughed and shivered. Since it was count time, a CO stood in front of the window, ticking them off on her fingers. "I got nine bodies in here!" Even though the Mental Health Center was home to the "sickest of the sick," it was still jail, and with misery etched on their faces, these patients sat passively, seemingly inured to the indignity of being counted like cattle.

A second, smaller pen served as the psychiatric waiting room, with three patients inside. "They were just bused in," George explained. One man was singing and rapping his hand against the window, while a rumpled older man paced back and forth. The third was curled up on the floor.

Next to the pen was the "on call" office, which was staffed twenty-four hours a day by a psychiatrist. The presiding doctor that morning was Dr. John Toussant. "Welcome aboard," Toussant smiled when George introduced me. "Three new arrivals," he said, pointing to the pen. "The older guy who's pacing, I just gave him a shot of Haldol. He should start calming down pretty soon, and then we'll get him over to the new admissions dorm."

"Sounds good," said George.

"Aaagghh, nothing wrong with that guy!" said a dour officer seated at a nearby desk.

"Putney!" George smiled. "Mary, I'd like you to meet Officer Putney. Not much happens around here without Putney!"

I extended my hand to a squat officer with a whiskered chin. But Putney simply glared at me. "There's a lot of knuckleheads in here, nothing wrong with 'em!"

"Oh, come on, Putney," George chided. "A lot of these guys are very sick, and you know it."

"Yeah—and a lot of 'em ain't."

George didn't have to explain this scenario to me. It was an all-too-familiar example of the tension between the Mental Health staff and the Department of Correction when it came to the mentally ill. For the most part, DOC was of the view that the mentally ill were faking it. They made their own frank assessments, which they were only too happy to share. To us, the mentally ill are patients; to them, they are inmates. To us, they are sick and often misunderstood; to DOC they are manipulators who are always trying to "get over."

With a wink from Toussant and a grunt from Putney, George and I departed Hart's Island. Across the hall was the new admissions dorm, which George explained was a temporary way station for the newly admitted. "Treatment begins here, and we also do a more in-depth evaluation before we move them into one of the other houses."

Inside the dorm, most of the patients were still dozing in their cots; others milled around in various states of dress, toothbrushes and soap in hand. A scruffy older man looked around with wide-eyed newness, awakening not just to the day but to lucidity. It was a familiar scene, complete with the morning cigarette haze, not at all unlike the Mental Observation Units at GMDC. In a little while, food wagons would arrive with lunch trays, and nurses would push in pharmacy carts laden with medication. The patients would line up for meals, and line up again for their Dixie cup full of pills. After that, there would be group therapy and maybe a staff-supervised game of bingo.

Off to the side were two small offices where Mental Health workers were meeting with the earlier arrivals. "We have a clinical meeting at eleven o'clock every morning, and they'll report on the newcomers," said George.

We then checked in on four more houses, which were more of the same—the jail system's sickest inmates rousing to another day of life and treatment behind bars.

Our only remaining business was a visit to Lower 1 and 3, the two houses not contained in our wing. "Hope you're up for a walk!" George said.

At the end of the wing, an officer unlocked the barred gate that separated our unit from the main jail. We stepped into AMKC's wide hallways, which were buzzing with morning activity. Navy blue–uniformed COs, two and three abreast, strode confidently down the corridor while a smattering of inmates, passes in hand, hurried along in a more subdued manner. The "beep-beep" of a motorized golf cart alerted us to step aside as an intent-looking CO with two captains aboard maneuvered through pedestrian traffic and zipped down the hall. A parade of linen wagons rumbled by, powered by white-uniformed inmate workers. Another crew swabbed the floors using string mops overly saturated with the jailhouse standard: pine-scented disinfectant.

We walked through seemingly endless corridors that narrowed down to thin passageways. Over the years, in order to accommodate a growing inmate population, the jails were enlarged using prefabricated extensions that resulted in mazelike structures, and this trip to Lower 1 and 3 revealed this haphazard design. We kept going until we reached a remote section of the jail. Finally, big black lettering spelled out "Lower 1 and 3." Its old oak doors reminded me of an elementary school classroom, except the panes of glass were cracked or missing altogether. With no electronic buzzers here, George pounded the door and a bored CO meandered over with his big key. When he pulled the door open and we stepped in, I was stunned by the deplorable condition of the house. The damp cinder-block walls were mottled with mildew, and wide swaths of peeling paint hung perilously over our heads. Two dreary dayrooms sat empty.

Tentatively, I followed George down a dimly lit tier. Upon peering into the cell windows, it was immediately obvious that these patients were much sicker than the men back in the main wing. Some were pacing and muttering; others, clothes in tatters, lay still on their narrow cots. A few yelled out to us, trying to get our attention, but it was hard to discern real concerns from psychotic rants. One man with a matted beard stared straight ahead through the window of his door, chanting, "My wife's a millionaire, but my hat doesn't fit!"

"Shouldn't they be sent to the hospital?" I asked George.

George shook his head. "Things are different now. Hospital runs are expensive."

"So what do we do? How do we treat them?"

"We wait. Even without meds, they often cycle in and out of psychosis, and when they straighten out a little, we try to persuade them to take the meds. A lot of times it works."

"Seems kind of primitive."

George shrugged.

I felt a terrible sadness for these tormented souls who've so long been misunderstood. Centuries ago, their odd behavior was attributed to possession by demons, and the afflicted were treated accordingly. Other horrible myths took hold, such as the belief that the mentally ill are impervious to temperature extremes and therefore were denied heat during the winter and chained to the walls of cold, dark asylums.

More recently, large state psychiatric hospitals took over the age-old problem of caring for the mentally ill. But over time, even these hospitals deteriorated and needed to be shuttered. With the advancement of powerful antipsychotic medications, the new hope was that mental illness could be managed with medication and supervised community housing. But that second, vital component—the supervised housing that the mentally ill needed and their families yearned for—never materialized, and medication alone often is not enough to support an independent life. Instead, massive numbers of mentally ill remain in a chronic state of psychosis, rendering them unable to attend to the simplest demands of daily living. In the absence of some kind of intermediary supervised care, they live on the streets, shuffle between family members, get into petty mischief, and wind up in jails and prisons, the new caretakers of the mentally ill.

While we waited for the CO to let us out, I couldn't help but think that despite all the recent breakthroughs in the treatment of mental illness, this dungeon-like facility of Lower 1 and 3 made it seem like we hadn't come very far at all.

27

OVER THE NEXT FEW DAYS, GEORGE INTRODUCED ME TO
my new administrative responsibilities: maintaining shift coverage,
figuring payroll, calculating the daily census, and tracking statistics. I wasn't crazy about these tasks, but I understood that they
came with the territory. More important, George and I were hitting
it off nicely. George was another seasoned veteran, and I hoped that
with his guidance I would ripen into a competent manager. But it
would never be. Less than a week into my new job, George called
me into his office and shut the door.

"I need to let you in on something, Mary," he said with a sheep-
ish look. "I'm quitting. Yes, I know this is a terrible introduction
for you, but I just don't trust this new outfit. I don't trust St. Barnabas. They don't know what the hell they're doing. I'm here close to
fifteen years; I helped to create this Mental Health Center."

"But they're new!" I protested. "Montefiore was here for
twenty-five years. You can't compare the two—St. Barnabas is still
learning. Things are going to get better."

"No, they're going to get worse. People are leaving here in
droves."

I was stunned. In an instant, all the good feelings about my
promotion were gone. I knew that hospital staff was leaving, but
I'd also assumed the exodus would taper off. My strategy was to
duck and dodge the chaos until things settled down. But there
was no more ducking and dodging. The reality of the hospital

changeover was hitting me in the face. Suddenly, I longed for the pre–St. Barnabas days and the Rikers life I'd known. I was half-tempted to run back across the street—back to GMDC. But there was no turning back. And even if I did, St. Barnabas was making sweeping changes, changes from which even GMDC would not be immune.

But George had one more shocker. "I need time to job hunt. As of next Monday, I'll be going out for a couple of weeks and you'll be in charge."

"But I just got here!"

"It'll be okay. You'll be able to reach me on beeper, and plus Karen will help out. We have a lot of systems in place. The place practically runs itself. It'll be fine."

I didn't feel like it was going to be fine, but there was nothing I could do. Other than resigning, which I was not ready to do, I had no choice but to ride out the storm. Tough days were ahead. But as I numbly left George's office, I never could have imagined just how tough they were going to be.

The following Monday morning arrived more quickly than I would have liked. One of the perks of my promotion was a coveted "Gate One" pass, which allowed me to drive directly to the jail, by-passing the parking fields and route buses. The small pleasure that I felt in passing the buses along the road vanished when I pulled into George's empty spot, a reminder that I was on my own. Although I'd been given a crash course on the workings of the Mental Health Center, I didn't know nearly enough to run the place with any authority. Nonetheless, I pulled the heavy door open and began the trek to our gate.

It was a busy morning in our wing; a long line of patients extended out of Hart's Island awaiting medical treatment. Two others stood outside a dorm while an officer fussed with keys. One bore a simple, childlike expression and I surmised he was retarded. The other rocked back and forth, an eager look on his face. The officer hollered to his colleague back at the gate, "I got two nuts here who need to go to the barbershop!"

I winced when I heard it, but this was everyday jailhouse jargon.

I had just about reached our office, eager to begin the day, when a loud voice stopped me in my tracks. "MAA–RRYY!"

A blonde-haired woman in a white shirt—a captain—was furiously headed in my direction. How did she know who I was? More important, *what did she want?*

"Are you in charge?" she demanded, adjusting a flashlight in her holster. The nameplate pinned to her shirt pocket read Sikorski.

"Yes, for the time being I am."

"Well, I'm the captain of the Mental Health Center, and I gotta tell you I'm not happy and the security dep's definitely not happy."

"What seems to be the problem?" I asked, a little less assertively than I would have liked.

"An inmate named San Filippo came in here last night. He's in the new admissions dorm right now. This guy's a major security risk! He's gotta be moved to a cellblock. Right away!"

Since cells provide higher security than dorms, DOC assigns general population inmates with more serious charges to a cellblock as opposed to a dorm. But Mental Observation Units, which were comprised of both cellblocks and dorms, were under our authority. Especially where suicide was a concern, we weren't going to place someone under our care into an isolated cell, high-security inmate or not. However, DOC highly resented our discretion in this area and challenged us every step of the way.

Because of George's quick departure, I wasn't prepared for dealing with DOC at this level. Regardless, this was my first challenge as an administrator, and I had to handle it. "I understand your concerns, Captain, and just so you know, our clinical team meets this morning to consider housing placements, and I'll definitely bring this up."

All things considered, I thought that sounded pretty reasonable. Besides, DOC was famous for perennially exaggerating security risks. But Captain Sikorski just rolled her eyes. "There's nothing wrong with this guy. Nothing! He's in a gang and just wants to get over. The deputy warden's not going for this, I can tell you that right now!"

DOC was always pressuring us to do things their way, but if this inmate was suicidal—gang member or not—and killed himself inside a cell, I'd be the one left to explain why he was in a cell, not her.

She continued to gape at me, but I didn't budge, and after a moment she backed off. "Well, all right—I'll let him know you're reviewing the case, but he needs to be in a cell," she emphasized one more time.

"Well, we'll see."

Inside our office, I immediately found Karen.

"Oh, Sikorski! She's always on the warpath. I mean, what are we going to do? Their mission and ours are completely different, and a lot of times they're right, but we still have to go through our own procedures and not be bullied by them."

Karen's take on it reassured me, and I decided to put the Captain Sikorski matter aside and delve into my morning chores, suddenly grateful for these concrete tasks. As I studied logbooks and calculated the census, I watched the clock, anxious for the start of the clinical meeting.

At precisely eleven o'clock, I joined Karen and Dr. Marvin Gardiner, the Rikers chief psychiatrist, while we waited for the new admissions team. Gardiner, a longtime Rikers veteran, was beyond retirement years; yet even though he moved slowly, his mind was keen and he was frequently called upon as an expert witness in court situations. Shortly, another psychiatrist and two clinicians made their way in, carrying stacks of charts. Over the weekend, sixteen patients had been referred to us for a higher level of care. The admitted patients basically fell into two categories: the severely depressed (those considered at high risk for suicide), and the "SPIMIs," those with severe and persistent mental illness such as schizophrenia, bipolar disorder, and dementia.

One by one, we read through the charts, making preliminary diagnoses and deciding on appropriate housing. Generally speaking, those in the throes of psychosis were better suited for a quiet cell, whereas dorms made more sense for the severely depressed. Finally we reached Jorge San Filippo's chart. The new admissions team reported that San Filippo said his mother had recently died, that he was facing a lot of time upstate and saw no reason to live. His chart also revealed a history of self-destructive behavior. I relayed Captain Sikorski's protests to the group, but given his mother's death and depressed mood when he was interviewed, a transfer to a cell was out of the question. The possibility of suicide needed to be taken seriously. It was the team's decision that he be transferred to a dorm for closer observation.

The remainder of the day was uneventful. If Captain Sikorski wanted to know the status of San Filippo, she never called to find out, and I was relieved to get out of the building without any further unpleasant encounters with DOC.

28

THANKFULLY, THE TWO WEEKS WITHOUT GEORGE PASSED by uneventfully. Although he returned as scheduled, his interest in work was halfhearted, and for an upcoming unit chiefs meeting, he asked me to go in his place. Every other week, the jail's unit chiefs met with St. Barnabas senior staff at "Central Office," their administrative base at the river's edge. I was a little excited to be tapped for this, recalling the years at GMDC when Pat had attended these meetings with the Montefiore brass and returned with news and directives for us.

I decided the occasion called for a suit, and it was with excitement that I drove over to Central Office. In the conference room, I grabbed a seat next to the unit chief of the Tombs, the Manhattan borough jail. Across the room, Charley waved to me. While we waited, everyone was whispering about the usual topic—who was quitting and who was trying to ride it out.

Shortly, the Central Office team made their way in, led by Dr. Alan Campbell, the new director of Mental Health, trailed by Hugh Kemper, a clinical psychologist, and Frank Nelson, a hospital administrator. Bringing up the rear was Suzanne Harris, the deputy director, wearing, of all things, a Yankees baseball uniform! In her pin-striped get-up, busting at the seams, the number-two person in charge of mental health services for the entire New York City jail system trotted to the center of the room, gesturing for all of us to get up and clap. I looked down at my patent leather shoes and glanced over at a shrugging Charley. Harris pumped her fists in the air: "Go Yankees! Go Yankees! Go Yankees! Come on, everybody—up!" Dutifully, we all rose and cheered the hometown heroes.

When the impromptu pep rally concluded, we cautiously sat back down. Time for business. (We hoped.) The first item on the agenda was departing personnel and the negative press that had dogged St. Barnabas since they'd arrived. Already they were making critical mistakes, mostly delays in sending sick and injured inmates to the hospital. Under ordinary circumstances this would have gone unnoticed, but because of the controversy surrounding the contract, their every move was being scrutinized; at every turn the media were swirling. A barrage of newspaper articles highlighted instances of poor patient treatment and questioned the quality of inmate health care provided by an inexperienced vendor motivated by profit.

All eyes were on Dr. Campbell, a big man with salt-and-pepper hair. "Look, folks," he started. "Any time there's a changeover, there's bound to be upheaval and resignations as new changes are implemented. It's to be expected. We're working toward a more streamlined, efficient operation. That's what we're known for. In the meantime, we just have to be patient and work a little harder. Don't worry, by the time we're through, things will settle down, the newspapers will go away, and you'll all have enough staff."

A few doubtful glances were exchanged, but nothing further was said.

He then switched to patient charts, impressing on us the importance of keeping chart entries up to date, neat, and legible. "Everything we're doing is being closely monitored, and it's being done through chart audits. It's critical that we do well on these audits."

With this news, I had no doubt everyone was silently groaning. In the past, audits were an annual event conducted by the State Department of Mental Health. But now, the city was performing its own audits as a way of keeping tabs on its new vendor. The frequency of these reviews threw us into a perpetual state of paper-work overdrive, which also had the unfortunate effect of changing the role of the clinical supervisor. Whereas supervisory sessions had historically been rich in education and a clinical review of cases, this precious weekly hour was now devoured by chart inspections. The paperwork demands had become so weighty that the clinical supervisors, many of them psychologists, were dubbed "chart jockeys," and we often lamented that the patients were becoming a mere footnote to the almighty chart.

Sensing the displeasure in the room, Hugh Kemper reminded us of St. Barnabas's plan to computerize the charts, which would make our paperwork lives that much easier. We nodded politely. Although it sounded promising, it was years in the offing.

After a few more routine matters were addressed, the meeting ended with a hearty, "Hang in there and keep up the good work. Everything's going great!"

Although that's what we all wanted to believe, I don't think anyone really did, and it was a depressing drive back to AMKC. Inside the jail, I walked into a pileup of civilians being held at the entryway gate while an alarm was in progress. In the main control booth, a soundless red "siren" was whirling around, its long red rays careening off the walls of the central corridor. Through the bars, a swarm of COs in helmets and carrying nightsticks silently marched three inmates to the receiving room. Two of the inmates walked with their arms behind their backs, wrists bound by white plastic handcuffs; the third inmate's hands were atop his head, fingers interlaced. I wondered what awaited them in the receiving room. Another depressing thought.

When I reached our wing, the usual line was backed up outside Hart's Island, and I nodded to the patients as I passed by. It felt strange that I didn't know any of them personally anymore. And to them, I was just the lady with the clipboard. Even though I'd only been an administrator for a matter of weeks, my close connection with the inmates was fading away. To try to stay connected, I decided to pop in on one of the houses before starting my day.

I stepped into a group session under way in the dayroom. About eight men were seated in a circle engaged in the usual topic, drug addiction. (My colleagues and I sometimes kidded that if drugs were ever legalized, there would be about ten inmates left on Rikers Island.) I stood back in the doorway and listened to the conversation. A middle-aged man had the floor and said, "It's okay while I'm in here. I feel good, I take my meds, but when I get out and go back home, there's drugs all around me. You start picking up, and you just forget all about the meds." The others nodded.

I tiptoed out so as not to disturb the process. These men were doing so much better than when they'd arrived. They'd be returning to their referring jails soon. It was a good feeling to see how far they had come. But I couldn't help but wonder what would happen when they left Rikers Island. This was a constant worry for them and for their families. There was a flip side to my conversations with Helen Tucker, whose son Michael I'd worked with at GMDC. As thrilled as she was by Michael's improvement, many of our talks had wound up with her in tears when she contemplated what was next. "What will happen to him when he leaves Rikers? There's no day program for him, no place to go. He'll be right back on the streets. Oh, dear God, what will happen? What will become of my son?" There was little I could say to comfort her. Upon release from Rikers, the inmates, mentally ill included, are simply dropped off at a bus depot in Queens. When I first arrived at Rikers, I was shocked to discover that there was no discharge planning for the mentally ill, that they were normalized on our Mental Observation Units and it all ended there.

But during my tenure at GMDC, a potential solution to this gap in care emerged. In the mid-1990s, a spate of crimes committed by the mentally ill drew media attention to the callous and potentially dangerous practice of dumping released mentally ill inmates onto the streets. Under public pressure, the city instituted the Link Program, a plan designed to "link" the mentally ill to outside programs prior to release. Enthusiastic Link counselors sat in at our staff meetings and explained the basics. Our job would be to identify the sickest patients—the SPIMIs—and refer them to the Link counselors, who would assess their appropriateness for a program. Since many of our patients fit the "severe and persistent mentally ill" category, the Link counselors were quickly inundated with referrals.

However, there were several catches, the first being that the legal charge had to be for a nonviolent, low-level crime. Unfortunately, many arrived facing serious charges, since it was common for initial charges to be inflated. In most cases, these charges were ultimately reduced, but the Link criteria were inflexible: the *initial charge* was what counted. This alone immediately eliminated most of our patients from consideration. The next problem was even thornier: the interpretation of "nonviolent, low-level." In one case, I filled out a Link referral for a paranoid schizophrenic charged with burglary, the particulars of the crime being that he'd swiped a broom from in front of an apartment building. Although interviewed by Link, he was ultimately rejected because of the "violent nature" of his charge. When I protested that burglary—by definition—is nonviolent, I was told that since there had been the *potential* for violence, he was disqualified. After numerous such rejections, I lost enthusiasm. The counselors themselves had grown discouraged, too, as the narrow acceptance criteria were not the designs of Link but of outside programs. The scarcity of outside resources meant that these programs could be picky and were skittish about admitting released inmates. I submitted dozens of referrals, and although doing so built up the patients' hopes that they were going to a program, it rarely happened. Of course, the irony is that if the patient who'd swiped the broom had been in supervised community treatment, it's unlikely he'd have been arrested in the first place.

The Link program had the right idea, but the complexity of providing psychiatric support for released inmates was simply beyond its scope. I thought it a tragedy that our patients were missing out on this, especially since most weren't dangerous and were charged with minor offenses.

Not everyone, however, fit the minor offense category. The ultimate tragic consequence for failure to care for the mentally ill occurred in January 1999, when Andrew Goldstein, a schizophrenic, shoved a woman named Kendra Webdale off a subway platform into the path of an oncoming train. Her death rocked the city, spotlighting the problem of the mentally ill roaming the streets.

To compound the tragedy, Andrew Goldstein knew he was ill and for years had sought help in coping with the taunting voices that flooded his every waking moment. Hospital records verified that Goldstein had repeatedly shown up at their doors, begging for help. The standard care he received was a prescription. Absent the necessary support and supervision, he was alone in the world and, in a severely compromised state, fended for himself as best he could. At his trial, the defense carped on this, laying partial blame for Webdale's death on the State of New York. Meanwhile, newspaper headlines portrayed him as a demon.

After his arrest, he wound up briefly at the Mental Health Center. But as he sat in our on-call room, there was nothing demonic about him. He was simply a tormented human being. But by the time Goldstein reached us, the whys and wherefores of his crime no longer mattered. Our sole objective was to get him out, and get him out fast. Since the Kendra Webdale story was front-page news, Andrew Goldstein was a "celebrity inmate." When headlines trumpeted particularly heinous crimes, the inmates, many guilty of serious crimes themselves, become righteous and indignant. This created a crisis, since neither we nor DOC wanted anything to befall a highly publicized inmate on our watch. Goldstein never made it past the on-call room; we hastily transferred him to a smaller, more secure unit in a city hospital prison ward.

After he was gone, we followed his case in the press. Ultimately, he was found guilty of murder and sentenced to twenty-five-to-life. Several years later, the conviction would be overturned on appeal, and in 2006 Goldstein pleaded guilty to manslaughter and was sentenced to twenty-three years. Kendra Webdale's death was all the more horrendous, and Andrew Goldstein's life all the more tragic, because Goldstein had tried to get help—help that does not exist.

But if any good could have come from this, it was Kendra's Law. Enacted in 1999, this law enables families and others to obtain court-ordered treatment for mentally ill people deemed at high risk for violence as a means of preventing future tragedies.

29

DESPITE CENTRAL OFFICE'S INSISTENCES TO THE CON-
trary, health-care services on Rikers Island were deteriorating, and
nowhere faster than at the Mental Health Center. My initial hopes
of supporting the staff in a meaningful way fell by the wayside as
my job was reduced to a scramble to plug empty shifts. My inter-
action with the overworked staff amounted to settling squabbles
and serving as a sounding board for tearful outbursts. Most were
already doing double shifts, yet we were forced to borrow staff
from other jails. But our biggest problem was a shrinking psychiatrist pool. As doctors resigned through normal attrition, there was
a long lag in replacing them. St. Barnabas was trying to replace
these physicians—most of whom had limited licenses—with fully
licensed doctors. The limited license doctors, the medical back-
bone of Rikers Island, were mostly foreigners. Like Alex, my former beau, they needed to pass stringent exams to become fully
credentialed here. While they studied, they practiced medicine under provisional state licenses. This arrangement had worked well
for years, providing the jails with a steady stream of physicians.
But in their zeal to snare the contract, St. Barnabas had naively
agreed to utilize only fully licensed doctors. For fully licensed doctors, with a wide array of employment options, jail is simply not
an appealing workplace.

Undaunted, Central Office was having some recruiting success with moonlighters, fully credentialed psychiatrists looking to

make extra money working overnight shifts. While their presence provided badly needed coverage, the presence of these anonymous late-night doctors only added to an overall sense of fragmentation. But worse, their arrival had unexpectedly dangerous consequences.

One morning, I got a call from a housing officer, reporting that a schizophrenic named Josiah Parker wasn't bathing and was behaving erratically. "I'm afraid he's going to get jumped," the officer warned.

When I arrived at the dorm to investigate, the patients were up and about, having just finished lunch. The remains of the meal still lay on the plastic trays. Somehow, the food never managed to resemble the mouth-watering fare depicted on the menu taped to the bubble window. Although standard and kosher meals are offered, both managed to look exactly the same: brownish glop, seasoned with packets of ketchup, washed down with the standard jailhouse beverage—Kool-Aid.

Wearing an array of hats, caps, and do-rags, the patients were returning trays to the food wagon, lighting up cigarettes, and milling around. A few talked on the phones, others waited their turn. In the dayroom the TV was blaring, and wet clothes were spread out on plastic chairs to dry (clothes were washed in buckets of water). A few of the more health conscious were doing push-ups. Contrary to popular jail folklore, I never saw a weight room or extravagant recreational facility at Rikers. In terms of outdoor recreation, some of the newer jails maintained spacious, evenly cemented yards with basketball hoops, but the older jails offered nothing more than small patches of grass and broken cement set aside for "recreating." Although entitled to one hour of outside "rec," not every house goes out at an optimal time of day. The rec time slot for this dorm was 7 a.m. Due to the early hour, most never made it outside at all, especially during the winter.

With lunch just finished, one of the highlights of the day was over and the patients were already curling back up in their cots. A common strategy for surviving jail was to try to sleep away the months between court appearances.

I was disheartened to see that nothing therapeutic was going on. The interview rooms were empty, and the scene throughout the day would differ little from this. Ordinarily, each patient would have had two mental health sessions a week, one with a clinician and the other with a psychiatrist, buttressed by daily group therapy. But now, all group therapy had ceased, and instead of being seen by both a psychiatrist and clinician, each patient was being seen just once a week—either by a clinician or by a psychiatrist, and the contacts were brief. The therapist had little time for more than a quick superficial dialogue, and the psychiatrist an even quicker medication renewal. Even worse, because we were borrowing staff from other jails, the patients rarely met with the same person. Although these contacts kept the treatment in compliance from an auditing perspective, quick encounters with different faces could hardly be called therapy. Far from a higher level of care, the Mental Health Center now provided the skimpiest care possible.

Since our staff presence in the houses was scarce, as soon as I arrived, I was surrounded by a sea of anxious faces with complaints ranging from medication side effects to requests for a return to GP. I jotted down names and issues.

At the head of the dorm, just outside the bubble, three cots were outlined by red tape on the floor. These were "enhanced suicide observation" cots, designated for those at high risk for suicide. Seated on the edge of a cot, a youth quietly wept, a thick pinkish scar circling his neck, indicating a previous hanging attempt.

I walked over to him. "What's wrong?" I asked.

He looked up at me sadly. "My mom's in the hospital and she's doing bad. She got sugar."

"Sugar" meant diabetes, which was rampant among the inmates and their poverty-stricken families.

"I need to make a long-distance call to talk to her. She's in a hospital in Jersey. I need to talk to her—she could die. How can I get to Social Services?"

Another anguishing situation. I had to tell him that Social Services was virtually nonexistent. Although we'd been able to arrange long-distance phone calls at GMDC, here we didn't have the same phone setup, so I was unable to help him with this. But I did tell him I'd pass his name on to the "Social Services Department" just in case something could be done. I also made a note to have his clinician and doctor check on him.

He wiped away the tears and thanked me.

Stepping away, I practically bumped into two young Latinos who'd patiently waited their turn. "Miss, look!" said the older, shorter one, pointing to his skinny sidekick. This was a translator situation, another common scenario. He chattered a quick command in Spanish, and his pal whipped up his T-shirt to display a gaunt rib cage, complete with a gunshot scar. "You see that?" said the shorter one. "He's losing too much weight! He needs to see the dietician so he can get double portions of food."

The dietician was just as overworked as the Social Services worker, but, regardless, I informed the inmate of the procedure. "Tell your friend to go to the clinic, and if a nurse or doctor says there's a problem, then they'll refer him to the dietician. They're the only ones who can make the referral."

"Oh, okay, miss, thank you." He translated the information back to his friend. The younger patient, who couldn't have been more than nineteen, backed away, bowing and muttering, *"Gracias, gracias."*

At the rear of the dorm, a foul smell was growing stronger, and I traced it to a rumpled-up patient who had to be Josiah Parker.

"He stinks," shouted one of his neighbors, who was holding his nose. "It's horrible to have to sleep next to him. He's up all night looking around the floor for cigarette butts."

"We take our meds, but he doesn't. Can't you get him out of here?" said another.

Parker, completely oblivious, continued his dialogue with no one.

"I'll take care of it," I said, pulling out a transfer form. He would probably wind up on the miserable Lower 1 and 3, since that's where we always seemed to have spare beds.

I was just finishing up the form when I noticed an older man who'd stood back, waiting to speak with me alone. With a cautious expression, he drew me away from the cots. Satisfied we were out of earshot, he whispered, "There's a gang in here and they're terrorizing everyone. They're taking commissary money, threatening to beat up anybody who doesn't do what they say, and they're running around at night torturing the really sick guys. You see that guy, Parker?"

"Yes," I nodded. "He's going to be moved out of here."

"Good, 'cause last night while he was sleeping and his feet were dangling off the bed, they were lighting matches and burning his toes. Everybody's afraid to go to sleep, that they're gonna get set on fire. It's really scary in here, especially at night."

"What's the CO doing while all this is going on?" I asked, already knowing the answer.

"Are you kidding? He isn't even on the floor. He's in the bubble sleeping and nobody better wake him! Even if you wanted to, nobody wants to be a snitch."

"Snitch" is the lowest form of jail life. "Snitches get stitches" is the oft-quoted, self-explanatory jailhouse mantra, and I knew this man was taking a big chance just talking to me about this. When I asked him to name the culprits, he didn't hesitate, nor was I surprised, as their names were always popping up as problems at our clinical meetings. I thanked him for the information, which gave me new ammunition in our efforts to discharge them.

I left the house with a growing sense of helplessness. There were so many moments when I'd felt frustrated by my inability to do something for those in a horrible predicament, such as the patient who couldn't make a simple call to his gravely ill mother. And then there was the kid who didn't speak English. I was sure he was Dominican; Rikers was full of inmates from the Dominican Republic. Through my sessions with them, they'd described impoverished lives in their native country, of growing up hungry with no medical care, of tapeworms and dilapidated shacks that flooded every time it rained, of no education, no government assistance—just poverty, sickness, and despair, with zero possibility for anything more. With nothing to lose and high hopes for America's opportunities, young Dominicans flocked to the United States in droves in the early 1990s. With legitimate jobs hard to come by, many resorted to drug trafficking. Despite their plans to make fortunes and return home as heroes, the drug trade usually only led to draconian sentences in US prisons, or a return home in a coffin.

What especially bothered me was that the jails were filled with so many ordinary people who simply had been born into circumstances that most of us couldn't begin to imagine, and they were just trying to survive. I constantly tried to figure out the whys and wherefores of life's gross inequities, but it was futile. But the one bright spot for me was always the valuable human attention we provided through our mental health support. In relating to these people with dignity, care, and respect, we were water on arid soil. But now, with all this cost cutting, even that was being chipped away. Maybe from a bean-counting perspective this fragmented style of care was working out well, but from the standpoint of anything meaningful, I feared that all was being lost.

30

THE DAY AFTER MY VISIT TO THE DORM, I PRESENTED THE
names of the predators during our clinical meeting. After a perusal
of their charts, it was agreed that they were all fit for discharge to
the AMKC general population. "Let them try to pull that fire stunt
in GP," Karen asserted.

Though our decision was swift, the real question was whether
or not we could keep them from returning. Virtually every time we
discharged malingerers, the following morning their names popped
right back up on our census. The problem was the new overnight
doctors, the moonlighters. With no connection to the larger or-
ganization, they ignored logbook directives, and when discharged
malingerers threatened suicide in the middle of the night, these
doctors simply readmitted them. When questioned, their defense
was that suicide risk put their licenses on the line. Although this
sounded plausible, there was no true threat of suicide, which they
would have realized had they been part of the larger staff working daily in the Mental Health Center with one biweekly overnight
shift, which had been the arrangement in the past. But these doctors simply finished up and left for the week. With this gaping hole
in our overnight defenses, the stage was set for infiltration by the
worst brand of malingerers, those who preyed upon the weak. And
in they came. Fights became daily occurrences, slashings common-
place, and extortion of the weak and sick was rampant. A steady
flow of patients with gashes, broken bones, and bloody noses

streamed through Hart's Island to be stitched and bandaged or, worse, wheeled out on gurneys.

One afternoon on a trip to Hart's Island, I heard a low, sickening moan. Alone and pushed to the side, a disheveled inmate lay on a gurney, writhing in pain.

"What happened to him?" I asked a nurse.

"The bone around his eye was shattered—very painful," she said. "We're just waiting for the ambulance."

One of the two COs sitting watch chimed in. "He didn't pay rent."

"He didn't pay *rent?*"

"That's right—didn't pay rent. They jumped him and broke his face to make an example out of him."

I felt sick. Without even looking at this inmate's chart, I knew he was mentally ill, that he rightfully belonged in the Mental Health Center, yet in this "protected house" he'd been brutally attacked. He'd have been better off in GP.

Alarmed by the violence, captains and deps descended upon George's office, imploring him to keep the predators out. Things got so bad that DOC informed us that the Mental Health Center, which held only 350 of AMKC's 2,500 inmates, was responsible for 75 percent of the jail's violence. Since we had sole authority as to the Mental Health Center's occupants, our inability to handle the situation was as demoralizing as it was embarrassing.

Since George had one foot out the door, he was disinclined to push the matter with Central Office, and even when he had tried, he was told that the recruitment of fully licensed doctors was a contractual obligation. Our new employers simply had little understanding of their unique domain.

But if I held out a single hope that this whole mess could be salvaged, it rested on George's departure. On a brisk November morning, George informed me he'd nailed down another job. With our leadership limbo ending, I looked forward to what the next chief might offer. With a little luck, we'd get a competent leader with experience and vision, someone who could forcefully communicate with Central Office, contractual obligations or no. Since George was giving a month's notice, I only hoped there was enough time to interview a battery of candidates before his final day. Some speculated there might even be a nationwide search to find the right person for this unique post.

But none of this was to be. George announced his resignation on a Monday, and by Tuesday a decision was made. Evidently skipping over any customary interview process, Suzanne Harris handpicked a newly hired St. Barnabas clinician to take over, someone with less than a year's experience at Rikers.

The stunning news was met with outrage. Not only were solid administrators with years of management experience passed over, they weren't even given an opportunity to apply for what was considered the crown jewel position. After this insult, there was loud talk of labor law violations, while everyone vowed to step up their job-seeking efforts and quit.

For me, this move was as disturbing as it was disappointing. With a relatively inexperienced person at the helm, nothing would change; in fact, it seemed likely that things would get worse. On the heels of George's farewell party, I contemplated a move to another jail.

But as luck would have it, there were no open positions on the island. I had to bide my time—and in the interim, run from one crisis to the next, often literally. Whether it was the arrival of a celebrity inmate, uncovered shifts, violence on the units, anxiety over audits, or bickering among staff, calamity was the norm. One morning, I arrived at work to find a rush of correctional personnel running in and out of Hart's Island. I found out why when I stepped inside. The medical side of the clinic had been trashed: desks upended, file cabinets on their sides, papers strewn ankle deep. One of the holding pens' Plexiglas walls was lying on the floor amid the debris. It looked as though a tornado had whipped through Hart's Island. A sea of officers were surveying the damage, including Captain Sikorski and Officer Putney.

"What happened?" I asked.

"They sent somebody over from the Bing last night," said Sikorski, "and when the psych told him there was nothing wrong with him—that he was going back—he went ballistic."

Since the Mental Health Center was the only facility that operated twenty-four hours a day, it was common for inmates held in solitary confinement to be bused over for evaluation if they threatened suicide during the night. While some were admitted for brief periods, most were diagnosed as malingering and sent right back.

"Whatever Bing time this guy was looking at before, he's looking at a lot more time now," commented Putney, referring to the tickets this inmate would incur for the tirade. "They gotta get a policy that these Bing monsters stay cuffed while they're being evaluated. They're the baddest of the bad—the worst of the worst."

"Bing monster" was the familiar term for inmates in solitary who resorted to desperate measures to get out. While their frantic attempts at relief rendered them a nuisance, Dr. Gardiner continually reminded us that their desperation only demonstrated the grueling nature of solitary confinement.

*　*　*

By April, I had been at the Mental Health Center for close to a year and I was miserable. In figuring the census, filling shifts, and calculating the payroll, I felt like nothing more than a well-educated clerk. Any type of meaningful management I'd hoped for had fallen by the wayside. But relief finally came when I received a call from a unit chief named Kelly Gordon. Since I only knew her casually, I was surprised when she asked if I'd be interested in joining her as assistant chief at the Otis Bantum Correctional Center, another of the men's jails. "It's pretty nice over here, as far as jails go," she said. "I'm trying to build a new team and I need an assistant chief. I think you and I could work well together."

I thanked her but didn't take the offer seriously. We had just learned that our new chief was pregnant, and I would be relied on to take over during her maternity leave. "There's no way they're going to let me go," I told her.

"I think this could really be great," she persisted. "It's a smaller building—1,600 inmates—and we actually have an adequate number of staff. I think it could be really good."

What she described was appealing, but the conversation was pointless, and when we hung up I gave it no further thought.

On a sunny day about a week later, I decided to weather all the time-consuming security checkpoints and go off the island for lunch. I drove down to the river and found a quiet spot near the Triboro Bridge. It felt nice to take in the open sky and wide expanse of the East River. With the lazy jangle of an ice cream truck in the distance, I watched as tugboats pulling tankers from around the world steamed into New York Harbor. I was just finishing up when my beeper went off. It was Central Office. I called in and was instructed to report to Suzanne Harris's office.

Hugh Kemper, third in command, greeted me. A diminutive man with a crinkly smile, Hugh was generally well liked. He ushered me into Harris's office, where the deputy director was lighting up a cigarette. A team picture of the Yankees smiled down from above.

Hugh cleared his throat and started, "Mary, as you know, we've been moving people around, trying to get the right fit for each jail—"

"Because," Suzanne interrupted, "each jail has its very own personality!"

"Yes," continued Hugh, "and we're trying to put the right managers into the right buildings. And we've decided that you would do well at OBCC. In fact, Kelly Gordon has specifically requested you as her assistant chief."

"Which is really quite flattering, Mary," Suzanne threw in.

I was stunned. They knew there was an upcoming maternity leave. I was familiar with the Mental Health Center's operations, I knew the staff, and I'd developed a decent rapport with DOC. None of this had happened overnight. I couldn't imagine how they were going to just throw someone else in here to learn all of this so quickly.

"Kelly needs you as soon as possible," Suzanne continued, "so as of Monday, you'll report to OBCC."

For a moment I struggled to figure it out, trying to understand their logic. And then it dawned on me that I didn't need to understand. All that mattered was that I was leaving a job I disliked, and this time their zany reasoning was working in my favor. Just like that, the Mental Health Center fiasco was over. Maybe things would be different at OBCC. It was a smaller jail and didn't have the high profile of the Mental Health Center. A smaller staff meant less time devoted to administrative tasks and more time for meaningful management. This was the break I'd been hoping for, and once again I found myself getting excited about my work. But as enthusiastic as I was, something was gnawing at me: within the confines of the Otis Bantum Correctional Center was the Central Punitive Segregation Unit—the Bing.

31

I SPENT MY LAST MORNING AT THE MENTAL HEALTH CEN-
ter clearing out my desk and saying hasty good-byes. At noon,
Kelly Gordon picked me up and we drove off the island for lunch
at a local Chinese restaurant. Though small in stature, Kelly was
an administrative dynamo. "We have a great staff," she said excit-
edly. "The last chief quit so the place has been in limbo. It'll be up
to us to rebuild and get things stabilized. We don't have a clinical
supervisor yet, but Hugh Kemper is interviewing for one now, so
when that spot's filled, we'll be in good shape. Hugh is our liaison
with Central Office, and we're lucky—he's okay. At least we're not
stuck with Yankee Doodle Dandy!"

With that, we both smiled and then started laughing. But when
the laughter subsided, Kelly fell silent, and in a measured tone, she
said, "Mary, there's something I should probably tell you."

This had the same ring to it as George's announcement when
I arrived at the Mental Health Center. "Let me guess. You're
quitting?"

"Well, not right away," she stammered. "I mean, I'm hoping
things will work out, but if something else comes up, I'm out of
here. Everyone's trying to get out—you ought to think about it too."

I just sighed. We drove back in silence.

But as we pulled up to the Otis Bantum Correctional Center,
my spirits picked up. The relatively modern building was bordered

by a neatly manicured lawn, and just down the hill the East River sparkled. I had a good feeling about this place. Maybe this was the new beginning I was searching for.

The lobby held the requisite pictures of Mayor Giuliani, Bernard Kerik—newly installed as correction commissioner—and Otis Bantum, the jail's namesake, a popular former warden. A couple of "trophy cases" showcased dozens of confiscated weapons. Made from odd scraps of metal sharpened to a razor's edge, some were long and pointy, resembling ice picks, while others were small and compact. The weapons were crude but deadly, a reminder that as nice as OBCC appeared, it was still jail.

Just inside the entryway gate, a picture window revealed an interior courtyard where inmates played basketball. Except for the watchful presence of correction officers, it could have been any city playground.

Kelly steered me to the clinic, where nurses in colorful uniforms that always reminded me of pajamas moved in and out of examining booths, loaded down with stacks of charts. In the center aisle, a row of hapless detainees awaited treatment. Keeping an eye on them was the clinic traffic cop, Officer Pepitone. Another gruff CO, he was on the phone, barking orders to an officer in an outer waiting room. "Send in three more bodies . . . no more than three!"

The clinic captain, standing next to Pepitone, fumbled with a hand-held radio. Two blue chevron patches stitched to the sleeve of his white shirt indicated at least ten years with the department. A chunky man in his late thirties, Captain Ryan put the radio down, and with a ruddy smile pumped my hand. "Welcome to OBCC!"

"He seems kind of nice," I said to Kelly, as we stepped away.

"He is—and everybody here likes him."

At the rear of the clinic, an inner recess led to our office, where I met Dr. Ismael Sackett, the chief physician. Wiry and nervous, he shook my hand with an iron grip and informed me he wouldn't be chief much longer, that he was just waiting on his "demotion." As a creative alternative to quitting, administrators distrustful of the new regime were lining up for demotions, seeking safety in the union ranks.

The Mental Health office was clean and comfortable, the cinder-block walls painted a soft blue. Around the perimeter of the rectangular room were three desks: one for Kelly, another for me, and a third for our eventual clinical supervisor.

Out in the clinic, Pepitone shouted the start of the afternoon count, and a few minutes later, the Mental Health crew meandered in, and it was with high hopes that I met our staff. Theresa Alvarez and Kathy Blakely, two recently hired young clinicians still fresh with ideals inculcated in school, were eager for managerial stability and support. Lynn Cosgrove, a longtime Montefiore veteran, was older and a bit jaded, but still friendly and receptive. Pete Majors was another clinician from the Montefiore days; he and I knew each other from GMDC, where he'd worked the night shift. Dr. David Diaz, a psychiatrist, was a hefty man in his early fifties who worked exclusively in the Bing. Originally from South America, his ability to flick into his native Spanish was a huge asset in treating the jail's large Spanish-speaking population. Another psychiatrist, Dr. Christian, was warm and chatty.

We pulled up chairs and, over the next hour, discussed our future work together. As ideas and suggestions were tossed about, it was with a sense of camaraderie and goodwill. An evening meeting with the night staff was equally encouraging. When we locked up the office for the day, I felt that this was it, that I'd finally found the team I was looking for.

*   *   *

Over the next few days, I became acquainted with the jail, starting off with its Mental Observation Unit, a single fifty-bed dorm. "We've got no cells here," Kelly said, "so if we get a paranoid schizophrenic who needs a cell, we have to send him to an MO in another jail."

Conveniently located across the hall from the clinic, the Mental Observation Unit was airy and spacious. An abundance of natural light streaming through the mesh-covered windows lent a mellowness to an otherwise depressing scene. Even the cigarette smoke wasn't as thick here. With the warmer weather, the windows were open, allowing a gentle breeze to flow across the rows of cots where the patients were reading, writing, or dozing. Toward the rear, a suicide prevention aide was engrossed in his paperback.

"It's calm in here," I noted. "Where's the gang? Where are the malingerers?"

"In general population!" Kelly asserted. "This dorm is for the mentally ill only—and I intend to keep it that way!"

"Good!"

In the dayroom, older men played cards while the usual bunch sat around the TV watching a kung fu movie, a jailhouse favorite.

Perched on the edge of a suicide observation cot, an older man with a trim build and closely cropped white hair smoked a cigarette. Behind his dark glasses, his right eye was distorted. "His name's Roy Evans, and he's one of those murder-suicide deals," Kelly whispered discreetly. "He's here for major depression." Roy Evans had apparently shot and killed his wife, but the bullet to his own head did little more than mildly affect his speech, disfigure his face, and put him in jail for murder. He nodded at me but did not smile.

Next to Evans, Teddy Gibson smiled shyly. Barely out of his teens, he was lying on his cot, jiggling his legs to the tune on his Walkman. Gibson's forearms were covered with pink crisscross scars. Kelly told me he was highly impulsive and that, after suffering chronic sexual abuse as a child, the undercarriage of his personality was so fragile that the slightest negative nuance sent him into a self-destructive tirade, as his cut-up arms attested.

As we toured the dorm, we'd acquired a quiet tag-along in the form of George LaRoche, who spoke like someone who was well educated. Wearing canary-colored sweat pants that draped from his thin frame, he became our unofficial guide. Ushering us up and down the rows of cots, he introduced me to Victor, a plump thirtyish fellow in a New York Mets baseball cap and a pair of oversized, jail-issued eyeglasses. When Victor looked up, his eyes went off in different directions. Mentally limited, he'd emptied out a bag of potato chips on a patch of smoothed bedding. "I don't think they gave me the right amount," he explained. As he lined up the chips, he told me about himself. "My mom got shot in the belly when she was pregnant with me. The bullet went right through my head. Yeah— that's what happened. Well, I have to count my chips now. Bye."

Kelly said that Victor had been arrested on a drug charge, either as a lookout during a drug deal or as an unsuspecting courier. It wasn't unusual for drug dealers to exploit those with limited mental faculties for various low-level tasks.

George steered us to Ruben, another pal of his with a Jamaican accent. Ruben jumped up to show off his inside-out jacket, its Ralph Lauren label barely clinging to the collar. "You see this?" he said, twirling around. "When I'm here, I wear it like this. But when I go to court," he said, removing the garment, turning it right side out and slipping into it, "I'm all ready for the judge."

"Very nice!" I applauded.

"He even wears that jacket to sleep," chirped the patient next to him.

In any other setting, I would have attributed this jacket routine to an eccentric aspect of Ruben's mental illness, but in here, I had to admit it was a creative solution to the problem of holding on to one's court clothes.

Off to the side were two small interview rooms cluttered with old furniture. "I don't know how they got to be so junked up," said Kelly, "but they need to be cleaned out so we can use them for sessions—if for no other reason than confidentiality. Right now, the sessions are taking place in the corners of the dorm—no good!"

Kelly also mentioned that group therapy had fallen by the wayside, and patients were only being seen individually. We agreed that we needed to get therapeutic groups back up and running as quickly as possible.

On our way out, we stopped by the bubble to visit the MO officers, a big, sandy-haired CO and his smaller, freckle-faced sidekick. Not exactly hard-nosed officers, Hartman and Burns came off more like a Laurel and Hardy comedy act.

"Welcome to the nuthouse!" Hartman grinned.

Burns, with one hand tickling the top of his head, and the other patting his stomach, hopped around the bubble. "Hooh, hooh, hooh."

"Meet our steady officers," Kelly said wryly.

"Sooo," said Hartman, "you just met a few of our nuts?"

"I prefer to think of them as our *patients*," I countered.

"You say *potahto*—we say potato!" joked Burns, with Hartman slapping his knee in laughter.

Although their sentiments were no surprise—the same as their correctional brethren—these two were essentially good-hearted and well-meaning, a very good sign for us.

As we departed the dorm, I figured managing these fifty beds would be a breeze compared to the 350-bed Mental Health Center. Of course, the tradeoff was that I'd be administering services to general population. And then, of course, there was the matter of the Bing.

I was anxious to finally see the infamous jail within jail, and after a meeting was coordinated with the punitive unit's newly installed deputy warden, Kelly and I set out for the five-story tower, which was structurally attached to OBCC.

"I'm glad we're meeting with him," said Kelly. "It's really important that we have a good relationship with the dep. I hate to tell you this, Mary, but our biggest challenge in here isn't the mentally ill or the guys in GP. Far and away, it's the Bing. Those five hundred cells are always full, and most of these guys are on psych meds—for hallucinating, crying, talking to themselves, defecating, refusing to eat."

"That bad?"

"I'm afraid so. All four of our psychiatrists carry heavy Bing caseloads. Thank God for the meds. But even with them, a lot of

times they reach a point where they can't hang on anymore, especially if they have long solitary sentences. They get to the end of
their rope and start banging their heads, cutting their arms, and
trying to hang themselves."

"And then what?" I asked uneasily.

"Well, obviously, we try to calm them down, talk to them,
maybe change the meds. But if we think somebody's really going to
die, then we pull him out and send him over to MHAUII."

"Sounds like a tropical island."

"Yeah, hardly. More like 'Mental Health Assessment Unit for
Infracted Inmates.' Sort of an MO for Bing inmates. All it really is
is eight cells in another one of the jails, but it's smaller and closely
monitored by Mental Health staff. It gives them a little relief. But
once they're better, they're bused right back here to finish the sentence. We're under a lot of pressure to keep them in, though, because once we send one out, they all start threatening suicide. On
the other hand, we can't have anyone dying. It gets tricky—you'll
see."

I got the feeling there was a lot I was going to see that I might
have preferred not to.

At the end of a long corridor, a lone officer sat in an elevated
Plexiglas booth. Heavy black lettering along the wall spelled out
the words CENTRAL PUNITIVE SEGREGATION UNIT. We held up
our ID badges and the officer inspected them closely. He nodded
and the heavy black gate started moving open on its track. We
stepped inside, turned a quick corner, and came to an elevator
bank.

"They connect to the higher floors," Kelly explained. "We
have a few minutes before our meeting, so let's peek in at the first
floor."

Kelly rapped on a long tinted window positioned between two
plain doors. "The door on the left is 1 South," she said. "The
one on the right is 1 Southwest—fifty cells on each side. It's the
same layout on all five floors." A CO thrust out a logbook and
we signed in. Kelly told the officer that we wanted to go into 1

Southwest. A loud buzz followed, and we pulled open the door on the right.

Cavernous and dimly lit, 1 Southwest was nothing more than rows of sulfur-colored steel doors, one after the next. At the top were little windows, and on the bottom a narrow flap for food trays. The windows were all empty. "They may look empty," Kelly whispered, "but it's full capacity in here—they're still sleeping. This is the only time it's quiet in here—the only time there's peace. They're in these cells twenty-three hours a day—no TV, no radio. They're entitled to one hour of rec, but most don't bother with it. They've got to be cuffed, shackled, and taken to an outside cage to stand alone and 'recreate.' It's a joke."

Along the walls, cameras were conspicuously mounted. All Bing activity was carefully monitored, the fallout from a class action suit brought against the city for brutality in the punitive unit when it was located in the House of Detention for Men, the original Rikers jail. Among other horrors, Bing officers had routinely inflicted "welcome beatings" as inmates arrived to serve their sentences. Reports of fractured skulls and perforated eardrums were rampant. As a result, the punitive unit in the old, decrepit jail was shut down and the infracted were transferred to this modern tower, where all activity was monitored by camera.

A set of stairs led down to a processing desk and shower area. At an empty shower stall, Kelly made a glum announcement. "*This*—is the Mental Health Office."

"A shower stall?"

"Yup. Pretty pathetic, huh? Up until recently, we've been seeing these inmates by going from cell to cell and talking through the doors, but Legal Aid's complaining that yelling through doors violates confidentiality. And they're right, but it's not an easy fix. So, the solution DOC came up with is to give us an escort to take these guys out of their cells and bring them down here for privacy. Problem is, we're not always getting this escort. That's what I want to bring up with the dep. Then maybe I can work on getting us a real office in here."

Kelly looked at her watch. "Let's go." We departed the eerie 1 Southwest, ducked into a side stairwell, and walked up to the second floor to the dep's office.

I don't know what I expected of someone in charge of a punitive segregation unit, but I definitely didn't expect the warm and friendly deputy warden Alfred Mancuso. Seated behind mountains of paperwork, a trail of cigarette smoke curling up from his ashtray, Dep Mancuso jumped up to shake our hands. "Hello!" he smiled. In his mid-forties, he was of medium build, sported a dark crew cut, and was well educated, as his framed master's diploma attested. Beside the diploma were citations, certificates, and ribboned medals for completed marathons; Mancuso was a dedicated runner. On the wall adjacent to his desk, five long rows of TV screens captured the activities on each floor of the Bing.

Pushing papers aside, he issued directives to a couple of captains who'd followed us in and motioned for us to sit down. "So, Mary," he said after we were introduced, "what do you think of the CPSU so far?"

"Kind of quiet," I replied.

"Quiet! Hah! It's still early. As soon as the meals start, the mayhem begins. Just as soon as we unlock the slots to put food trays through, out come the arms—swiping, hitting, grabbing. And lately it's been really bad. They all know I'm new here, so I'm being tested. We're getting a big increase in use of force. At the beginning I expect it, but once these guys see I'm consistent and mean what I say, the numbers should come down. That's what usually happens when there's a change of guard—least that's what I'm hoping. I've been with the department for close to twenty years, and nothing prepares you for this. But there's no getting around this post if you want to become a full warden. You first have to prove yourself in the Bing. Let's see if I survive it," he smiled.

He paused as a scene on a monitor caught his attention. His eyes narrowed and he dragged hard on his cigarette, watching as a handcuffed inmate was led out of his cell. Satisfied with how it was being handled, he returned to us. "Okay, where were we?"

"Well," said Kelly, "our immediate problem concerns confidentiality." She outlined our dilemma and explained that the warden had promised us an escort. "The thing is, the escort isn't always showing up."

"Well, now, I can see how the cell-to-cell arrangement would work well for the department. It's a hassle to pull these guys out—they've got to be searched, cuffed . . . but if the warden's made that commitment, then I guess that's how it's got to be." He thought for a moment and said, "How's this: I'll make sure you get an escort every morning. If nobody shows up, call me immediately."

"That's great," Kelly said with a note of relief.

"Happy to help. After all, it's the psych meds that make this place even slightly manageable. Plus, I'd really, really like to avoid suicides. So, if you have any issues in here—anything at all—my door is always open."

"Thank you," we said.

With business concluded, Mancuso dared us to sample some of the hot peppers he kept in colorful jars on his desk and told us a couple of corny jokes. As we laughed, I was uncomfortably aware that just outside his office, hundreds of human beings were awakening to another day of grim isolation.

32

SHORTLY AFTER MY ARRIVAL AT OBCC, KELLY TOOK A
weeklong vacation, leaving me to run things alone. Given my administrative experience at the Mental Health Center, I felt okay
with it, and things started off smoothly. The office coffeepot was
the early morning gathering place, and I enjoyed chatting with the
crew before the day began. Theresa and Kathy prepared to assess
the morning GP referrals while Lynn Cosgrove, wearing a taboo
Montefiore lab coat, would start off on the MO. While we sipped
coffee, Dr. Diaz, keeping one ear attuned to the early morning
chatter, puttered with the plants that sat atop the file cabinets. Pete
Majors, the primary Bing clinician, had the longest commute, and
he and Dr. Christian were the last ones to rush in and join us before
things got under way.

After everyone had cleared out, my first order of business
was the basket of referrals. I logged each one in, careful to ensure they'd be evaluated within the seventy-two-hour mandatory
timeframe. Toward the bottom, one referral puzzled me. A Bing
inmate named Rafael Ramirez was complaining of numbness and
tingling, which struck me as a medical issue. I pulled his chart and
was surprised to see that he'd recently been evaluated by Mental
Health three times, with chart notes indicating nothing more than
irritability and anxiety. The attending psychiatrists must have considered even that to be mild because they'd prescribed no medication. I took it up with the chief physician, who was also baffled as

to why the referral was given to mental health, and he agreed that medical should check him out.

The following day, Dr. Sackett informed me that the medical team's efforts had been thwarted because Ramirez was in court. On Wednesday morning, he'd completed his Bing sentence and was transferred out of OBCC.

By Thursday morning, I'd forgotten all about Ramirez when I got a disturbing call from Janet. "Mary, did you hear the news? There was a suicide, a hanging at AMKC, general population." I sat up straight. While suicide attempts were an everyday occurrence on Rikers, completed suicides were infrequent and, for the Mental Health Department, particularly upsetting. Although our interventions kept suicides down to a handful a year, we could not prevent them all.

"And I hate to tell you this," she added, "but he was just transferred from the Bing."

"The Bing! What was his name?"

"Rafael Ramirez."

Rafael Ramirez! How in the world did numbness and tingling translate to suicide? I got off the phone with Janet and started pacing the room. This was terrible. What happened when he'd gone to court? Maybe he'd been given a stiff sentence. I just didn't know.

Even though I'd never met Ramirez and he'd killed himself in another jail, this was the closest I'd come to a suicide. When I'd been a clinician, I was fortunate that, of the hundreds of depressed inmates I'd worked with, none had killed themselves. But when it had happened to others, Montefiore Hospital, our former employer, was always supportive, bringing staff together, allowing us to talk and grieve. But it was a new day, and the phone had yet to ring with a call from St. Barnabas.

As the day wore on, I learned through the grapevine that his chart had been found in proper order, with all protocol followed. This brought a certain relief, but of course it would not bring the dead young man back. I kept reviewing the sequence of events, wondering if there might have been a different outcome if I hadn't referred him back to medical. But even if I'd scheduled him for another evaluation, his appointment wouldn't have been until the tail end of the seventy-two hours, at which point he would already have been gone from OBCC. It would have made no difference. Still, I felt I needed to talk this out with my superiors, so I stayed close to the phone. But by Friday afternoon, when there was still no call from Central Office, I realized that the support we'd been afforded by Montefiore was a thing of the past. Instead, I simply said a quiet prayer for the soul of Rafael Ramirez.

The following Monday Kelly returned, to my great relief. The suicide had unnerved me, and I didn't want to run things alone anymore. But it wasn't to be. Just as George had sat me down when I started at the Mental Health Center, Kelly did the same. No, she wasn't quitting, but she was taking time off for a surgical procedure. Recovery would be anywhere from two to eight weeks.

Kelly's announcement hit hard and, in hindsight, was my strongest cue to get out. But I didn't see it. What I saw was that we had a great staff, a manageable building, and with it the potential for high-quality work. If this was the final hurdle before things settled down, I could do it—especially if Kelly was only gone for two weeks, although in my heart I knew that was unlikely. Kelly had already had several run-ins with St. Barnabas and wouldn't be rushing back anytime soon. Realistically, I was looking at the full eight weeks—if she returned at all. In a phone conversation with Hugh Kemper, he tried to be encouraging. "Kelly'll be back before you know it. And don't forget, I'm interviewing for a clinical supervisor, so that spot could be filled before she even returns. Let's think positive, Mary!"

I wanted to believe him, but when we hung up, I knew I was in for a long, hot summer.

33

ON MONDAY, JUNE 14, 1999, I TOOK OVER AS ACTING
chief of Mental Health at the Otis Bantum Correctional Center.
Despite my nervousness, I was buoyed by the staff; they rallied
around me and even pitched in with some of my administrative
tasks.

In some ways, things got off to a promising start. I was especially pleased with developments on the MO, where Theresa
tackled the problem of the dorm's unused interview rooms. Since
cleaning them out required DOC's assistance, and because DOC
dragged its heels with anything beyond its own security concerns,
I wasn't overly optimistic. But when Theresa approached the MO
captain, he responded favorably. Captain Catalano, an eager young
man, agreed to have the junk removed and the rooms painted. Although Theresa explained that a cheerful environment would be
beneficial to the patients, I think he was far more interested in Theresa than the mentally ill. Regardless, he fulfilled his promise, and
we now had two usable rooms for individual sessions. Building on
this, with Catalano's permission, Theresa and Kathy brought in
plants and old paperbacks for the patients to read.

We kept the momentum going by devising a weekly schedule
of group therapy that included the topics of community living, violence reduction, and substance abuse. During my daily rounds, I
was delighted to see that our Mental Observation Unit was developing into a true therapeutic environment and that our patients

were no longer lolling around on their cots and watching TV but were now participating in mandatory group sessions.

When it came to general population, my biggest challenge was ensuring that referred inmates were evaluated in a timely manner. The last thing I wanted was for someone to fall through the cracks, especially after the Ramirez suicide. The GP sessions took place in the clinic, where it irritated me that our quarters were crowded and cramped, especially since the medical staff was allotted roomy space. Our doctors and therapists were doubled up in booths that served as makeshift offices, so when an inmate arrived for his session, one person had to vacate the booth to maintain privacy. It rankled me that the treatment of intangible maladies such as depression—easily as agonizing and devastating as the worst physical pain—were always given such short shrift. But considering everything else I was faced with, now was not the time to challenge the existing arrangement.

It was the Bing, however, where I wasn't feeling so confident. Almost every morning, I received a call from the punitive unit informing me that someone was threatening to kill himself. Thankfully, Pete and Dr. Diaz were accustomed to these situations, and I would dispatch them to investigate. Diaz would adjust the meds, and he and Pete would talk to the inmate, trying to cajole him into enduring the punishment. But it wasn't long before Diaz called me from the Bing, asking that I come up to 4 South. This meant there was a tough decision to be made, and it was a nervous walk through the jail. When I reached the punitive unit, I stepped into an elevator car, and since I was going to the fourth floor, I held up four fingers to a corner camera, waiting to be spotted on a TV monitor. As the car lifted, the errant cries of the punished echoed throughout the cavernous tower, and I winced at the sound of a particularly piercing howl. When the door opened, a swarm of officers were hovering around a captain who was pressing a radio to his ear. From what I could glean, an inmate on the floor above had set fire to his mattress. The captain and COs disappeared into a stairwell and pounded upstairs to extinguish the fire. The inmate would be "extracted" from his cell and "arrested" for arson. Despite the heat, despite the additional legal charge—despite, even, the possibility of death—I was already learning that setting fires is a common ploy to gain relief from the torment of solitary. But I had also noticed one aspect of fire-setting that was never discussed: Who supplied the matches?

My arrival at 4 South was a far cry from my first quiet visit. The noise level was ferocious; the inmates were wide awake, railing violently against their confinement. Bodies thumped against the doors and faces were pressed into the small windows. As I walked past the cells, they cried out to me, *"Miss! Help! Please, miss!! Please!"* Fighting my natural urge to rush to their aid, I reminded myself that they'd done something to warrant this punishment—hurt another inmate, perhaps, maybe cut someone.

I kept my eyes trained on Diaz and Pete, who were standing in front of a cell with its door slightly ajar.

"Welcome," Pete said wryly.

Diaz motioned me to the side of the cell. "His name's Leonard Putansk. He's been going downhill for a while. We've done the usual, upped his meds, talked to him, but we've got to make a decision here. I don't think he's ready to come out yet, but we're getting close—there's a lot of blood. I think you need to take a look and then we'll decide. You ready?"

I steeled myself and nodded.

The officer pulled the door open to reveal a claustrophobic cell, the cement walls smeared with crimson stains. A burly young man in a sweat-soaked T-shirt sat on the cot and sobbed, his back to me. But he turned around quickly, his forearms slathered with blood.

"Please, miss! Please! Help me! My family, they're in Kosovo—I don't know if they're dead or alive with all the fighting going on over there!"

"I'm sorry about your family," I said softly. "That must be very hard."

"It is—it is! I've already been in this cell for three months now. They've got me down for another six. They wouldn't do this to a dog! I'm going to kill myself. You gotta get me out of here! I can't take this anymore, I can't. I'm telling you, I can't."

"Okay, just a minute now," I managed, stepping back out.

Diaz motioned me out of Putansk's earshot. "It looks worse than it is," he said. "He's picking at his skin. It's superficial. He's trying to make it as dramatic as he can so we'll pull him out."

"He's doing a pretty good job," I said. "So, why don't we pull him out, send him over to MHAUII?"

"It's not that simple," said Pete. "He's desperate, but they all are. We can't pull them out just because they're miserable; that's the whole idea. We only intervene if we think his life is at stake, and at this point, I don't think it is, although he's going to up the ante."

"Well, if we know he's going to do something more drastic, why wait?"

"Because we can't give in," Diaz replied. "If we do, they'll all start cutting themselves and threatening suicide. It's a tug of war, Mary. Welcome to the Bing."

As his words resonated, a sick, weak feeling washed over me. But I had to push it aside and stay focused. "But he's already been in there for three months! With *six* more to go!"

"That's nothing," said Pete. "In these supermaxes they're building all over the country, they throw people in a cell for the rest of their lives. *'Here's your life—a square box.'*"

I shuddered at the thought. A human life—relegated to a box.

Since Diaz and Pete were disinclined to pull him out, I deferred to their experience and the three of us went back into the cell and informed Putansk of our decision. In response, he howled and beat the walls with his fists. "We'll get someone from medical to take care of those cuts," said Pete. Diaz nodded to the CO, who shut the door and locked it up. As we made our way out, Leonard Putansk's agonized wails seemed to follow us.

As the day wore on, I tried to focus on other matters, but I kept thinking about Putansk. I just hoped he was doing a little better. When we didn't hear anything more from the Bing, I relaxed a little. But the following afternoon, the call came: "They're cutting someone down, a Leonard Putansk."

My stomach knotted at the words—*cutting someone down.*

I pushed my paperwork aside and put my head in my hands. I was not cut out for this. The phone rang again, and this time it was Dr. Campbell, the new director of Mental Health. Somehow, the news had already reached him at Central Office. "Find out if he's dead or alive and call me back," Campbell snapped.

I forced myself out into the clinic where a swarm of officers, keys jangling at their sides, were running the gurney down the main aisle. In the examining room, Putansk was quickly surrounded by a sea of white lab coats. In the thick of things was Diaz, who waved me in from the doorway. As I reluctantly approached the table, Diaz put his big arm around my shoulders and ushered me up to the semiconscious inmate, pointing to the thick pink welt where the sheet had dug into his neck.

"He's okay," Diaz smiled. "Don't worry, he's going to be fine. I knew he was going to do something, but he timed it for when a CO would be walking by. We'll send him to the hospital and when he comes back, he'll go to MHAUII."

"He's going to be okay," Diaz reiterated, in response to what must have been my ashen face. For him this was everyday stuff, but for me it was all new—and all horrifying. As Leonard Putansk was stabilized with a neck brace and wheeled out to a waiting ambulance, I wondered how I could ever come to terms with any of this.

34

DESPITE MY APPREHENSIONS ABOUT THE BING, I PLOD-
ded on, doing my best as OBCC's sole Mental Health administrator, supervising every aspect of the operation—from monitoring
referrals to figuring the payroll to compiling statistics.

There were also many, many meetings to attend: warden's
meetings, unit chief meetings, quality assurance meetings, staff
and clinic meetings. I barely had a moment to breathe, and at one
unit chiefs meeting, the pressure shot up. Dr. Campbell outlined
the upcoming summer audit schedule, emphasizing its importance.
"The audits are our report card," he said solemnly, "and we expect
them to be perfect." I scribbled the date for OBCC's audit, hoping
Kelly would be back or that we'd at least have a clinical supervisor
to spearhead the necessary chart reviews.

Next was the distribution of forms for staff to sign—
everything from absentee policies, dress codes, and parking procedures to our relationship with DOC—plus countless forms on
patient care. Taking a page from the Giuliani administration's
touted policy of accountability, St. Barnabas was churning out the
paperwork. If the audits were less than successful, then we, the
unit chiefs, would be accountable. In turn, we were to make our
staff accountable. When staff deviated from policy, they would be
confronted with their signed understanding of that policy. Management, even of such an inherently complex situation, was reduced to

a simple maxim: everyone had a job to do, and if something went wrong, then the faulty link in the chain would be identified and corrective measures taken.

Although the accountability theory made sense in the abstract, its application was less than tidy. The premise that everyone had a job to do was turning a blind eye to the fact that many were doing more than one job. In my case, I was doing my job, Kelly's job, and the job of the clinical supervisor. The staffing levels in most of the jails were inadequate, yet we were treated as if we had reasonable workloads. But as a fresh stack of forms was distributed, we silently accepted them.

Campbell finished up with a dreaded announcement: "We're getting ready to fire all the limited license doctors. We've got enough fully licensed doctors, so we're going to move ahead on this. We'll let them go in waves. The transition should be completed by the end of summer."

With this news, we all cringed. Most of us had worked side by side with our doctors for years and were rooting for them to pass their exams and stay. Besides, we suspected that all Central Office had in store was a fresh supply of moonlighters.

Defensively, the deputy director, Suzanne Harris (wearing civilian clothes), reminded us once again that this was a contractual obligation. "It's not going to be any surprise to these doctors—they know. But just in case, you're not to say anything about it. Not a word. We'll handle it!"

I suspected that all four of OBCC's doctors had limited licenses, but when Harris confirmed it, I felt sick. I tried to explain to the Central Office team that it would be no simple matter to place a new doctor in the Bing, but that was brushed off. They had no clue about the Bing, and my only hope was that Kelly would be back before any of this began.

But a week later, with no sign of Kelly, Hugh Kemper called. "Two new doctors are starting at OBCC next week. The first is Tarra Grant, and the second is Katherine Ketchum."

"What about our own doctors?" I nervously asked.

"Well, just sit tight. We're not going to let them go just yet."

The following Monday, Drs. Grant and Ketchum arrived on schedule. If our doctors suspected what was up, they didn't let on. They welcomed the women, perhaps assuming they were with us for training purposes. Despite my misgivings, on a personal level I found both new doctors quite likeable and was pleasantly surprised to learn that they weren't moonlighters but dedicated, interested physicians. Ketchum, a petite blonde in her fifties, was an eager perfectionist. But after a tour of the Bing, she was horrified and refused to return. Fortunately, she took an immediate interest in the Mental Observation Unit, where she assumed the role of primary psychiatrist.

Grant, a feisty younger woman with a short Afro, was obligated to work in an undesirable setting like jail for two years to satisfy the terms of her student loan. Grant was warm, affable, and competent. Unlike Ketchum, she was game for the punitive unit and began accompanying our doctors to the Bing.

Both new psychiatrists, unaware that they'd been hired to replace the team that was training them, quickly assimilated, and I tried to blot out what would happen next.

* * *

As we approached the Fourth of July weekend, we were heading into one of the hottest summers on record, and in no time the jails were stifling. The scorched rec yard, usually teeming with inmates, sat empty under the blazing afternoon sun. The clinic was slightly cooler but by no means comfortable. The COs lugged through the halls in their polyester uniforms, drenched in sweat. But at least officers and civilians could look forward to going home and cooling off; for the inmates, there was no relief. Of particular concern were the mentally ill, whose medications interfered with the body's ability to cool itself. Extreme heat could kill them. Each day the pharmacy cranked out lists of those on the questionable meds, and in the few cases where they could be replaced by something more benign, our doctors did so. Besides that, there was little else to do besides push them to drink plenty of water and to take cool showers. Considering the health hazard, air-conditioning on all Mental Observation Units should have been mandatory, but this was jail—there would be no such indulgence. Instead, two oscillating floor fans stood at either end of the dorm. Since DOC relaxed the rules prohibiting bare chests, mostly everyone was shirtless. The lucky ones had shorts; the others lay very still on their cots in dark jeans. Although I offered to have the heavy pants cut into shorts, no one took me up on it. Owning only one pair of pants, they had to look ahead to the fall and winter, when they'd be needed for warmth. When I realized my well-meaning offer was more of a taunt than a realistic option, I dropped it.

As hot as it was on the MO and in GP, nowhere was hotter than in the Bing. Trapped inside sweltering cells, the only salvation for the punished was that each had a small sink and access to cool water. One afternoon when the mercury skyrocketed past 100 degrees, Pete and Grant called and asked me to come up to 2 Southwest.

By now, going over to the Bing was a regular part of my day. There was no avoiding it. The Leonard Putansk encounter was my introduction to a daily onslaught of suicide threats and gestures. To cope with these cell-door visits and the gut-wrenching decisions that ultimately rested on my shoulders, I started bumming a cigarette here and there. I would steal away to the restroom for a quick smoke to brace myself for the walk over to the punitive unit. Solitary confinement was far worse than I'd imagined. Behind so many of these doors were blood-smeared cells, makeshift nooses, and the agonized, shell-shocked faces of people begging for a reprieve. As I walked through the halls that afternoon, I rehearsed the mental drill that I'd started relying on to help me keep walking: I reminded myself that solitary confinement was standard punishment in jails and prisons across the country. Thousands of mental health workers were doing exactly what I was doing. It was legally sanctioned and carried out in a nation that prohibits cruel and unusual punishment. Therefore, I told myself that none of this was really as bad as it seemed. Yet as I approached the big barred gate, my legs were wobbling anyway.

At the elevator, I bumped into Diaz. The sweat-drenched psychiatrist whipped his head to the side, throwing off a spray of droplets. "It's brutal in there," he said. "I've got to get water."

When I stepped into 2 Southwest, it was as though I'd stuck my head in an oven to remove a roast—and kept it there! As I made my way toward Pete and Grant, sweaty palms were slapping and sliding down the windows. *"We're dying in here, miss—we're dying!"*

"Shut the fuck up!" the officers shouted. *"Shut up, motherfuckers!"*

I kept going, aware of a growing stench. Midway down the floor, Pete and Grant were covering their mouths. The COs were darting away, pinching their noses. As I drew closer, I was also holding my hand to my mouth.

"Have a look," said Pete, pointing to the open door.

I peered into the cell, where a young Black man was staring ahead blankly, all the while humming. Lathered in sweat, he was completely naked. With his cupped right palm, he raked his hand across his neck and chest, smearing himself with feces. The excrement was in his hair and slathered around his neck and ears.

"Send him out!" the officers yelled. *"He's lost it! You gotta send him out!"*

The three of us retreated down the floor.

"Oh, my God!" I said.

"Pretty bad," said Pete.

"What do you think?" asked Grant. "MHAUII?"

"Sure," said Pete. "But we know what MHAUII's going to say: that he's malingering, that this is just a ruse to get out, that it isn't life and death."

Pete was right. This was not life and death, yet in accordance with anything decent and humane, we needed to provide this man with relief.

"Look," I said, "as far as I'm concerned, a line's been crossed. This could be calculated, but even so, if you're willing to go to this length, then as far as I'm concerned, you win."

"I'm with you," said Pete.

"Me too," said Grant. "Besides, the COs are going to lynch us if we don't get him out of here."

"All right then," I said. "Let me go down and call MHAUII."

As I bolted from the floor, leaving behind the heat, the stench, and the anguished cries, I felt like I was departing the gates of hell. As I hurried through the halls, all my carefully crafted rationale about solitary confinement being okay because it was legally sanctioned went right out the window. This punishment was absolutely cruel! And anyone who said otherwise had obviously never set foot inside one of these horrific units.

Back at the clinic, I prepared to do battle with MHAUII. The removal of a Bing inmate came in two parts: our decision that he should come out, and MHAUII's agreement to accept him into one of their specialized cells. Since their small unit wasn't only for Bing inmates but also for high-profile and otherwise odd cases, their eight cells were never empty. The arrival of a Bing inmate meant that an occupant of one of these cells needed to be relocated. For the MHAUII staff, these bumps were disruptive and time-consuming.

Sure enough, when I reached the MHAUII chief, he had a different take on things. "Smearing feces is the oldest trick in the book. You can't let him manipulate you."

"Listen," I countered, "it's over 100 degrees in there, he's naked, and he's covered in shit. He needs to come out."

"This isn't life and death. If you give in every time these Bing monsters act out, then you're going to wind up with five hundred empty cells."

Bing monsters! There it was again, and from our own staff! Though I heard these dehumanizing terms every day, I never got used to them. It seemed to me that when you can call someone a *monster,* or a *skel,* or a *body,* then it suddenly becomes okay to do whatever you want to them because they're not really human beings. Yet the inmates I met with were not *bodies*. They were people. And when I stepped into these cells, what I saw was real blood, real thudding skulls, and actual human torment.

I didn't care what the MHAUII chief said. Not having seen this man, not having felt his desperation, it was so easy to peg him as a malingerer. In some ways, the MHAUII staff was as removed as the public, who learn about solitary confinement in the newspapers by reading how some convict is "locked down twenty-three hours a day" and then turn the page. People have no clue what solitary means. But one prominent American knows exactly what it means. Senator John McCain was famously held as a POW during the Vietnam War. During his five-and-a-half-year captivity, he was beaten regularly, sustaining broken arms and broken legs. Two of those years were spent in solitary. Despite the trauma of his limbs being deliberately broken, what McCain found *even worse* was solitary confinement. He said, "It crushes your spirit and weakens your resistance more effectively than any other form of mistreatment." Worse than beatings and broken bones! We're horrified by what happened to McCain, yet somehow we don't equate it with the treatment that we mete out every day right here in the United States!

The MHAUII chief and I had reached an uncomfortable impasse. But I wasn't going to back down on this one. Even if they didn't keep him for long, I was determined to get him out, even if it was for nothing more than the lousy bus ride to the other side of the island—"bus therapy," as we called it.

"Fine, fine!" he said abruptly. "I'll start the paperwork to bump somebody."

"Thank you."

When these conversations ended and my wishes prevailed, I always felt like a villain who'd just gotten away with something, and I resented being made to feel that way. Nonetheless, I was glad the call was over and the matter settled. Yet I knew my peace was short-lived and that within a day or two we'd rush to the cell of another desperate human being.

35

AS THE DOG DAYS OF SUMMER WORE ON, THE SUFFER-
ing in the Bing weighed heavily on me, but I still needed to address
practical concerns. Vacations had begun, and I had to scramble to
maintain coverage by borrowing staff from other jails. But mostly
I was worried about the audit. Ten days before the targeted audit
date, I received a fax advising me to have thirty charts ready for review. Preparing for an audit involved a massive amount of detailed
paperwork, and I called Hugh to see if it could be postponed until
Kelly returned or at least until we had our clinical supervisor.

"Gee, Mary," he said, "I'm sorry, but requesting a postpone-
ment sends the wrong message."

"I'll do the best I can," I sighed.

"The best you can? Mary—it *has* to be good . . . it has to be
perfect."

I knew Hugh felt bad that Kelly wasn't back, and although he
offered to send an administrator from another jail to help me out,
nothing came of it, and I was on my own in identifying thirty charts
that could stand up to the scrutiny. For the next couple of weeks I
stayed late into the night, studying charts, checking dates, reading
written entries, looking for necessary signatures and required forms.
The work was painstaking, but finally I had the files I needed.

On the appointed day, four hot and grumpy auditors showed
up. Things immediately got off to a bad start when there was no
place for them to sit. I never expected four of them, and I had

grabbed only two spots in the clinic. Since clinic space was scarce, I was lucky to get that. The head auditor, Leslie, solved the problem by plopping down at Kelly's desk and instructing her colleague to sit at the clinical supervisor's desk. I was uncomfortable with this arrangement, but there were no other options, and I began my day while they worked a few feet away.

For a few moments, all was quiet, save for the whirring of fans. Suddenly, Leslie began flipping rapidly through the charts, one after another. Something was wrong. She turned to me and said, "What we want are charts on inmates who've been here six months, so we can gauge continuity of care. Can you please get us a batch of charts that reflect six months of treatment?"

"No, I can't," I said, surprised by my own abruptness. "No one said anything to me about this."

"Well, we're telling you now," Leslie said assertively.

"It's too late," I said, just as assertively. Enough was enough.

Just then the phone rang. It was the Bing. Always the Bing. "You're needed up here—second floor."

While I was relieved to be getting away from Leslie, the Bing was not an appealing alternative. I hurried to the bathroom and lit up a cigarette. I took a couple of hard drags, my muscles slackened, and I slumped against the wall where the cold cinderblock felt good on my warm cheek. I looked up at the mirror, caught my reflection, and for a moment searched for the traces of the idealistic intern I'd once been. So much had changed. But there was little time to think about that now. Another crisis awaited. I flushed the butt, splashed cold water on my face, and headed up.

A wild scene awaited outside the second floor elevator. Officers in riot gear, led by Dep Mancuso, were converging on a cell. "Pull him out!" Mancuso shouted. No longer looking confident and composed, the dep was bedraggled. "Get him out, and onto the goddammed bus!"

Later on, I would learn that the occupant of the cell was refusing to come out because the bus would take him to court, where he was to receive a sentence of life in prison.

I sidestepped the commotion and started down the hall to see Dr. Christian, who was talking through the crack in the cell door to the distraught person inside. Although Mancuso had kept his word with the daily escort, considering the hundreds of inmates needing medication, a single escort could only ensure that a small number of inmates could be met with privately. Of necessity, we fell back on the cell-to-cell method.

"It's going to be okay," Christian shouted through the crack. "You're going to be all right, my friend."

"I'm gonna die in here, I'm gonna die!" came the muffled sobs from within.

"No, you're not. We're starting you on medication right now and it'll calm you down. You'll see. We're just waiting for the nurse."

"I'm going to take the cop-out! It'll get me off Rikers Island and out of here."

"Don't make any big decisions. You've only got ten days in here—some people are in here for years—you're going to be fine. You're going to be fine."

"I didn't even do anything to get a ticket! I swear, I didn't! I didn't do a thing."

Christian stepped to the side of the cell and said, "It's okay, Mary, false alarm—I've got this one."

A reprieve. But my mind was already racing. This inmate's protest, *I didn't do a thing!* made me wonder. Several days earlier, a friendly officer nicknamed Smitty had stopped by my office for a cup of water and a quick break. As he was leaving, he pulled out his infraction pad and revealed something stunning. "I've got to go write up tickets. The way they're loading up this island, they're scrambling for beds. With five hundred beds in the Bing, they can't afford to let one of them sit empty. Every time somebody goes into the hole, a GP bed opens up. We have our orders: 'Write 'em up! Write 'em up!' Let me go find some poor schmo. See you later, Miss B!"

Now, I wondered if the person in this cell was one of those "poor schmos."

Although we're led to believe that inmates in solitary confinement are the baddest of the bad, I found that claim to be highly exaggerated. In the beginning, I had actually hoped it was true as a means of helping me to justify this brutal punishment. But in the short time I'd been working in the Bing, I'd discovered that many of these cells' occupants suffered from impulse control disorders. It's not so much that they won't behave, it's that they *can't*. I wondered if someday we wouldn't look back at this primitive punishment and shake our heads. And then there are those in solitary like poor Keith Bargeman, who acted out in the hallway because his court suit had been stolen. Hardly the worst of the worst! And in terms of the most serious jailhouse infraction, "Assault on Staff," after speaking with these offenders, I learned that the infraction usually came about when correctional personnel struck first and the inmate hit back. An unprovoked assault is rare, if for no other reason than there's no escaping the most violent retribution for such an act, and every inmate knows it.

And even in cases of the very worst sociopath held in solitary, the question still remained: How could it be that a punishment that drives *any human being*—criminal or otherwise—to attempt suicide to escape it not be considered cruel and unusual?

Years later, the United Nations Special Rapporteur on torture would state that solitary confinement beyond fifteen days should be absolutely prohibited. Yet instead of reducing or seeking alternatives to solitary confinement, the nation has been on a chilling march to build more. Supermax prisons, made up solely of isolation cells for supposedly high-risk prisoners, house human beings inside these cells—not for thirty, sixty, or ninety days, but indefinitely, *as a matter of routine*. In supermaxes, things have been designed very carefully. For instance, the cells are padded, so that an inmate in desperate need of relief could bang his head continuously without risk of injury. In these more sophisticated, sinister units, the "problem of head-banging" has been overcome. For twenty years, these specialized prisons have been cropping up across the United States, the morality of their use unquestioned, unchallenged.

I headed back down to the clinic, more confused and despondent than ever.

When I arrived, the auditors were packing up, the audit complete. With the Bing still fresh in my mind, the audit now seemed trivial. Leslie curtly informed me that Central Office would be getting the results in two weeks. I mumbled polite good-byes as they left. Two weeks came and went, and true to form, Central Office never disclosed the results. But operating under the old adage that no news is good news, I presumed we had done well.

36

WITH THE AUDIT BEHIND ME, I BREATHED A LITTLE EAS-
ier, but not for long. The termination of the limited license doctors
was beginning, and our first casualty was a shocked Dr. Christian.
As I had suspected, our doctors never knew they were being termi-
nated. Dr. Diaz vowed to start calling in sick. "Let Central Office
come over here and handle the Bing!"

I felt terrible for our doctors, but I didn't want them to do anything rash. "Hold on," I said. "You have every right to be angry,
but right now they're looking for reasons to fire people. Let's not
give them any. Let's see if we can ride this out."

Maybe it didn't matter. Maybe by the end of the summer
they would all be axed anyway. But there was a little hope. Even
though Central Office had procured a cadre of fully licensed doctors, whether they would actually stay on remained to be seen. All
over the island, there were growing reports of newly arrived doctors quitting just as soon as they comprehended the bleak reality of
their new workplace.

Although Drs. Grant and Ketchum had acclimated surprisingly
well, jail had been a disaster for our other new additions, Fernando
Dayrit and Vivian Tierney. Tierney didn't last a week. After finishing one of her shifts, she waited outside for the route bus to take her
to Control. Although a Gate One pass was part of her hiring pack-
age, it was still being processed. After an hour went by, Tierney began the forbidden walk to Control. She actually made it pretty far

along the road before a security detail spotted her and ordered her into their jeep. Whisked into nearby AMKC, she was interrogated by a security captain. She quit the next day.

With similar incidents occurring, the installation of fully licensed doctors was falling apart fast. In my view—contract or not—we would of necessity be falling back on the services of the limited license doctors. In the meantime, my plan was to lie low and keep our remaining limited license doctors out of the firing line until the whole thing blew over.

As if this wasn't enough, the doctor crisis coincided with yet another, more mundane one: a shortage of parking space. Due to an increased allotment of Gate One passes, cars with the privileged pass had exceeded OBCC's parking lot capacity. Spillover vehicles were parking in a fire lane, and DOC's security unit was issuing tickets.

"I'm not paying these!" Dr. Grant yelled. "I don't think it's asking too much to have a place to park my car!"

When the clinic manager told her to tone it down, reminding her of our status as "guests in their house," Grant only became louder. "I'm sick of this 'guests in their house' crap! This isn't *their* house! These jails are owned by the taxpayers! I'm not paying for these, and Central Office needs to do something about it!"

I liked Tarra Grant. And she was a good doctor. When she and Dr. Ketchum had learned of the physician replacement plan, they'd been extremely upset. Grant's patience with Central Office was wearing thin.

I reported the parking problem to Hugh, who sighed heavily.

In protest, the entire clinic staff took to driving around the parking lot each morning in a procession, waiting for spots to open up. Inside, a nervous Captain Ryan was on his radio with the warden. "I've got fifty inmates signed up for sick call, another one having seizures in the Bing—and our doctors are driving around the parking lot."

After a week of this, a beleaguered Captain Ryan gathered the clinic staff. "Look, folks—I think you need to write a petition to the warden." Although directly approaching DOC was strictly taboo, everyone was too disgusted to care, and a petition was circulated. But when word of it got back to Central Office, our superiors were livid. Suzanne Harris informed us that Central Office had been working on a deal with DOC to resolve the parking problem, but because of this "highly inappropriate" action, the deal was off.

Of course, no one believed any deal was in the works to begin with, and our best hope was still the petition. But in the end, it was ignored, and we were simply left to duck out of the jail and try to move our cars in advance of the despised ticket writers.

* * *

By the end of July, I was exhausted. Since Kelly's departure six weeks earlier, I hadn't taken a day off, many evenings were spent in the office, and I was becoming concerned about a stubborn ache in my side that wasn't going away. Weekends brought little relief, as I was contacted about various crises. At night, I barely slept. By now I was chain-smoking. Furtive trips to the bathroom were over: a big ashtray sat right on my desk. But I was determined to make it to Kelly's return. If I had been a conscientious therapist, I was an equally conscientious employee, doing my best on all fronts. But it was the Bing that continued to be my biggest worry. Each day, I entered a cell with our team and faced a human being unhinged by the rigors of solitary. Some babbled incoherently, others cowered in a corner. One man was trying to tear off an ear. We talked to them, evaluated their injuries, examined makeshift nooses, and then stepped out for the huddle, asking ourselves: *Is he malingering? How far will he go? Could he lose the arm? Will he make it to tomorrow? Will he be dead tomorrow?* As we looked into each other's eyes, trying to make the right decision, I had an awareness that I was now a monitor of human suffering, and that all of us were making decisions that no person should ever be asked to make.

Just a couple more weeks, I told myself, just a couple more weeks. Kelly would return, and then I knew not what. But somehow Kelly's return was the finish line.

In the meantime I had to hold it all together, and I was especially concerned about keeping medication for the Bing inmates from expiring, which was a disaster. The meds needed to be renewed in face-to-face encounters every two weeks, and with most of our regular psychiatrists out on vacation, I reluctantly turned to Fernando Dayrit, our newest staff member. Although he was starting to acclimate to the punitive unit, earlier in the week, the timing in a staged suicide was off; although the inmate survived, he'd broken his neck. When Dayrit learned about it, was understandably skittish about going back into the tower, but I was desperate to have the meds renewed. With clipboard in hand and an attached list of notes, I pleaded with him to go back in. I handed the clipboard to him and said, "Listen, it wasn't that bad."

"The guy broke his neck!" Dayrit replied.

"Yes—but it was just a little bone—not an important bone."

What I remember most in that moment was the sound of the clipboard clattering to the floor. Then Dayrit stepped back and eyed me as if I was a monster. He turned and walked out. I retreated to my office and broke into sobs. I kept seeing his face and the look that mirrored back to me just how desensitized I'd become.

After I'd composed myself, I dried my eyes and finished out the day as best I could.

That evening, I called my father. He seemed to be the only person who could handle what this job was really about. With friends I was quiet and withdrawn. No longer did I feel the need to educate people about life behind bars, not only because they wouldn't understand or believe it, but because talking about it meant reliving it, and I needed every moment that I was away from Rikers to forget about it so I could go back in.

My father listened quietly as I told him about what happened. "I can't believe those words came out of my mouth," I said. "I was just trying to do my job."

"Mary," he said. "This job is destroying you."

I couldn't disagree.

"And this could get worse," he continued. "Much worse. Have you thought about what happens if someone steps into a noose and really dies? It takes seconds. You have people stepping into nooses every day. You're so immersed in this, you don't even see how perilous this situation is. If someone hangs for real, fingers will be pointed. Guess who'll be blamed?"

The thought of someone actually dying was a dark cloud that accompanied me into the cells and followed me home at night. It was my worst fear. But I hadn't been overly concerned for myself. After all, Central Office was always thanking me for the great job I was doing. Would they really turn on me?

"You bet they will!" my father insisted. "Someone will have to take the rap. Everyone will run for cover, and you'll be the one left standing. Now listen to me. You've done everything you can for these inmates. The person you have to worry about now is yourself. I want to put these people on notice. I'm dictating a memo outlining their failure to provide adequate administrative coverage. If somebody dies in there, they're going to have a tough time pinning it on you. Do you have a pen?"

I hesitated. To send a memo like this would likely seal my fate with St. Barnabas.

"Mary, listen to me . . . you can't change the world!"

Tears were streaming down my cheeks, and I thought I detected a quiver in my father's voice as he said, "But I will say this to you, my dear girl: God bless you for trying."

We sat in silence for a while, and then he said, "Do you have a pen?"

Somewhere deep within, I knew my father was right. Another silence followed. And then I said yes.

The memo was sent. Needless to say, it was not well received by Central Office, but the following morning another administrator arrived at OBCC to assist me until Kelly's return.

* * *

The memo to Central Office went out not a moment too soon. A couple of days later, my worst fear was almost realized. "Mental

Health!" shouted Pepitone. "Somebody's getting cut down in the Bing!"

I met up with Grant and the two of us headed up. Just outside the Bing's mini-clinic, a CO briefed us. "His name's Luis Morales. He'd just stepped into a noose when an officer was walking by. He was swinging. They were able to get in and cut him down fast. Medical says he's okay, but if the CO hadn't passed by, he'd have been a goner."

"Did an inmate tip off the CO?" I asked. "Tell him what Morales was up to?"

"No, that's just it. The officer *happened* to be walking by. He didn't tip off anybody. This was for real."

Inside the mini-clinic, Luis Morales, in an orange jumpsuit and his hair in a ponytail, was slumped over the countertop.

"Mr. Morales," said Grant.

Luis Morales looked up, his tear-stained face devoid of expression.

"Why did you do this?" she asked.

"I don't give a shit anymore," he said flatly. "I'm a loser. I've been in and out of jail my whole life. The only good thing I had going for me was my wife. She said she'd always stick by me, but now I'm going upstate for a long stretch and she's had enough. I can't live without her and my kids. Without them, there's nothing. *Nothing*." With that, he buried his face in his hands and convulsed into sobs.

Even the CO was touched by his despair. "Hey, you don't want to kill yourself—it's not that bad."

But it was that bad, and Grant and I both knew it. There were no silver linings here. We tried to comfort him as best we could.

I was so engrossed that I didn't hear the phone ring. "Miss Buser," whispered the officer. "It's for you. Pepitone in the clinic—he says it's important."

I took the phone and stepped outside. "Yeah, Pep?"

"Listen, Mary, they're getting ready to tow your car. I got a buddy in security and I was able to buy you ten minutes, but you better get down here before they come back."

They were getting ready to tow my car! Caught in the cross-hairs of the tragic and the absurd, I asked Grant to step out for a moment and explained the situation.

"Un-believable!" she said.

Although torn, we both agreed that Luis Morales was stable for the moment and that she would stay with him while I moved the car.

"I'll be right back," I told her.

I bolted out of the Bing and ran through the halls, wriggling through gates one after the next just before they slammed shut. Outside the jail, I raced across the sunbaked lot, my sandals sinking into the mushy tar. I jumped into my car and backed out of some-body else's designated spot that I'd grabbed in desperation. Driving up and down the rows, I scanned the cars for an empty spot. Noth-ing. I drove around again, hoping I'd missed something. I hadn't. At the jail's main entrance, I waited for someone to come out. Nobody did. Finally, I turned onto the perimeter road, drove down a hill and rounded a bend that put me at the water's edge, where there were always a few spots. The problem was that I now had to wait for the route bus to get me back up to the jail. I looked helplessly up at the Bing. It would have been such an easy walk back, but I dared not risk it. Anxiously I waited, willing a route bus to appear. But none came, and I realized that I wouldn't be rejoining my colleague any time soon. Grant would have to handle the situation alone and get Morales to MHAUII or the hospital.

I sat down on a wooden mooring and lit up a cigarette. Across the way in a field of reeds, a rusted-out paddy wagon that looked like a leftover from the Eliot Ness days lay on its side. It was a hazy, sunny morning, and I leaned down to dip my hand in the East River's cold water. In the distance was the bridge, where a parade of buses rumbled across the span, shuttling the detainees to court. And just around the river's bend was the big city. From the glitter of Broadway to the corporate hustle of Midtown, careers were launched and fortunes made. That energy and promise might as well have been on another planet. Shortly, a car came around the bend, its three occupants studying me. It was Suzanne Harris, Hugh Kemper, and Frank Nelson headed down the road to Central Office. The car slowed, and the three of them looked at me curiously, undoubtedly trying to figure out what OBCC's Mental Health chief was doing sitting at the river's edge. And I would have gladly told them, had they stopped. But they didn't, and I can't say I was surprised. They knew that whatever the problem was, they didn't have an answer. In some ways I actually felt bad for them. The bravado of their early days was long gone. Between the demands of their own superiors, being bullied by DOC and the city, and trying to manage an angry staff, their jobs were unenviable. But while the Central Office team might have been having a tough go of it, St. Barnabas Hospital itself was doing quite nicely. Newspaper reports estimated that profits from the Rikers contract were already well into the millions.

37

A COUPLE OF DAYS LATER I WAS AT MY DESK WORKING
on OBCC's daily statistics, my cynicism growing. Although the
form was never without incidents of arm cutting, head banging,
and attempted hangings, once I faxed it to Central Office, most of
this data would disappear. Self-injurious behavior was considered
strictly in terms of suicide attempts. If it was deemed that the *motivation* for self-harm was "goal-directed"—as opposed to a bona
fide wish to die—then it would simply be deleted. In the case of
Leonard Putansk, despite the fact that he was taken to the hospital
for an attempted hanging, because the gesture came on the heels
of his demand to be released from solitary, it was not considered a
true suicide attempt. Using this formula, the big numbers of claw-
ing, cutting, and attempted hangings that were so pervasive among
the detainees were whittled down to a mere one or two a month,
serving as the island's official numbers—the numbers that were
served up to the public. I never trust statistics.

I was just finalizing the form when Theresa Alvarez burst into
my office. "Mary! They're ransacking the MO! They think somebody's got a razor! I was in the middle of running the community group when the squad came in with nightsticks, helmets, riot
gear . . . *and everything!*"

"Wait here," I instructed her and dashed across the hall to the
MO. I don't know why I went over—a sense of protectiveness, a
reflex, I guess. But when I got to the door, I could go no farther.

Mental frailties notwithstanding, a razor blade was a security matter, and I had no business being here; if spotted, I would be solidly reprimanded. But no one had seen me just yet. The door was slightly ajar and I edged in closer, just close enough to see the helmets and to hear a nightstick crack against a metal cot. An angry voice yelled, "Listen up, ya motherfuckers! You're nothing but sorry pieces of shit—not one of you should have even been BORN! Maybe you think you're fooling the doctors with all this mental illness CRAP, but you're NOT"—*crack!*—"FOOLING"—*crack!*—"ME! Now I want my razor back—and I want it back NOW!"

Heavy boots were pounding down the hallway. It was the Emergency Response Services Unit—the Ninja Turtles. I didn't dare stay a moment longer and darted back across the hall, but not before I caught sight of an oversized angular chair being rushed toward the MO. It always reminded me of an electric chair on wheels. One of DOC's most favored security apparatus, it detects weapons stored within the body. This was going to be bad.

Back at the clinic, we all buried ourselves in paperwork; no one talked about what was happening across the hall. I looked up at the clock—three-quarters of an hour had ticked by. Ten minutes later, Pepitone stuck his head in and told us the search team had just left.

We ran over to the MO. It looked like a bomb had been dropped. Lockers lay on their sides, family pictures were strewn about, the bookcase that Theresa had set up was on its side, books scattered on the floor. Mattresses were everywhere. The patients were rocking on their mattressless cots, too devastated to start the cleanup. A few sobbed. Victor, the mentally retarded inmate, sat on the edge of his cot; at his feet were his big eyeglasses, the frames twisted and the lenses nothing more than shards of glass.

At the bubble, the usually good-natured Officer Hartman was dazed. Hovering over him, arms flailing, was Burns, who alternated between berating Hartman and then trying to prop up his flagging spirits.

"What were you thinking?" asked Burns. "Mary, he calls security and tells them a blade's missing. Why'd you tell them it was gone? All you did was get yourself in hot water. What are you? Stupid?"

"Well, what was I supposed to do?" Hartman said glumly. "I was just following procedure."

Every morning disposable razors for shaving are dispensed from the bubble. In exchange for the razor, the inmate must turn in his all-important ID card. To get the card back, the blade must be returned.

Apparently, Hartman sent the inmates out to rec without checking IDs and without realizing he was still holding one ID card in the bubble, meaning that someone had walked out of the house with a razor blade. Only after the inmates were gone did Hartman notice the remaining ID. Following protocol, he called security and the squad arrived to search the inmate who'd left the ID behind. A strip search revealed no blade. He claimed he'd dropped it in the house and had simply forgotten about his ID. He was hauled off to the receiving room, and that's when the search team swarmed in.

In the meantime, a grim-looking Captain Catalano, the MO captain, told me the culprit was still in the receiving room and advised me to transfer him to an MO in another jail. Since he'd brought this upon the house, he was in danger of being soundly beaten if returned to the dorm. I filled out the paperwork promptly.

The following day, the blade had not yet turned up and the house was still "on the burn." Once again, the dorm was ransacked.

Afterward, we decided to gather the inmates in the dayroom and try to comfort them. At first, only a few would get up, but once we got the group going, they started trickling in. They were initially reluctant to talk, but once they started, the floodgates opened. They repeated the speech I'd heard at the door. Then they said they were ordered to strip, lined up against the wall with legs outstretched and palms against the wall, and warned not to make a sound while the team ransacked their belongings and inspected their rectums. They told us their arms were aching, but they all knew the officers were waiting for one of them to flinch—so someone could be made an example of. They said one of them looked at Victor and said, "Hey, Goofy," pulled off his glasses, and stomped on them.

Back in our office, Dr. Ketchum was beside herself. "For God's sake, why are they doing this? They're torturing these fragile people! The razor's gone—that guy got rid of it in the hallway. Don't they realize that?"

Even Catalano thought the searches were going too far but told me it was out of his hands. But he did have an interesting take on the whole thing. "The problem here is that it was our mistake. Nobody should have left that dorm without an ID. Now if somebody gets cut up with that razor, especially in an MO house, it would look very bad for the department. That's why they're pushing so hard to find it."

Buzzie Taylor, an older inmate with a long history of drug and alcohol addiction, was a permanent resident on the MO who suffered from major depression. After the third search, we had to console a shaken Buzzie, but not because of the search. He told us he was heading into the bathroom: "I was just going to take a pee and try to forget about everything. I went around a corner and a pair of sneakers banged into my head, and I said, 'What?' and then I look up and it's Teddy—hanging!"

Teddy Gibson, the patient with the crisscross scars who'd been sexually abused as a child, was barely clinging to life. He was already being intubated when the gurney was rushed through the clinic. The ambulance arrived quickly. It was only after a week that we got word that Teddy had survived. I told a much-relieved staff, and they in turn shared the news with the patients. However, there were murmurings that there'd been brain damage. We would never know for sure, as he never returned to OBCC, but after Teddy Gibson's attempted suicide, the searches ended.

38

AFTER I HAD SPENT EIGHT WEEKS RUNNING OBCC ALONE,
the heat let up, the summer vacations ended, and the audit was history. Even the calls from the Bing had fallen off. But best of all, Kelly returned. The long nightmare was over. As soon as Kelly got settled, I took a badly needed vacation and did my best to forget all about Rikers Island. While I was out, I saw a doctor about my abdominal pain. After a series of tests came the diagnosis: duodenal ulcer. He told me that most ulcers are caused by a virus, but further tests ruled out any virus. He said that some ulcers are, indeed, caused by "good old-fashioned stress." I didn't doubt it for a second.

When I returned to work, Kelly's presence felt luxurious. Together, we oversaw the unit, compiled statistics, traded off on meetings, and handled the daily crises. In short, the place became manageable. And then, an exciting development: we got a clinical supervisor! The enthused psychologist set up shop at the third desk, and our office was complete. Everything was finally coming together. I was well rested and should have felt great—but strangely, I did not.

About two weeks into Kelly's return, we were catching up on paperwork when the phone rang and Kelly answered it. I wasn't paying attention to her conversation, but when she got off she softly said, "Mary."

I was distracted and didn't respond.

"Mary!"

I swiveled around in my chair, but by now she was busy reading something.

I turned back and resumed assigning referrals. A few minutes passed before she said, "I have an interview."

I took a deep breath and said nothing.

"Well, it's just one interview." But there was a sparkle in her eye, and I knew the interview would fall into place and that she, too, would be gone.

Sure enough, one week and two interviews later, Kelly had a job offer. "I'd have to be crazy not to take it," she said. "Things here are too ridiculous."

"I know, Kelly. I wish it wasn't so, but I understand."

"You'll be taking over here at OBCC, Mary. You'll be the new chief."

I wished I could have been excited at the prospect, but I wasn't sure about it at all. But I needn't have worried about any agonizing decision.

When Kelly returned after tendering her resignation, she said that Suzanne Harris asked her who she thought should take over. "I was a little surprised," said Kelly. "After all, it's obvious you'd be the next chief. But she said they'd have to think about it, maybe consider candidates from outside."

I couldn't have been more stunned if Kelly had slapped me across the face.

"Listen, don't get upset," said Kelly. "It was just talk."

Just talk! Yes, I had sent an unwelcome memo. But I had also singlehandedly pulled the unit through a horrendous summer—overseeing the Bing, guiding us through a successful audit, maintaining staff coverage during a lengthy vacation cycle, not to mention managing a psychiatrist crisis—in every way demonstrating my ability to supervise OBCC's Mental Health Department. How dare they! My world was coming apart. I grabbed my jacket, ran out to my car, and drove off the island and down to the Triboro Bridge. The beastly heat had finally relented, and summer's green leaves had changed colors and fluttered to the earth. I walked down a leaf-covered path and sought sanctuary at the river's edge. The dark water, buffeted by stiff winds, crashed along the rocky shoreline. I looked out on the water, and as I did, a powerful realization was taking shape: *It was over.* There was nothing left of the meaning and fulfillment I had once found on Rikers Island. *It was over now.*

I lifted my face up to the wind and felt the soft spray of water. Images from the beginning started flashing through my mind—I smiled at the memory of the mothers and babies in the Rose Singer nursery. I thought of Lucy and Annie Tilden and Rhonda Reynolds. Where were they now? I recalled my first day at GMDC when Janet and Pat had met me in the lobby, and how enthused I'd been. I thought of my first case, Antwan Williams; of Chris Barnett, the motorcyclist; Alex Mora, whose brother had been shot; and Alex Lugo, forced to be a prison gladiator. I recalled Michael Tucker and his mother, and the many worried families of the mentally ill that I'd tried to comfort. Countless others flashed through my mind, hundreds of people struggling, trying to find their way. Maybe my father was right—maybe I couldn't change the world. But in some small way I'd always tried. I'd shaken hands with every single person I'd met. I'd looked the disdained, sick, and forgotten in the eye, listened with an open heart, and treated all with dignity. Despite everything I'd been through, I still believed in the dignity of all life.

Yes, it was over now. St. Barnabas may have just done me a favor.

I started back to my car, and then I stopped. I turned around and walked back to a trash bin and reached into my pocket. I pulled out my cigarettes and tossed them away for good.

*   *   *

When I woke up the next morning, my heart was immediately flooded with the ugliness of the previous day, the bitter sting of rejection. Yet I also felt a deep sense of peace at the thought of my decision to leave. For the remainder of the week, I kept things to myself, allowing the staff to first process the news of Kelly's departure. When she'd gathered everyone to inform them, they were surprised and disappointed. And then, inevitably, conversation turned to talk of the new chief. Everyone looked in my direction. "Don't assume it's going to be me," I cautioned. But my warning wasn't taken seriously. "Oh, Mary," Theresa said, waving her hand, "you're so modest!" Under the pressure of summer's events, we had forged a strong bond. This whole group had grown dear to me, and the thought of telling them that I would also be leaving was almost unbearable.

But at the first opportunity, I called over to my old friends Janet and Charley. "Now, don't do anything rash, Mary!" Janet said. But by now, even Janet's admonitions were drowned out by the roar in my own heart; my time on Rikers was done.

The following day, I typed up my resignation letter. My first stop at Central Office was Hugh Kemper's office. As soon as he saw the envelope, he knew. "Why, Mary? Why?"

I liked Hugh and knew he'd been in my corner. "I just feel it's time to move on."

"Does this have to do with not being asked to replace Kelly?"

"Honestly, Hugh? No . . . not that I wasn't upset about it, but I think it was a catalyst, the push that I needed."

"I'm sorry, Mary. I'm really sorry."

Next was Dr. Campbell's office. When I handed him the envelope, he seemed mildly surprised but received the news politely, wishing me well in my "new endeavors."

Thankfully, Suzanne Harris was out that day.

39

MY LAST DAY ON RIKERS ISLAND BROUGHT UNEXPECTED gifts that I will never forget and will always treasure. My goal was to get through what would be an emotional day of tying up loose ends. Kelly was already gone, and predictably, Central Office had yanked our new clinical supervisor, saying she was needed in another jail. Had I not been leaving, I would have been seething, but now I simply took it as another sign that my decision to leave was the right one.

I was assigning my last batch of referrals when Hugh Kemper appeared at the door with two overstuffed briefcases, the contents of his desk, in each hand. St. Barnabas had a new idea. Because of a recent suicide at Rose Singer, it occurred to them that the Central Office administrators were out of touch with the jails. Their overnight solution was to physically relocate their staff to the jails themselves. Hugh was assigned to OBCC. I cleared off a table for him, and he started digging into the briefcases, searching for papers that had been filed in his desk.

The phone rang, and it was the Bing. Someone had just cut himself, and another was threatening suicide. I called Pete Majors into the office. Hugh looked up. "I'd like to go over there," he said. "I'd like to see the Bing."

"Coming with us, Mary?" asked Pete.

"No. Looks like there's enough of you to handle it." I would never again set foot in the punitive tower.

After they left, I went out to the fax machine and noticed a band of DOC brass making their way through the clinic. With their white shirts and colorful medals, this was a high-ranking crew. In the middle was a short, well-dressed man in a business suit whom I did not recognize. They were coming closer, looking in my direction.

"Who's Mary Buser?" asked the man in the suit.

"There she is," said one of the deps, pointing to me.

The man in charge thrust out his hand. Although puzzled, I reached out and shook it.

"I'm Deputy Commissioner Paris," he said.

I recognized the name immediately; he worked just under Commissioner Bernard Kerik.

"On behalf of the New York City Department of Correction, I want to thank you for the work you've done on Rikers Island."

I was stunned. Hardly a word of gratitude from my own employers, but recognition from this unlikeliest of sources.

"Everyone I've spoken to is complaining about what a loss it is that you're leaving," he said. "This is a tough building, with the Bing, and you've done a great job."

"Thank you," I said. "Thank you!"

"If you ever want to come back to Rikers, you call me directly, do you understand?"

"Yes," I nodded.

"Good," he said smiling. "See that she gets one of my cards," he said to one of his deps.

I floated back into my office with a smile I couldn't erase. That was my first wonderful gift.

When Hugh got back, he was looking a little wan but said nothing about his trip to the Bing. Instead, he wanted to meet the warden. With Kelly gone and my own departure imminent, Hugh needed to do a little damage control. I walked him over to the warden's office, where Warden Cooper was barking out orders. Big, loud, and streetwise, the warden eyed Hugh warily. "I don't know why there's such a turnover of Mental Health staff here, I really don't," Cooper said. "We were all very happy with Kelly and Mary, and first Kelly quits, and now Mary. I don't get it."

"Yes, I know, Warden, and we're not happy about it either," said Hugh, "but I want to assure you that we have someone very experienced who'll be stepping in to take over."

"Well, I hope so," he said skeptically. "We're getting into Christmas. Bad time of year for these inmates, and I'd like to know that I've got a solid Mental Health team to handle the holidays. Because let me tell you something, okay? I don't want a call at four in the morning that somebody's hanging for real. I do not—no, no, I do not."

"Warden, I totally understand your concern, and that's why I'm stopping by to personally assure you that you'll be very satisfied with the next chief."

"Well, I hope so," Cooper repeated dubiously. "I hope so. Because let me tell you something," he said, wagging a finger at Hugh. "When all is said and done, these inmates, okay—these inmates, here—they're still human beings."

*   *   *

Back at the clinic, Theresa was looking for me. "Oh, Mary, there you are. I know it's your last day and all, but I just need you to sign off on a couple of chart notes. I have them spread out in the lounge. It'll only take a minute."

"Okay," I sighed. "Last time." I followed her into the darkened lounge. The overhead lights suddenly flicked on and the packed room yelled, "Surprise!!!" I stepped back in shock as a forbidden camera bulb flashed. The room was full of OBCC's health-care team—doctors, nurses, pharmacy techs, dentists, and our own staff. Tables were spilling over with home-cooked food, buckets of fried chicken, soda, cakes, pie, and cookies. I wished they hadn't done it, but at the same time, I was delighted. One by one, those who knew me and those who didn't made their way over to wish me well, asking why I was leaving. I politely told them that it was time to move on—which was the truth. While I was uncomfortable in my starring role, I was moved that so much thought and effort had been put into this celebration.

Whenever there's food, word travels quickly, and there was a line of COs vying their way in for the goods. I eased out of the crowded lounge with a plate of food and made my way back to the office with the Mental Health crew. My decision to quit had come as a shock and they had not taken it well. Hugh had been dispatched to meet with them and smooth things over. Telling them I was leaving was one of the hardest things I'd ever done. But now it was over and I cherished these final moments with my team.

Throughout the day, the phone rang with well-wishers from around the island, and I appreciated every call.

I wanted the day to end, yet I wanted it to never end. But soon it was dark, and after final hugs and good-byes with staff, I sat quietly and worked on my final payroll. Finishing up, I gathered up my bags, shut off the lights, punched out for the last time, and walked out through the clinic, where the usual crowd awaited treatment. Out in the hall, busloads of inmates returning from court were spilling out of the receiving room. In their dark hoodies, they squinted as their eyes adjusted to the glaring fluorescent hallway lights.

I decided to walk over to the MO one last time for a final moment with the most innocent of the inmates. I didn't go into the dorm, but through the big window I said a silent good-bye to our mentally ill patients, who were huddled around the TV in their laceless sneakers and torn pants, watching the happy Huxtables.

In the lobby, I opened up the big logbook and took my time signing my name for the last time. Then I signaled to the officer, who popped the front door.

Outside, the night air was cold and fresh. After a hectic day in which I hadn't had a moment to myself, I suddenly felt very alone. Plumes of clouds silently moved across the early winter sky. Driving around the perimeter road for the final time, I felt like I was in a dream. I passed the road that led down to the women's jail.

Another lifetime. The jails were lit up with Christmas lights. "Season's Greetings" read the lettering in front of the adolescent jail.

At the exit booth ahead, an officer spotted me and stepped out as I pulled in. I waited while he checked underneath the car and then shone a flashlight about the trunk for the last time. Across the way on a grassy knoll, a pine tree bedecked in colorful lights swayed in the wind. For a blessed moment, all was quiet. Even the air traffic above was still.

The CO slammed the trunk and walked up to my window, rubbing his hands together. "Gettin' cold!"

"It feels good," I said.

"Feels good?"

"It was a hot summer."

I took one last look around and then drove straight ahead, up and over the long narrow bridge that connects Rikers Island to the Borough of Queens.

EPILOGUE

BY THE LATE 1990s, THE RIKERS POPULATION HOVERED at a record high 24,000 inmates. But by 2014, this number had dropped by half to roughly 12,000 inmates on any given day. This was due in part to the easing of drug laws.

The harsh Rockefeller drug laws, enacted in 1973, mandated sentences of fifteen years to life for people caught trafficking as little as four ounces of drugs. Although these laws were ostensibly designed to take down drug kingpins, the result was mass incarceration of the lowest-level street players, primarily poor minorities, and did nothing to stem the flow of drugs. In 2004 under pressure to reform these draconian laws, New York governor George Pataki signed the Drug Law Reform Act, which reduced mandatory sentences for the same crimes to eight to twenty years.

Despite the drop in numbers, the island remains plagued with violence, brutality, and callous indifference to human life. In February 2014 a homeless veteran suffering from mental illness, who had been arrested for trespassing, died in an overheated cell. In the summer of 2014 the *New York Times* published a series of scathing articles that exposed systemic guard-on-inmate brutality, leading to an investigation by the Justice Department.

In April 2014 New York City mayor Bill de Blasio appointed Joseph Ponte as correction commissioner, with a mandate to bring reform to the troubled complex. In his first year, Ponte addressed the issue of solitary confinement and enacted new protocols that include prohibiting this grueling punishment for those with serious medical or mental health issues, as well as limiting its use to no more than thirty consecutive days for all others.

Despite the increased public scrutiny, in January 2015 the *New York Times* reported that brutality persists at Rikers and cited incidents of ongoing abuse of the inmates, particularly the mentally ill.

In a trend that began in the mid-1980s, following the shuttering of state psychiatric hospitals, Rikers Island continues to be the prime caretaker of New York City's unsupervised mentally ill, who are typically arrested for low-level crimes and petty mischief. There have been no efforts to make good on earlier political promises of community-based housing and supervision for the mentally ill, measures that would likely prevent the bulk of these arrests in the first place.

Rikers Island continues to be populated by poor detainees who cannot afford bail as they await trial. Because the pathway to trial is far more daunting for the incarcerated, the detainee who might have been exonerated at trial will often accept guilt in the more expedient plea bargain process, often as a means of escaping Rikers Island. No efforts are underway to address this gross inequity.

GLOSSARY OF TERMS

ABBREVIATIONS USED IN THE BOOK
Department of Correction—DOC
Correction Officer—CO
Deputy Warden/Assistant Deputy Warden—Dep
Mental Observation Unit—MO (housing unit for the mentally fragile)
Mental Health Center (higher level of care than standard MO)
Central Punitive Segregation Unit—CPSU, aka the Bing
Mental Health Assessment Unit for Infracted Inmates—MHAUII

FACILITIES ON RIKERS ISLAND
Rose M. Singer Center—RMSC, aka The Women's House
George Motchan Detention Center—GMDC
Anna M. Kross Center—AMKC
Otis Bantum Correctional Center—OBCC
George R. Vierno Center—GRVC
Eric M. Taylor Center—EMTC, aka The Sentenced Building
Robert N. Davoren Complex—RNDC
North Infirmary Command—NIC
James A. Thomas Center—JATC (formerly House of Detention for Men,
    the first jail on Rikers)
West Facility—WF, aka West

ACKNOWLEDGMENTS

AS A FIRST-TIME AUTHOR, I WOULD LIKE TO ACKNOWLEDGE Karen Wolny and the amazing team at St. Martin's Press, who believed in this book and so capably guided me through the publication process. A special thanks to Emily Carleton and Donna Cherry for their editorial expertise. I am also grateful to Laura Apperson, Meredith Balkus, and Yasmin Matthew; and to Gabrielle Gantz and Christine Catarino in publicity and marketing. Thank you also to copy editor Bill Warhop.

For recognizing the potential in my manuscript and providing his expert guidance in seeing it to publication, I am grateful to my literary agent, Adam Chromy of Movable Type Management. I would also like to thank Michele Matrisciani of Bookchic, who first took note of my work and shepherded it into the appropriate channels.

There were many long years that preceded publication, and I am grateful to so many who cheered me on. First, I would like to acknowledge my mother and my father, who listened to my endless stories about Rikers and encouraged me to write this book. I am proud to say they were my first editors. My great sadness is that they are not here to see it published, yet somehow I believe they know.

For their love and support throughout this journey, I would like to thank John, Charlie, Danny, Thomas, Peter, Mary Lou, and "Aunt Mary Lou." A special thanks to Mary Farry and my Ohio 'cuz, as well.

To the readers who so generously gave of their time in reading earlier versions of the manuscript (and encouraged me to keep going!): Mary Lou Buser, Anne Ashley Quinn, Kathy Loughlin, Helen Burguiere, Dominick Bencivenga, Liz Weber, Kelly Caldwell, the late Harry Cronin, and Evelyn Neleson.

To my dear friends who've been with me through the highs and lows of this process: Susan Reeves, Karen Goldman, Karen Cassidy, Janet Cocchi, Evelyn Soto, and Wolfgang and Patricia Demisch. For her friendship and expert advice, a special thanks to Bettina Faltermeier.

My coworkers have also been so helpful and supportive—thank you to Jeanne Logan; her father, Jerry Logan; to Robin Rich, Erin Sherwood, Lanethia Spence, and Rich Thomas.

Sister Marion Defeis, Rikers Island chaplain and activist of twenty-three years, has been an indomitable force in seeing this story told. Thank you, Marion!

Finally, a theme of this book is the importance of listening and being heard. I don't know if I could have written this book were there not someone to listen to me. For believing in my ability to tell this story, even when I couldn't always see it, I am eternally grateful to Janet Lee Bachant.